THE POLITICS OF AGRICULTURAL COOPERATIVIZATION IN CHINA

Mao, Deng Zihui, and the "High Tide" of 1955

Frederick C. Teiwes
Warren Sun

Editors

An East Gate Book

Routledge
Taylor & Francis Group

LONDON AND NEW YORK

An East Gate Book

First published 1993 by M.E. Sharpe

Published 2015 by Routledge
2 Park Square, Milton Park, Abingdon, Oxon OX14 4RN
711 Third Avenue, New York, NY 10017, USA

Routledge is an imprint of the Taylor & Francis Group, an informa business

Library of Congress Cataloging-in-Publication Data

The Politics of agricultural cooperativization in China : Mao, Deng Zihui, and the "high
tide" of 1955 / Frederick C. Teiwes and Warren Sun, eds.
p.   cm.
An East Gate book.
Seelction of documents from Chinese sources.
ISBN 1-56324-382-2
1. Agriculture, Cooperative—China—History—20th century—Sources.
2. Agriculture and state—China—History—20th century—sources.
3. Mao, Tse-tung, 1893–1976.
4. Teng, Tzu-hui, 1896–1972.
I. Teiwes, Frederick C.
II. Sun, Warren.
HD1491.C6P64   1993
334′.683′0951—dc20
93-6434
CIP

ISBN 13: 9781563243820 (pbk)

Contents

FREDERICK C. TEIWES AND WARREN SUN

Editors' Introduction

The dramatic acceleration of agricultural cooperativization in the second half of 1955 has long been recognized as one of the key turning points in the history of the People's Republic of China (PRC), yet in crucial respects the nature of this policy reversal has been poorly understood. While scholarly analysis has achieved high standards when examining this "high tide" from the perspectives of overall policy dilemmas, the process of mass mobilization, and the movement's impact on China's villages,[1] the treatment of leadership politics and the broader political process at this critical juncture has been decidedly deficient. Indeed, surprisingly little research has been done on these aspects, and where the cooperativization debate has been discussed analysts have largely followed the flawed "two-line struggle" interpretation promoted by the Chinese Communist Party (CCP) itself during the Cultural Revolution.[2] Although post-Mao party history materials that call this interpretation into question have been available since at least 1981,[3] they have had only minimal impact on scholarly understanding.[4] A rich new vein of sources published during the past four years, however, allows a much deeper and more accurate understanding of the politics of cooperativization than was hitherto possible.

The standard view[5] holds that the fluctuating pattern of speed-ups followed by retrenchments in the cooperativization movement over the 1952–55 period reflected an ongoing struggle between radical and conservative positions. The radical view, emphasizing the dangers of rural class polarization if the individual peasant economy was not transformed and the possibility of rapid development by mobilizing the subjective desires of the peasants for change, was articulated above all by Chairman Mao Zedong. In the opposing camp were a wide array of party officials who worried about the disruptive effects of rapid advance on agricultural production, believed that full collectivization had to wait until agricultural mechanization was well advanced, and advocated a prudent process of steady advance closely linked to favorable objective conditions in the vast countryside. The chief spokesman for this position was Deng Zihui, the head of the Central Rural Work Department, but the grouping encompassed more powerful figures including the party's number two leader, Liu Shaoqi, and Secretary-General Deng Xiaoping. This group, moreover, was powerful enough to thwart Mao's wishes and in the first half of 1955, and after forming a consensus on the current situation, imposed a cautious policy of consolidating cooperatives. To overturn this situation, Mao circumvented the higher party bodies where he was in the minority and appealed directly to provincial leaders for support. The result was his famous July 31 speech to a conference of provincial party secretaries that led directly to the "high tide."

Inevitably, certain aspects of the above interpretation have some validity, but the new documentation provided in this issue of *Chinese Law and Government* demonstrate once and for all the fundamentally distorted view resulting from the application of the "two-line struggle" model to the cooperativization debate. Moreover, these documents, together with additional post-Mao party history materials[6] and information obtained through interviews with Chinese scholars and former officials,[7] provide a richly detailed if still incomplete history of the unfolding cooperativization issue in its two related aspects of the pace of development and the dissolving of Agricultural Producers' Cooperatives (APCs) during the first seven months of 1955, as well as new information on the question before 1955 and after Mao's July 31 speech. (A Chronology of Events has been included so that the complex unfolding of events that have often been presented out of sequence in the translated documents can be more easily understood.) Simply put, in the first three and one-half to four months of 1955 a strong conservative consensus did exist, but it was a consensus fully shared by Mao. Subsequently, by late April or May Mao began to change his mind and conclude that more rapid expansion was feasible and essential. This development went through two stages, with the chairman's initial call in May for more rapid growth of APCs accommodated by both Deng Zihui and a party Secretariat meeting chaired by Liu Shaoqi. By late June, however, Mao had concluded a further increase in the pace of guiding cooperatives was necessary, but now Deng Zihui, playing a lone hand, attempted to continue arguing a more cautious line only to be overwhelmed by Mao's late July initiative. The fascinating detail now available makes not only for compelling political history, it also allows for a rigorous analysis of key aspects of the Chinese political system in the mid-1950s.

The debate on agricultural cooperativization: A concise history

In planning for the coming victory in early 1949 the CCP leadership declared collectivized agriculture a fundamental goal, but one that would be realized gradually. In the immediate future China would have to complete the "New democratic revolution" and restore a shattered economy, and in both respects the individual peasant economy would play a major role. Not only were small peasant owners the main beneficiaries of land reform, but the need to revitalize production required concessions to potentially hostile elements as demonstrated by Mao Zedong's June 1950 advocacy of "maintaining the rich peasant economy."[8] A clear tension existed in this situation:

The need to reassure rich peasants and other rural productive elements argued for a go slow approach, but failing to move ahead toward collective agriculture would, in the eyes of the elite, disadvantage the party's poor peasant constituency, prevent firm political control of the vast countryside, *and* delay the achievement of a purportedly more productive planned economy. (See Document 1 for greater detail.)

In the pre-1953 period this tension produced only one major leadership conflict, a conflict that was more the result of Mao's reaction to events than the product of a clearly articulated debate. In a July 1951 comment on a Shanxi provincial report, Liu Shaoqi sharply attacked as "agrarian socialist thought" a proposal to launch a campaign to convert mutual aid teams, the lowest form of cooperative agriculture, into fully socialist collectives of the Soviet type. Liu's action, although consistent with existing policy, reportedly angered Mao both because he had not been consulted and due to his wish to push cooperativization forward. He then set out to accomplish that end by drafting a resolution on developing mutual aid and cooperativization that implicitly rebuked Liu but at the same time avoided the dramatic step advocated by the Shanxi authorities. Instead, Mao outlined the intermediate step of the semi-socialist lower stage cooperative for a smoother transition to socialist agriculture. Moreover, Mao's resolution that was distributed in December 1951 for trial implementation set relatively modest targets with rural organization focusing overwhelmingly on mutual aid teams.[9]

Although no major policy conflicts were apparent in 1952,[10] the increasing salience of the cooperativization issue was indicated by a November decision to establish a Central Rural Work Department to oversee the process. Significantly, in filling this position Mao called on one of his oldest and most trusted colleagues, Deng Zihui, who had stood with him in difficult circumstances in the late 1920s and early 1930s. When Deng assumed his post in early 1953 he was faced with major disruptions in the villages. While the policy guidelines of December 1951 that would be approved formally in February 1953 were comparatively moderate, as would again prove the case several times in the following years, the dynamics of implementation produced such excesses as blindly setting targets for mutual aid teams and APCs, impatiently seeking higher forms of organization, overaccumulating common property, and using coercive methods to deal with the peasants, all of which produced widespread discontent and panic. To deal with these problems, with the backing of the party center and of Mao who warned against excessive interference in the small peasant economy[11] Deng initiated a program of "opposing rash advance" (*fan maojin*) that both slowed the movement and saw the dissolution of several thousand APCs. (See Document 2 for details.)

The overall policy context was in the process of change, however. As in other areas, Mao's articulation of the general line for the transition period in June 1953 meant greater emphasis on the socialist transformation of agriculture. In policy terms this resulted in a December resolution on developing APCs that emphasized cooperatives rather than mutual aid teams as the "key link" of the whole movement and approved a target more than doubling APCs to 35,000 by fall 1954. Politically, by the time of the October-November conference on mutual aid and cooperativization Mao found fault with Deng Zihui's handling of *fan maojin* earlier in the year, conveniently ignoring his own support for that policy. In particular, Mao sternly criticized the dissolution of cooperatives in the spring that was "wrong no matter what the circumstances," although there is nothing to indicate that he had objected at the time. Thus the political temperature had been raised and Deng underwent self-criticism, albeit one that, according to his biographer (see Document 3), Deng regarded with reservation. Nevertheless, at the end of 1953 cooperativization policy was still of a centrist cast that warned of both the Left and Right and regarded "rash advance" as well as "rash retreat" as mistakes to be avoided.[12]

Although Mao had clearly been angered by the "antirash advance" of 1953 and cooperativization became an issue of even higher salience in 1954, the framework of opposing both the left and right seemingly helped to avoid major leadership differences throughout the new year. In actuality, 1954 was a period when the movement was pushed ahead forcefully both to increase agricultural production through the allegedly more efficient use of resources and to prevent rural class polarization. In broad strategic terms this was reflected in the new understanding that full collectivization could proceed before the mechanization of agriculture.[13] In immediate terms it was seen in the overfulfillment of plans and the setting of even bolder targets: the 35,000 APC target of December 1953 was more than doubled to 90,000 by spring 1954, in April, the Rural Work Department called for a big expansion to 300–350,000 cooperatives in 1955, and in October the department again increased the target to 600,000 by spring 1955. Deng Zihui, his normal pragmatism notwithstanding, was in the thick of these developments. Not only was he a key figure at the April and October conferences that set the ambitious goals, his statements called attention to the importance of cooperativization for the rural class struggle.[14] From the perspective of spring 1955, Deng concluded that he had been overoptimistic the previous year and had "misinterpreted" Mao's class policy by being overly harsh to middle peasants (see Document 11). By the end of 1954, however, it was becoming clear that campaign dynamics were producing similar excesses to those of 1952–53, and that rural tension was further exacerbated by the overpurchase of grain under the new state monopoly purchasing and marketing policy. (See Document 4, chapter 9, parts I and II, for details.)

The major initiative for dealing with these problems apparently came from Deng Zihui at the start of 1955. Deng spoke to Liu Shaoqi and wrote to Zhou Enlai (Document 6) about the escalating rural tensions in the first days of January, and his recommendation to shift the cooperativization movement to a stage of consolidation and controlled development was quickly endorsed by the Politburo that then issued a circular drafted by Deng to realize this objective (Document 7). This circular called on provincial authorities, who had in many cases been setting even higher targets than those approved at the October 1954 conference, to stop development where the plan had been overfulfilled and, in places like Zhejiang and Hebei where APCs had been set up without appropriate preparations, to reduce the number of cooperatives. In these moves the role of Mao is obscure although on balance it seems likely he was informed and, at the very least, did not object.[15] But expansion continued apace despite the efforts of the Rural Work Department, which focused on Zhejiang, Hebei, and Shandong, and some intermediate organs such as, ironically given subsequent developments, the Shanghai Bureau of Ke Qingshi, to cool down the movement. Apparently because of the enthusiasm of the lower levels, the total number of APCs grew to 580,000 by early February and 670,000 in April.[16]

By early March, however, Mao's presence began to be forcefully felt on the side of the conservative program. Indeed, in his 1991 *Reflections* (Document 5), Bo Yibo, at the time the head of the State Construction Commission, commented not only that Mao didn't hesitate to believe Deng Zihui at this point and that their views were basically identical, but also that the chairman backed a pace of cooperativization so slow that sometimes Deng was caught by surprise. From early to mid-March, Mao signed an urgent directive on grain work that had been discussed by virtually the entire top leadership including Liu, Zhou, Chen Yun, and Deng Xiaoping, lowered the target for peasant households in cooperatives by the end of the First Five-Year Plan from 50 to 33 percent despite Deng Zihui's protests, coined the three-word policy of "stop, shrink, develop" (*ting, suo, fa*) that became the slogan for efforts to reduce the pace of the movement, approved the reduction of APCs in Zhejiang and Hebei, and (perhaps slightly later) called for a halt in developing cooperatives until fall 1956.[17] The cautious policy orientation was further confirmed at the National Party Conference in late March where the chairman reasserted that cooperativization would take three five-year plans to complete. Mao's direct role was undoubtedly the source of a more thorough effort to carry out the policy of consolidation.

These efforts had two main aspects, slowing the overall pace of the movement and dissolving poorly run APCs, especially in Zhejiang where the phenomenon was most serious. Concerning Zhejiang, a study meeting to deal with the matter was convened on March 24 by Deng and Tan Zhenlin, the head of Second Office of the Secretariat that was responsible for agriculture, a meeting also attended by Zhejiang First Secretary Jiang Hua.

These discussions resulted in a telegram to the Zhejiang Provincial Committee (Document 9) that called on the local authorities to stop the development of APCs and selectively reduce those cooperatives lacking adequate conditions. The scope of the contraction was indicated by the estimate that 30,000 APCs could be successfully consolidated, a figure implying the dissolution of more than 20,000. To make sure of Mao's consent, Deng asked the chairman's secretary, Chen Boda, to check with him, and Chen reported by phone that "the center agrees." Deng then departed on an overseas trip leaving this matter in the hands of Tan Zhenlin who also happened to be the former top leader in Zhejiang. Tan was vigorous in following up particularly by dispatching Du Runsheng and Yuan Chenglong to Zhejiang. There they pressured the provincial leaders to adopt the conservative policies, calling on local cadres to "get off the horse" of cooperativization, and on April 11 cabled the Rural Work Department and Secretariat in Beijing (Document 10) advocating a policy of resolute contraction (*jianjue shousuo*) for Zhejiang. These recommendations gained the support of Tan Zhenlin and Jiang Hua in Beijing, and in the circumstances the provincial committee "unanimously" agreed and over the next month dissolved 15,000 cooperatives.[18]

Meanwhile the Rural Work Department had moved to slow the overall pace of the movement with a March 22 circular (Document 8) that emphasized respecting the will of the peasants, declared that no additional APCs should be established regardless of locality, and called for a reasonable reduction (*heli jianshao*) in the number of cooperatives and the proportion of peasant households in them. This general policy thrust continued through April and into May and was decidedly in evidence at the April 20 Secretariat meeting chaired by Liu Shaoqi and the subsequent rural work conference. At the Secretariat meeting Liu called for halting cooperative development for a year (a shorter period than Mao had called for) while, by implication, indicated a willingness to see as many as 170,000 to 270,000 APCs dissolved.[19] Deng floated a more limited proposal to reduce the number of APCs by 50,000 to 100,000 at the rural work conference, while his opening and concluding speeches (Documents 11–12) emphasized consolidation and guarding against "rash advance." Interestingly, Deng—who met with Mao several times in this period—both cited the chairman's authority for the moderate program *and* cautioned against "rash retreat" such as had occurred under his aegis in 1953; moreover, the suggestions he and Liu had made to cut substantially the number of cooperatives were not adopted. In arguing for "active consolidation" rather than "passive contraction" Deng reflected the general principle of avoiding both right and left deviations, but whether or not he was aware of it, the inherent tension in this guideline was already intensifying as Mao began to reconsider his position.

In what became known as the "change in May" (see Document 4, chapter

10, part I [2], and Document 5, part IV), although it most likely began in late April, Mao moved to a position that placed greater emphasis on the development of cooperatives. While there is uncertainty as to precise timing, the chairman's new outlook undoubtedly began to form during several inspection tours of the countryside in April and May, and it had reached a definite stage by May 17 when he demanded a change in policy implementation at a specially convened conference of provincial party secretaries. A number of factors seemingly came together over this period. First, Mao encountered peasants and local officials expressing enthusiasm for cooperativization during his tours. Moreover, concrete evidence of rural progress seemed to present itself in the form of "wheat that has grown to a person's waist," evidence that led to doubts about the more measured views of Deng Zihui. In particular, Deng's conclusion that badly run cooperatives were the main cause of rural tension, a view expressed privately to Mao on the eve of the rural work conference and publicly at the conference's conclusion (Document 12), seemed increasingly at odds with the situation as the chairman understood it.

Meanwhile, other "objective" evidence indicated that the second main source of tension in the villages, the grain shortage due to overpurchase under the state's new monopoly, was not as severe as thought and of a quite different nature. According to reports reaching the center, in many cases "grain shortages" were the result of better-off peasants demanding grain from the state while hiding their own surplus. This not only led to late April measures to overhaul grain work, it also further contributed to Mao's disenchantment with the Rural Work Department for its warnings about grain deficiencies that he criticized as "blowing a wind of rumors." More broadly, this development led Mao to start addressing the overall rural situation more from the perspective of class struggle, a tendency abetted by concern about the "bitter life" of the peasants on the part of nonparty figures and, most ominously, by the view of Shanghai's Ke Qingshi, apparently put to Mao on one of his tours, that 30 percent of party cadres including senior officials were unwilling to pursue socialism in the countryside.[20]

While the timing is somewhat unclear,[21] the first apparent indication to other leaders of Mao's changing views was his late April or early May warning to Deng "not to repeat the 1953 mistake of dissolving a large number of cooperatives." The chairman was clearly concerned with the 15,000 APCs dissolved in Zhejiang and another 11,000 in Hebei and Shandong, an attitude that Bo Yibo viewed three and one-half decades later as misinterpreting Deng's strictures against particularly shoddy cooperatives in specific areas as reflecting a negative attitude toward cooperativization as a whole.[22] Even more suggestive of Mao's growing impatience, but also of the formative nature of his thinking, was a May 9 meeting with Deng and a number of other concerned officials. On this occasion Mao called for a lowering of the target for grain purchase while at the same time asking whether it would be possible to lift the target for peasant households in APCs to 40 percent by the end of the five-year plan. After Deng reminded him that he had set the current 33 percent target in March and advocated sticking to it, the chairman reluctantly agreed. In raising the issue, however, Mao did more than indicate his desire for a more rapid pace. He rejected Deng's contention that poor cooperatives were the chief cause of rural tension, instead pointing to the grain problem and suggesting the reduced grain target would be a concession to the peasants that could be "exchanged for socialism." His political concerns were further indicated by a reference to Ke Qingshi's claim that 30 percent of party cadres at all levels disagreed with building socialism.[23]

If Mao's May 9 discussion was a sign of shifting views, his new outlook was more forcefully and publicly indicated in his May 17 speech to provincial secretaries (Document 13). Although reaffirming the three-word policy of "stop, shrink, develop," the chairman stressed development while his previous injunction to halt expansion was conveniently brushed aside. Moreover, he spoke in a very assertive, critical tone that took to task the "passive sentiment" toward cooperativization and warned it would be a "big mistake" if this were not changed. This critical tone apparently contributed to some tension at the meeting as a number of provincial leaders, presumably smarting at treatment they had received earlier in the year, made complaints about the Rural Work Department that assertedly further raised Mao's doubts about Deng. In addition, Mao proposed some concrete targets totaling 340,000 APCs in seven key provinces while the conference as a whole called for one million nationwide in 1956. But while a clear change of emphasis had taken place, the overall policy remained comparatively moderate with the voluntary nature of cooperatives stressed, middle peasant interests affirmed, and the continuing dissolution of APCs where necessary allowed.[24]

The revised program was speedily accepted by the relevant party bodies. The Rural Work Department formally proposed the one million target of the May 17 conference to a Politburo meeting chaired by Liu Shaoqi on June 14, and the meeting approved this "big expansion" for the coming year.[25] Meanwhile, local committees altered their plans as in the case of Liaoning (see Document 16b) where a decision to stop development was aborted after the local leader returned from the May 17 gathering. The reaction in Liaoning, however, was typical of the comparatively limited adjustment of policy Mao had asked for. From the perspective of August, the provincial committee criticized itself for still being timid in June. The same phenomenon was seen at the center. In a June 21 report on his investigations in Zhejiang (Document 14), Tan Zhenlin, who apart from his agricultural responsibilities and links to Zhejiang was significant for his long and close association with Mao,[26] focused on the need to protect middle peasant interests. And as late as July 6 a comment on a Hebei directive in the name of the "center" (Document 15) emphasized a pragmatic approach toward private property in advancing cooperativization.[27] Yet while these developments indicate a party that was both responsive to Mao *and* still relatively cautious in policy orientation, in the same period the chairman's outlook was in the process of changing even further.

Less is known about the specific factors influencing the change of June-July than for the change in May, but two seem significant: the results of further inspections of cooperatives undertaken by Mao in June, and his increasingly critical focus on the performance of the Rural Work Department. While there is little information concerning the chairman's June investigations, upon his return late in the month he summoned Deng Zihui for a talk. In their discussion Mao ventured that the recently approved expansion to one million APCs seemed too small and instead proposed an increase to 1.3 million. Deng, however, insisted that the existing plan was better and made a detailed argument of his case noting the desirability of keeping in step with the pace of industrialization, the heavy task of consolidating existing cooperatives, and the need to complete that task in order to lay the basis for full cooperativization in the future. The meeting apparently ended in disagreement.[28]

A more ominous encounter took place on July 11. By now Mao had begun a two month retreat to study further the cooperativization issue. On the day in question the chairman called in Deng and other Rural Work Department leaders together with Tan Zhenlin to reiterate his views and severely criticize the assembled group. Deng, however, apparently alone among those present, held his ground during the tense five-hour session causing Mao to exclaim that his mind "needed to be shelled by artillery." Now the chairman began to delve deeper into the affairs of Deng's department by calling for its files, concluding that the department was "rightist and short of enthusiasm," and starting to draft his landmark July 31 report. In all this Deng seemed completely isolated despite the broad consensus at the top concerning his program for most of the year. When he discussed the clash with Mao among colleagues in the department they were astonished that he dared "offend Chairman Mao merely over hundreds of thousands of cooperatives."[29] At a more prominent level Tan Zhenlin and Minister of Agriculture Liao Luyan apparently avoided major difficulty by abandoning their previous views,[30] while the very highest leaders were reportedly called in for discussions and seemingly offered no resistance to Mao's latest shift of position.[31]

Mao's July 31 report clearly was a seminal event, but not in the sense of overcoming entrenched resistance at the center. Right up to the eve of his speech, the chairman's position was evolving and not clearly understood by his colleagues. Indeed, as one Chinese scholar who has written on the matter observed orally, to most leaders at the time (like Deng's nervous departmental colleagues) Mao's argument with Deng seemed to be about numbers of APCs rather than policy direction, and only in hindsight did the significance of the differences become clear.[32]

In any case, no source, written or oral, provides evidence of explicit opposition to the new course either before or after the July 31 speech apart from Deng Zihui in June-July.[33] The seminal nature of that speech, as has been demonstrated in earlier studies,[34] was less in the policy prescriptions that remained reasoned and moderate even with the new target of 1.3 million cooperatives, than in the political pressure of the chairman's presentation. Beginning by ridiculing Deng for "tottering [along] like a woman with bound feet," Mao treated the dispute as one of political line with "some comrades . . . [who] proceed from the stand of the bourgeoisie, the rich peasants, and the well-to-do middle peasants with their spontaneous tendencies toward capitalism."[35] With such ominous rhetorical flourishes, an entirely new political atmosphere had been created.

No one could withstand the pressure generated by Mao. Even that most redoubtable of figures, Deng Zihui, supported Mao's criticism of his "passive" approach after the chairman spoke, and on August 1 Mao reciprocated by declaring the debate with Deng resolved.[36] The provincial leaders returned to their localities to convene meetings and relay the chairman's report. This produced expressions of complete agreement with the chairman, self-criticisms of rightist mistakes earlier in the year, and significantly increased APC targets (see Documents 16a-e). For the remainder of the year the campaign dynamic took over with central targets being outstripped by the provinces, the center setting new and higher targets, and the localities once again surpassing Beijing's plans.[37]

At the same time when lower level leaders strove to prove their loyalty to Mao's line, Mao himself adopted an increasingly strident posture toward the mistakes of the first half of the year. He not only approved use of the right opportunist label and dwelt repeatedly on class struggle themes, the chairman also became increasingly harsh in his attitude toward the Rural Work Department leading to Deng's denunciation by name at the October Central Committee plenum that formally endorsed the "high tide."[38] All of this further increased pressure for an even more rapid expansion of cooperatives.

By the end of 1955 cooperativization had far outstripped Mao's July target, a development leading him to observe that the movement's success had made him even happier than the victory of 1949.[39] Mao had indeed launched, and the party machine carried out, a high tide that would soon collectivize agriculture a decade and a half earlier than he had believed possible.

The politics of cooperativization

The clearest lesson of the above review of the debate on agricultural cooperativization is the virtually unchallenged authority of Mao. Apart from Deng Zihui's June-July attempt to argue the case on its merits with the chairman, there is no evidence of party leaders at any level opposing a clearly articulated view put forward by Mao. Thus Mao's ability to alter the terms of the debate and the course of policy was not only apparent in the two shifts toward an intensified pace of development in May and July, but equally if less dramatically in the conservative orientation of the first four plus months of 1955. In January through March the momentum of development continued despite the efforts of the Rural Work Department and the center to cool things down in the absence of Mao's explicit and public (in the inner-party sense) support. Once that support was manifest in March with, among other measures, his coining of the "stop, shrink, develop" policy, the pace of cooperativization slowed and substantial numbers of poorly managed APCs were dissolved.

Mao's authority was apparent in other senses as well. Deng Zihui reported to the chairman at key junctures, sought to ascertain his approval of new measures such as the policy of contraction in Zhejiang, and used the chairman's views to bolster his own case in party forums. Clearly the general perception was that Mao's words had to be obeyed. At both the May 17 and July 31 conferences of provincial secretaries, his views were presented as suggestions but in an assertive manner. As one senior party historian commented, with Mao it was hard to distinguish a suggestion from an order, and in these cases the assembled officials had no doubt that the only viable course open to them was to return to their localities and carry out his wishes as they understood them. Most dramatically, when Deng Zihui persisted in his views after Mao's forceful reassertion of the desire to increase the APC target to 1.3 million, Deng's rural work colleagues were astonished that he would risk "bringing disaster" by continuing to argue with the chairman.[40]

In many respects the cooperativization debate can been seen as another example of court politics surrounding Mao, a type of politics that had marked the leadership power struggle culminating in the 1953–54 purge of Gao Gang and Rao Shushi—a case that was well fixed in the minds of CCP leaders and only formally settled at the March 1955 National Party Conference.[41] The effort to influence Mao to adopt one's policy preferences went beyond the normal effort to persuade an authoritative decision maker; as Bo Yibo observed with regard to Ke Qingshi's reporting to Mao that 30 percent of cadres were unwilling to practice socialism, Ke "figured out very well Chairman Mao's thinking and what he liked."[42] Moreover, in a situation where the "emperor" was also the "great leader" of a successful revolution, the impulse to obey had elements of faith and belief as well as fear and calculation. Indeed, if Bo can be believed, Deng Zihui himself was eventually convinced of the correctness of Mao's position after studying the chairman's analysis of class trends in the countryside (see Document 16d), and acknowledged in his self-criticism to the October plenum that the root of his "mistakes" lay in the "lack of correct class analysis."[43]

A disconcerting aspect of court politics was arbitrary actions by the leader, something that had already surfaced in Mao's behavior and would become ever more prominent in subsequent years. Indeed, in the historical assessments of the chairman's leadership after his death, Mao's escalation of the conflict with Deng into a struggle of political lines and the application of the right opportunist label to a loyal colleague is seen as a serious mistake.[44] In fact, Mao's behavior in 1955 was probably less arbitrary than various of his actions during the Gao Gang affair,[45] not to mention the period from the late 1950s on. Nevertheless, he was apparently unbothered in making assertions which, by available evidence, both distorted history and shirked his own responsibility. The clearest case of this was Mao's attempt to make the Rural Work Department solely responsible for dissolving cooperatives in Zhejiang "without the approval of the center" despite not only his general policy guideline that allowed for "shrinking" the number of APCs, but also his specific approval relayed through Chen Boda of the March 25 telegram (Document 9) that implicitly sanctioned the cutting down of 20,000 APCs in that province—a document he later denounced as being "decided on in a state of panic."[46] This was not novel in the chairman's handling of the cooperativization question either; as we have seen in attacking "opposing rash advance" in late 1953 he turned a blind eye to his own support for that program earlier in the same year.

The above court phenomena notwithstanding, the debate on cooperativization in major respects had the features of a regularized political process. Although at the crucial mid to late July stage the decision making circle had largely narrowed to Mao, those immediately around him like Chen Boda, and the highest ranking CCP leaders who seem to have been more informed than consulted, for the first half of 1955 and earlier the responsible bureaucratic organs in Beijing and local authorities charged with implementing cooperativization were systematically involved and policies were discussed in appropriate inner-party bodies. The initiative for dealing with the deteriorating situation in the countryside at the start of 1955 apparently came from the Rural Work Department, and the cautious program adopted was thoroughly reviewed at the late April-early May rural work conference.

Moreover, the debate in the first half of the year, and in important respects after July 31, was a rational discussion of complex problems. While, in the period from late April to the end of July, Mao's position was ambiguous and unclear to other actors—in August the Hubei authorities (Document 16a) criticized themselves for failing to understand the gist of his May 17 speech while the Yunnan party leadership pointed to the chairman's "unambiguous" July 31 message as ending their vacillation[47]—this ambiguity was different from the often frustrating and ominous type that marked the chairman's behavior on so many other occasions.[48] Unlike the Gao Gang case where power at the top level was involved and the chairman's contradictory views on issues and individuals left his colleagues in a state of high uncertainty and anxiety, in 1955 Mao's ambiguity was part and parcel of coming to grips with a major policy problem and gradually working out a new position. That there was a lack of clarity was fully understandable in terms of inherent contradictions in the widely accepted guidelines of avoiding right and left deviations, making use of the individual peasant economy while transforming its basis, and relying on poor peasants while uniting with middle peasants. Significantly, while in political terms Mao's July 31 report bore the earmarks of a demand from on high, substantively it contained a reasoned argument addressing key regime concerns.

Mao's individual role in July notwithstanding, the above considerations give some support to the official claim that until 1957 political processes were relatively "democratic" in the restricted CCP sense.[49] Certainly and somewhat surprisingly, given the recent Gao Gang affair where Mao demonstrated the ability to transform fairly technical policy issues into questions of political orientation,[50] until the chairman clearly demanded change in mid-July other leaders were fairly open and even incautious in pushing their ideas, albeit normally within the framework of the agreed policy. This was clearly the case with Deng, undoubtedly an almost unique colleague in terms of his boldness in dealing with Mao,[51] who on several occasions before the July 11 confrontation took contrary positions in discussions with the chairman. But it was also found in the actions of others, perhaps nowhere more strikingly than in Liu Shaoqi's April suggestions to dissolve 100,000 or 170,000 or 270,000 APCs. While no one apart from Deng (briefly) was willing to challenge Mao's clearly expressed views, the implicit assumption in the first half of 1955 apparently was that one could energetically carry out duties and articulate views without any undue danger of courting political "disaster."

To the extent this picture of a regularized and relatively democratic debate before mid-July is accurate, it undoubtedly was linked to the relative absence of radical and conservative camps, at least at the center. While such statements as Mao's 1958 observation that, in contrast to earlier unity, "on the question of forming cooperatives [there were different] attitudes" and Vice Premier Chen Yi's fall 1955 assertion that Mao's intervention "settled the debate of the past three years"[52] have led analysts to believe the issue was hotly debated, the evidence from the newly available sources suggests that on the whole a process of shifting consensus marked policy at the top. Of course, at key junctures as in July-September 1951 regarding the Shanxi cooperatives and in October-November 1953 concerning rash advance, Mao's personal intervention served to alter the consensus. The point, however, is that it is not possible to identify groups of central leaders arguing sharply different views either before or after Mao acted. Of particular relevance is that Deng Zihui and his department played a leading role in the overambitious policies of 1954.[53] Moreover, there is little to indicate any significant differences opinion within the rural bureaucracies[54] or the top leadership as a whole[55] during the first half of 1955. Policy clearly did fluctuate from mid-1951 to early 1955, but it was more in response to Mao's initiatives and relatively unified assessments of changing circumstances than due to consistent advocacy on the part of even loosely formed policy groups.

While a reasonably regularized bureaucratic process functioned in the first half of 1955, this process had some particular characteristics. The most general of these was the relatively narrow range of institutional actors involved. Apart from the periodic involvement of Mao, other key individuals such as Liu Shaoqi, the Secretariat, and the Politburo, cooperativization policy in Beijing seemed largely restricted to the key responsible bodies, Deng Zihui's Rural Work Department and Tan Zhenlin's Second Office of the Secretariat. Here there was an anomaly indicative of the revolutionary origins of the regime: in strict bureaucratic terms Deng's department was subordinate to Tan's office, but it was Deng with his superior party status who was clearly the main mover in conducting cooperativization policy.[56] Other bureaucratic units seldom participated; there is little evidence of their role in the documents, and two quite separate oral sources with access to archives on the period agree there was a reluctance to become involved. The main exception occurred when APC policy was being considered in conjunction with the related issue of the purchase and marketing of grain. Thus when Mao called in a group of officials on May 9 to propose reducing the grain target "in exchange for socialism," Minister of Finance Li Xiannian and Vice Minister of Grain Chen Guodong were among those summoned.[57] Otherwise, given the importance placed on cooperatives for increasing agricultural production that was viewed as crucial for the overall industrialization effort, it is striking how minimally the State Planning Commission features in the story.[58] And while Bo Yibo, then a key economic official, goes into considerable detail on his personal involvement in other key events of the early and mid-1950s in his *Reflections*, his discussion of the cooperativization debate is almost entirely from the perspective of a well-supported researcher.[59]

Several explanations of this situation can be offered largely on the basis of discussions with party historians. One consideration concerns the personal relations among leaders. Given both the high revolutionary status of individual leaders and the cultural proclivity to indirection and separate circles, a reluctance to interfere in the affairs of institutions headed by such high-status leaders was understandable.[60] A somewhat different angle was advanced by one historian who observed that relations among longstanding party leaders tended to be either very good or very bad, and in either case there was an unwillingness to become involved in the area outside one's own direct responsibilities.[61] Another consideration is that cooperativization policy was seen as a question of implementing a broad policy that had already been determined and thus as something that should be left to the Rural Work Department and the center for quick decisions. Moreover, however important the development of APCs would be for production, policy in this area did not involve concrete economic targets that would involve the planning and financial agencies. Finally, and perhaps most tellingly, the institutional practices of the time that emphasized a strict division of labor discouraged wide-ranging involvement in the affairs of other units. In particular, the abolition of Zhou Enlai's central government party group secretaries conference (*dangzu ganshihui*) in 1953 removed a coordinating forum where various bureaucratic perspectives could be aired.[62] Government organs now reported directly to the party center (i.e., Mao), a procedure that encouraged them to stick to their own duties.

Cooperativization, however, had to be implemented by local authorities from the regional[63] and provincial levels to the grassroots, and here the situation was rather different from that at the center. First, at the lowest levels there was the repeated phenomenon of overly responsive policy implementation, whether in the blind pursuit of targets without attention to policy restrictions during expansionary phases or in the form of rash retreat when a slowdown was decreed. As an oral source put it, local cadres were not well-educated and their main function was to do what they were told. At the provincial level, judging from the case of Zhejiang and other rapidly expanding provinces in late 1954-early 1955, there apparently was a more complex relationship to the Beijing authorities. Without Mao's personal and prominent involvement, the center sometimes had difficulty in getting its way, with considerable effort required and some friction resulting. This was clearly the case in Zhejiang where despite the center's January circular (Document 7) suggesting "reasonable reduction" of local APCs, the Shanghai Bureau's February report calling for the province to "mark time" and consolidate cooperatives, and the Rural Work Department concentrating much of its effort on the province, only several hundred APCs were dissolved and overall growth actually accelerated before Mao's involvement.[64]

An important aspect of the equation was that, unlike the comparatively high albeit shifting consensus at the center, there were apparently significant differences of outlook both among provinces and within individual localities. As a well-placed party historian observed, there were divided responses to the contraction policy ranging from going along to strong opposition. In cases like Zhejiang, he said, local authorities strongly resented being pressured to comply, asking "why us?" and "aren't we trusted?,"[65] and such sentiments undoubtedly fueled the provincial complaints directed at the Rural Work Department at the May 17 conference. A number of factors apparently caused the diversity of views. Particular local contexts were important as in Zhejiang where the local campaign against Rao Shushi reportedly generated blind enthusiasm for cooperativization.[66] More broadly, certain individual provinces seemed to reflect more long-term political orientations of their leaders. Thus the Guangdong authorities not only pushed the consolidation policies before Mao's May 17 speech that came to them as an unanticipated bolt out of the blue, but even in October adopted an approach that leading party historians have characterized as "relatively 'sober.' "[67] Even more dramatic was the apparently consistent radical bent of Anhui. In its August report to the center (Document 16c) the provincial committee claimed to have fought conservative orders from above going back to 1952 as well as having rejected a spring 1955 directive to cut local APCs by 20 percent. While the details that might illuminate these claims are not available, the likelihood of a persistent left inclination is further enhanced by the fact that the local leader, Zeng Xisheng, subsequently became one of the leading provincial radicals of the Great Leap Forward period.[68]

These difficulties for the central authorities notwithstanding, the role of the localities was secondary in the overall course of cooperativization yet at the same time significant. To a certain degree influence was exerted through regular bureaucratic reporting,[69] but clearly the main local influence came via Mao. The change in May and again in June-July were to an indeterminate but important extent the result of Mao's investigation tours. The glowing reports the chairman received on those occasions, whether reflecting the conscious putting of the radical view as perhaps in the case of Ke Qingshi or simply the impulse of lowly cadres and peasants to demonstrate loyalty to the great leader, certainly led Mao to begin reassessing the situation. It was in this influence on Mao's thinking, not any political support at the July 31 conference, where the significance of the localities lay. The circumvention of the center must be understood in terms of political style rather than power. While Mao could have walked into the Politburo and got his way, as one historian observed, this would have been inconvenient to his democratic image particularly in view of the recent June 14 decision to set a target of one million APCs that his own demands had brought about. Much better, then, to create a political atmosphere that would achieve his goals on the basis of the "enthusiasm" of the masses from below.

We then return to Mao as the decisive factor. But what ultimately determined his volte-face in April-July 1955? In part, Mao was influenced by relatively objective information as in the reports showing the grain crisis was not as serious as previously thought. The turnabout also reflected distorted evidence such as reports of local officials trying to impress the chairman on his investigation tours, a situation leading Bo Yibo to the wistful observation that the party's line of "seeking truth from facts . . . is not easy to carry out."[70] Yet it can be argued that political factors extraneous to the actual issues played a surprisingly significant role. The comments of nonparty personages about the bitter life of the peasants clearly angered Mao, and arguably enhanced his inclination to view the issue in class terms. Even more telling, ironically in terms of his aims, was Deng Zihui's willingness to argue with Mao after the chairman's position, at least with regard to numbers of APCs, was clear. This led to Mao's investigation of the Rural Work Department and a further hardening of his views. While clearly the pace of cooperativization would have increased if Deng had immediately conceded the argument, it is unlikely the same overblown political rhetoric would have been required on July 31, if indeed a conference would have been convened at all. Without that rhetoric the frenzied pace of the high tide, which both outstripped in speed and avoided the pattern of growth followed by consolidation of previous upsurges, would also have been unlikely. Given the significance of the high tide as a model for future radical adventures, the pique of even the "democratic" Mao of the mid-1950s over someone daring to oppose his edict conceivably was crucial to bringing about a far more fundamental disaster than that envisioned by Deng's nervous rural work colleagues.[71]

A note on the documents and translations

The documents translated in this issue consist of two types, party history accounts written during the post-Mao reform era and original documents from 1955. The party history accounts (Documents 1–5) are presented to give both general context and blow-by-blow detail on the unfolding cooperativization debate. Such accounts not only express the reversal of verdicts on leaders such as Deng Zihui whose reputations were blackened during the Maoist period, they also reflect the need to reassess the policies of that time. This is clearly the case in Document 1, a journal article from the era of decollectivized agriculture that provides a broad if not totally satisfactory overview of policy toward the individual peasant economy during 1949–57. Document 2, another 1980s journal offering, focuses in detail on the main precursor of the 1955 events, the conflict over "opposing rash advance" in 1953. Document 3 consists of selections from a highly laudatory biography of Deng Zihui; the excerpts chosen deal with the 1953–54 period as well as 1956, leaving the critical events of 1955 to the more richly detailed Documents 4 and 5. This account is undoubtedly somewhat biased in its view of Deng as a consistent pragmatist, but it provides a good feel for the man and his concerns nevertheless.

The major party history accounts in Documents 4 and 5 are what makes possible a near definitive reassessment of the 1955 debate. Document 4 is the bulk of two chapters of a major 1989 book by three senior party historians, Lin Yunhui, Fan Shouxin, and Zhang Gong, while Document 5 is from the 1991 *Reflections* of one of the CCP's most important figures then and now, Bo Yibo. While these two selections cover much of the same ground, they are different in significant respects. First, Lin Yunhui et al. give greater attention than Bo to the 1954 background to the 1955 debate, and more generally to the actual problems in the villages and the responses of local officials, particularly after Mao's July 1955 speech. Bo, on the other hand, as one would expect given his much higher status in the party, clearly had greater access to inner-party records and presents a more detailed and more finely nuanced account of leadership interaction. This is perhaps most clearly seen in his analysis of the "change in May" where he chides "some historical works in recent years" (clearly a reference to the Lin, Fan, and Zhang book) for "not exploring or explaining clearly the causes of the change."[72] In addition, Bo is more concerned not only with interpreting political developments but also with systematically analyzing the policy differences between Mao and Deng. Finally, Bo is much more sensitive to upholding the reputation of Mao. While the more matter-of-fact account of Lin Yunhui, et al., implicitly assumes Mao was wrong in both policy and politics, Bo seeks to strike a more subtle balance. On cooperativization itself, he not only notes Deng's "correct" views but also indicates where Deng made policy errors and Mao's views were superior.[73] On the political issue, however, Bo adheres to the post-Mao consensus—the chairman erred seriously in raising a policy dispute to the level of political principle. The differences of the two accounts notwithstanding, together they raise our understanding of the 1955 turning point to a new level.

The original 1955 documents (Documents 6–16[a-e]) allow the reader to follow the story from January to September through the key circulars of the party center and Rural Work Department, reports from central officials in the field, speeches by Mao and Deng Zihui, and provincial reports following Mao's July 31 speech together with the chairman's comments on them.[74] With the exception of a section of one of Deng's speeches and parts of the provincial reports, these documents are translated in full, i.e., the original source is completely translated although the Chinese text itself may be an excerpt. Virtually all key central documents, apart from those previously available in English such as Mao's July 31 report and his speech to the October plenum, are included, with the exception of Deng's March 21 speech to the National Party Conference that was not translated in view of its similarity to his subsequent offerings to the rural work conference in

April-May. While other local reports are available, Documents 16a-e provide typical examples of such reports after July 31.[75]

A few points about the translations are in order. An effort has been made to be as faithful to the Chinese texts as possible although overly long paragraphs have been broken up. Square brackets have been used for editors' notes, when supplying information such as dates not in the actual text, and to convey meaning that is clearly implied but not explicitly stated. When deletions are made by the editors a note is provided briefly summarizing what has been left out; all other deletions are in the original texts. As there are frequent references to the original 1955 documents in Documents 4 and 5, a consistent practice was adopted to avoid unnecessary repetition while at the same time retaining the integrity of the party history texts. The practice was to delete and cross reference in the 1955 documents only passages that are quoted exactly rather than paraphrased, and only in cases where very substantial and easily identified sections of the original document are used.

Finally, the editors would like to thank the Australian Research Council and the Ian Potter Foundation for supporting the research on which this translation project is based.

Notes

1. Longstanding examples are Kenneth R. Walker, "Collectivisation in Retrospect: The 'Socialist High Tide' of Autumn 1955-Spring 1956," *The China Quarterly* (*CQ*), no. 26 (1966); Thomas P. Bernstein, "Leadership and Mass Mobilization in the Soviet and Chinese Collectivisation Campaigns of 1929-30 and 1955-56: A Comparison," *CQ*, no. 31 (1967); and (somewhat more recently) Vivienne Shue, *Peasant China in Transition: The Dynamics of Development toward Socialism, 1949-1956* (Berkeley: University of California Press, 1980).

2. Studies from the Maoist era briefly questioning this interpretation on the basis of restricted evidence are Frederick C. Teiwes, "Provincial Politics in China: Themes and Variations," in John M. H. Lindbeck, ed., *China: Management of a Revolutionary Society* (Seattle: University of Washington Press, 1971), pp. 140-44; and idem, "Chinese Politics 1949-1965: A Changing Mao," part II, *Current Scene*, February 1974, pp. 7-9.

3. For example, see Qiang Yuangan and Lin Bangguan, "Shilun yijiuwuwu nian dangnei guanyu nongye hezuohua wenti de zhenglun" (A discussion of the debate within the party in 1955 concerning the question of agricultural cooperativization), *Dangshi yanjiu* (Research on party history), no. 1 (1981).

4. The major effort to reassess the debate is Frederick C. Teiwes, "Establishment and Consolidation of the New Regime," in Roderick MacFarquhar and John K. Fairbank, eds., *The Cambridge History of China*, vol. 14 (Cambridge: Cambridge University Press, 1987), pp. 110-19, largely on the basis of the source in note 3. While capturing essential aspects of the political process, this study is significantly limited by its sources and misleading on key points.

5. While not every account follows the below in every detail, it is a fair summary of the accepted argument. Undoubtedly the two most detailed statements of the standard view are Parris H. Chang, *Power and Policy in China* (University Park: The Pennsylvania State University Press, 1975), pp. 10-17; and Maurice Meisner, *Mao's China and After: A History of the People's Republic* (New York: The Free Press, 1986), chapter 10. Neither of these analyses is based on sustained primary research; Chang's treatment is basically background to the main focus of his study while Meisner's book is a broad-gauged thematic history.

6. Informative articles on the 1955 debate in addition to that cited in note 3 include Bian Ruqun and Han Sheng, " 'Ting, suo, fa' fangzhen yu nongye hezuohua de yichang bianlun" (The "stop, shrink, develop" policy and the debate on agricultural cooperativization), *Dangshi yanjiu*

ziliao (Research materials on party history), no. 5 (1981); Wang Shuixiang et al., "Nongye hezuohua yundongzhong Zhejiang guanche 'jianjue shousuo' fangzhen chutan" (A preliminary exploration of Zhejiang's implementation of the "resolute contraction" policy during the agricultural cooperativization movement), *Dangshi yanjiu ziliao*, no. 1 (1985); and Chen Wei, "Deng Zihui Tongzhi dui nongye hezuohua de gongxian" (Comrade Deng Zihui's contributions to agricultural cooperativization), *Dangshi ziliao tongxun* (Party history materials bulletin), no. 23 (1982). An invaluable recent collection of Mao's writings from the period including new references to the APC question is *Jianguo yilai Mao Zedong wengao* (Mao Zedong's manuscripts since the founding of the state), vol. 4 (January 1953–December 1954) and vol. 5 (January–December 1955) (Beijing: Zhongyang wenxian chubanshe, 1990, 1991), while an extensive documentary collection on cooperativization is *Nongye jitihua zhongyao wenjian huibian* (A collection of important documents on agricultural collectivization), vol. I (Beijing: Guojia nongye weiyuanhui bangongting, 1981). Official chronologies are of great use in piecing together developments. See Ma Qibin, et al., *Zhongguo Gongchandang zhizheng sishinian (1949–1989)* (The CCP's forty years in power, 1949–1989) (Beijing: Zhonggong dangshi ziliao chubanshe, 1989); Party History Research Center of the Central Committee of the Chinese Communist Party, comp., *History of the Chinese Communist Party—A Chronology of Events (1919–1990)* (Beijing: Foreign Languages Press, 1991); and He Ping, ed., *Mao Zedong dacidian* (Dictionary of Mao Zedong) (Beijing: Zhongguo guoji guangbo chubanshe, 1992).

7. From 1986 to 1992, and especially since 1989, more than a dozen individuals were interviewed concerning the cooperativization issue.

8. *Selected Works of Mao Tsetung (SW)*, vol. V (Peking: Foreign Languages Press, 1977), p. 29.

9. On these events, see Frederick C. Teiwes, *Politics at Mao's Court: Gao Gang and Party Factionalism in the Early 1950s* (Armonk: M. E. Sharpe, 1990), pp. 42–43; and Document 1, pp. 53–54.

Collectivization and cooperativization refer to the same process of the socialist transformation of agriculture that involved three stages. The initial stage of mutual aid teams involved peasants pooling their labor while retaining ownership rights over land and other productive forces; next came elementary or lower stage APCs where productive property was controlled by the cooperative but each peasant received a dividend according to the relative contribution land, tools, and animals; and the final form was the advanced or higher stage APC (the full collective) where the dividend was abolished and payment was strictly according to labor.

10. While we have found no source indicating such a conflict, it should be noted that in May 1952 Gao Gang's Northeast Bureau introduced a somewhat strident note in attacking spontaneous rural capitalism. See *Nongye jitihua*, I, 64–70. This evidence suggests that Gao may have had a more leftist view on cooperativization than could be discerned when *Politics at Mao's Court* was written. In any case, the party center endorsed the Northeast Bureau's views.

11. *SW*, V, 91. See also Teiwes, *Politics at Mao's Court*, p. 43.

12. For an overview of these developments, see Teiwes, *Politics at Mao's Court*, pp. 43, 87–91.

13. See the analysis of Walker, "Collectivisation," pp. 6–8. This was a long-term consideration as immediate plans focused on lower stage APCs but it was significant for cadres' general understanding. The new documentary evidence supports Walker as mechanization is barely raised in the debate. Nevertheless, while it was accepted that progress could be made toward full collectives, it was still the case, acknowledged by Mao even in July 1955 (see *SW*, V, 203), that the completion of collectivization would be coordinated with mechanization. There were, however, differences between Mao and Deng in 1955 over how closely the overall speed of cooperativization should be tailored to objective factors such as the pace of industrialization; see Document 5, part II.

14. See Deng's statements of April 1, July 15, and September 10, 1954, in *Current Background (CB)*, nos. 305, 306, and 320 (1954–55).

15. While there is no direct evidence of Mao's involvement with the January documents, oral sources believe that he must have seen them. This is persuasive given the fact that Mao "really cared about APCs" and bureaucratic procedures since 1953 required all central documents to be sent to Mao for vetting when he was not on leave (see *SW*, V, 92). In this case Mao had revised a document concerning the October 1954 cooperativization conference on

December 30; see *Mao wengao*, v. 4, pp. 641–43.

16. See Document 4, pp. 95–96; and Document 5, p. 125.

17. Document 5, pp. 146–47, 149–51.

18. See Document 4, pp. 95–98; and Document 5, pp. 125–28.

19. Document 4, p. 99.

20. Document 5, pp. 151–53. For an excellent analysis of the grain issue, see Thomas P. Bernstein, "Cadre and Peasant Behavior Under Conditions of Insecurity and Deprivation: The Grain Supply Crisis of the Spring of 1955," in A. Doak Barnett, ed., *Chinese Communist Politics in Action* (Seattle: University of Washington Press, 1969).

21. See Document 5, p. 129. Mao's account, that the warning came in April, gains some indirect support from Tan Zhenlin's claim that he (Tan) gave this same warning to Deng on May 1; see Jin Ye, ed., *Huiyi Tan Zhenlin* (Remember Tan Zhenlin) (Hangzhou: Zhejiang renmin chubanshe, 1992), pp. 533–34. Tan would have been unlikely to do this on his own, but it is conceivable that he picked up the view from Mao before Mao personally conveyed it to Deng.

22. Document 5, p. 133.

23. Document 4, p. 103; and Document 5, p. 148.

24. Document 5, pp. 148–49, 153; Document 13; and Bian Ruqun and Han Sheng (note 6), p. 703.

25. Document 5, p. 134; and Bian Ruqun and Han Sheng (note 6), p. 703.

26. Tan's ties to Mao went back to the 1927 Autumn Harvest Uprising and, according to an authoritative oral source, he regarded himself as "Mao's man."

27. The center in this case apparently was not Mao since this comment is not included in *Mao wengao*, vol. 5. Given Mao's intense interest in cooperativization at the time, however, it is unlikely the comment escaped his notice.

28. Document 4, pp. 104–105; and Document 5, pp. 134–35.

29. Quan Yanchi, *Zouxian shentande Mao Zedong* (Mao Zedong who became a God) (Beijing: Zhongwai wenhua chubangongsi, 1989), pp. 204–206; Document 4, p. 107; and Document 5, pp. 136, 142–43. Deng's recalcitrant behavior continued right up to July 31. After the July 11 confrontation he prepared a draft speech elaborating his views, apparently for the July 31 conference; Document 5, p. 142.

30. *Mao wengao*, vol. 5, pp. 222–23, and oral source.

31. According to a source who was a junior official in Mao's office at the time, in mid-July Mao met with a small number of people including most if not all top central leaders. Another oral source reported that accessible central archives contain no documents dealing with the views of these leaders in the period from the June 14 Politburo meeting to Mao's July 31 report.

32. At the provincial level, as late as July 28 Zhejiang leader Lin Hujia reported that the policy of "resolute contraction" had been correct even though shortcomings had occurred. At the central level, although the speeches of Chen Yun and Liao Luyan to the National People's Congress in late July were notable for their strident defense of cooperatives, Liao spoke matter-of-factly about the elimination of APCs from a text approved by Mao (see *Mao wengao*, V, 222–23) while Chen still affirmed Mao's earlier 33 percent target for households in APCs by the end of 1957 even as the chairman decided on a new 50 percent target. See Document 5, pp. 128–29, 131; and *CB*, nos. 339 (1955), pp. 9, 11–12, and 352 (1955), pp. 4–8.

33. In September Mao claimed that "there is still a lack of unity of will within the party" on cooperativization (*SW*, V, 238), but this almost certainly referred to lingering doubts about the policy rather than political opposition.

34. See Walker, "Collectivisation," pp. 30ff; and Teiwes, "Establishment," pp. 115–17. The treatment by the latter study (p. 115) of Mao's May speech rather than the July 31 report as decisive is clearly mistaken.

35. *SW*, V, 184, 201.

36. Document 5, p. 137.

37. See Teiwes, "Provincial Politics," pp. 142–43.

38. Document 5, pp. 137–40. For all the harsh words, however, Deng was still treated more leniently than the rhetoric implied with Mao declaring during the October plenum that the Politburo considered his self-criticism at the session satisfactory, and no further action was taken. See *SW*, V, 224.

39. Dong Bian et al., *Mao Zedong he tade mishu Tian Jiaying* (Mao Zedong and his secretary Tian Jiaying) (Beijing: Zhongyang wenxian chubanshe, 1990), p. 24.

40. Document 4, p. 107.

41. See Teiwes, *Politics at Mao's Court*, especially the Conclusion.

42. Document 5, p. 153.

43. Ibid., pp. 144–45.

44. This point was made in the important 1980 report by Liao Gailong (Liao Kai-lung), "Historical Experiences and Our Road of Development," Part I, *Issues & Studies*, October 1981, p. 77; see also Document 5, p. 122. However, the significance of this event in the degeneration of Mao's leadership style is somewhat obscured by the official view that he "gave full play to democracy" from 1935 to 1957; Liao, Part II, *Issues & Studies*, November 1981, pp. 91–92. For an overview of arbitrariness in Mao's leadership style, see Frederick C. Teiwes, "Mao and His Lieutenants," *The Australian Journal of Chinese Affairs*, no. 19–20 (1988).

45. In particular his ahistorical criticisms of Liu Shaoqi and harsh denunciation of Bo Yibo; see Teiwes, *Politics at Mao's Court*, pp. 41–44, 62–70.

46. See Document 4, pp. 107–108.

47. Ibid., p. 112.

48. The difficulties other leaders faced in coming to terms with Mao's ambiguous behavior over the entire 1949–65 period is a major theme of the new introduction to Frederick C. Teiwes, *Politics and Purges in China: Rectification and the Decline of Party Norms 1950–1965*, 2nd ed. (Armonk: M. E. Sharpe, 1993).

49. The new introduction to ibid. provides an overview of the changing state of inner party democracy before the Cultural Revolution.

50. Especially concerning Bo Yibo's new tax system; Teiwes, *Politics at Mao's Court*, pp. 62ff.

51. This is the assessment of an authoritative oral source; cf. Teiwes, "Mao and His Lieutenants," pp. 13–15.

52. Stuart Schram, ed., *Mao Tse-tung Unrehearsed, Talks and Letters: 1956–71*, p. 122; and *Xinhua yuebao* (New China monthly), no. 12 (1955), p. 160.

53. While Deng's biographer attempts to downplay his responsibility (see Document 3, pp. 76–79), both Deng's self-criticism during the 1955 rural work conference (Document 11, pp. 173–77) and the department's activities in 1954 (see Chronology of Events, pp. 33–34) indicate his activist role.

54. Mao claimed in September 1955 that Deng refused to listen to "*slightly* different opinions at [his] department" (Document 5, p. 139 [emphasis added]), but oral sources know of no evidence of significant differences among any of the leading figures in the department. One such source said there was some indication that Mao's reference was to the head of an office (*chu*).

55. Oral sources believe that all top leaders backed the early 1955 policy. According to one senior party historian, however, although supportive, Chen Yun played a lesser role due to ill health than that asserted in Teiwes, "Establishment," p. 114, a view supported by Chen's virtual absence from the documents in this collection.

56. While both Deng and Tan joined the CCP in 1926 and played important roles in the Jiangxi phase of the revolution, the older (by six years) Deng clearly had higher status when the PRC was established as reflected in his selection by Mao in 1952 as one of the twenty-one most significant party leaders. See Teiwes, *Politics at Mao's Court*, pp. 98–101.

57. Document 5, p. 148.

58. One oral source with access to the central archives noted the absence of planning commission submissions in relevant documents. While a January-February planning conference and Li Fuchun's early July report on the First Five-Year Plan did discuss cooperativization (see Ma Qibin et al., *Zhizheng sishinian*, p. 89; and *CB*, no. 335 (1955), pp. 19, 31–32), our source believes such instances were restatements of overall regime policy rather than an institutional position.

59. The sole exception is Bo's reference to his unduly harsh criticism of Deng at the October Central Committee plenum; Document 5, p. 139.

60. This is the editors' own observation based to a substantial extent on leadership behavior during the Gao Gang affair. See Teiwes, *Politics at Mao's Court*, pp. 45–47, 144ff and passim.

61. Another party historian, however, felt that personal relations only became a major inhibiting factor from the late 1950s, i.e., when Mao's behavior began to undermine more significantly inner-party democracy.

62. See Ma Qibin et al., *Zhizheng sishinian*, pp. 61–62. Another oral source specializing in

Zhou Enlai, however, believes that the abolition of this organ made little difference as it was seldom used when it existed.

63. Following the dissolution of the great regions in 1954–55 only one regional party bureau was left, the Shanghai Bureau that replaced the old East China Bureau. The reasons for the continued existence of this body are unclear.

64. Document 4, pp. 95–96; and Document 5, pp. 125, 131–32. It should be noted that the poor response here and elsewhere may have been related to the comparatively low-key manner in that the call for consolidation was made and the seeming emphasis on persuasion. Thus Shandong, Henan, and Hebei reportedly "willingly reduced [their targets] after consultation with us"; Document 6, p. 156.

65. The source in question based his views primarily on the circulars of provincial conferences that were much more revealing about local sentiment than provincial reports to the center.

66. Document 5, p. 125. This reaction is understandable in light of Rao's alleged rightist mistakes on rural policy; see Teiwes, *Politics at Mao's Court*, p. 269.

67. See Teiwes, "Provincial Politics," p. 142; and Document 4, pp. 116–17. Ironically, however, Guangdong leader Tao Zhu subsequently became a very radical figure during the Great Leap and also in the 1962–66 period.

68. See Teiwes, *Politics and Purges*, pp. 307, 309n, 367.

69. See Document 4, pp. 86–88.

70. Document 5, p. 154.

71. This proposition was put to a senior party historian who demurred by saying that cooperativization would have sped up in any case. But the point, although necessarily hypothetical, is that the political packaging of the new upsurge was decisive to what occurred, and without Deng confronting Mao it is unlikely the chairman would have felt such packaging was required.

72. Document 5, p. 149.

73. See Ibid., pp. 130–31.

74. The documents have come from two collections. Documents 7, 8, 9, 10, and 13 appeared in *Dang de wenxian* (The party's documents), no. 1, (1989) pp. 19–28, while the remainder were taken from the party history study collection compiled by Zhongguo Jiefangjun Guofang Daxue dangshi dangjian zhenggong jiaoyanshi (The party history, party building, and political work teaching and research office of the national defense university of the Chinese People's Liberation Army), *Zhonggong dangshi jiaoxue cankao ziliao* (CCP history teaching reference materials), vol. 20 (April 1956), pp. 478, 545–50, 569–74, 600–601, vol. 21 (April 1986), pp. 32–33, 60–69, 88–92, 97–100.

75. Deng's speech to the National Party Conference can be found in *Dangshi cankao ziliao*, vol. 20, pp. 526–31. A few additional central documents of lesser significance and further provincial reports from August-September (most of which are excerpted in Document 4, pp. 111–13), are collected in *Nongye jitihua*, vol. I. Some of these same documents and other relevant pieces are in *Mao wengao*, vol. 5.

Chronology of Events

1949

March 5–13

The Second Plenary Session of the Seventh Central Committee called for the development of collectivized agriculture but in a cautious and gradual way that recognized that individual farming would play a key role for a relatively long period of time.

1950

June 6–9

The Third Plenary Session of the Seventh Central Committee reaffirmed the gradual approach to rural change and emphasized completing land reform. It stressed individual farming for restoring production as graphically illustrated by Mao Zedong advocating "maintaining the rich peasant economy."

June 14–23

The Chinese People's Political Consultative Conference endorsed Liu Shaoqi's "Report on the Question of Land Reform" and the draft land reform law. These documents implemented Mao's views on supporting the "rich peasant economy" and declared the main aim of land reform to be "freeing the rural productive forces" rather than assisting the poor.

1951

April 17

The Shanxi Provincial Committee proposed to the party center "upgrading mutual aid and cooperative organizations in old liberated are as" to the form of APCs in order to "keep in check the spontaneous tendency of the peasants toward capitalism."

July 3 and 5

Liu Shaoqi twice criticized the Shanxi document, saying "such a view is agrarian socialist thought that is mistaken, dangerous, and utopian." Mao *subsequently* endorsed the Shanxi view and indicated displeasure with Liu.

September 20–30

The party center convened the First National Mutual Aid and Cooperation Conference. The conference passed the "Resolution on Mutual Aid and Cooperativization in Agriculture (Draft)" that set a target of having 40 percent of the rural population "organized" largely into mutual aid teams by the end of 1952. While implicitly critical of Liu Shaoqi, the resolution still recognized the importance of individual farming and did not endorse a direct leap from mutual aid teams to full-scale collectives. Instead, it approved an intermediate step of semisocialist lower stage cooperatives devised by Mao where the land and means of production were still owned by private peasants but used collectively.

December 15

The above document was distributed to party committees at various levels for trial implementation.

1952

May 10

The center issued a report by Gao Gang's Northeast Bureau that warned that, if unchecked, "the spontaneous development of capitalism" fostered by the individual peasant economy would "lead to a capitalist future."

October 6–21

The Ministry of Agriculture convened the National Agricultural Work Conference that demanded that 60 percent of the rural population be "organized" by the end of 1953.

November 12

The party center decided to establish the Rural Work Department under the center.

1953

Early January

Deng Zihui arrived in Beijing and was asked by Mao to take up the appointment of director of the new Rural Work Department.

January 31

North China party Leader Liu Lantao in a letter to lower levels criticized the tendency of "rash advance" as manifested in striving for more and larger cooperatives. This was followed on March 2 by a North China Bureau directive requiring correction of the tendency.

February 15

The "Resolution on Mutual Aid and Cooperativization in Agriculture" was formally approved by the Central Committee following a year's trial implementation and a few amendments of the 1951 draft. It stipulated that the approach to be used in the socialist transformation of agriculture was one of step-by-step advance. It also pointed out that any leftist tendency to impetuosity and rash advance would be regarded as an adventurist mistake.

March 8

The party center issued an instruction to the large administrative regions requiring local authorities to curb rash advance in mutual aid and cooperativization.

March 16

The party center issued an instruction on spring plowing and production to various party committees drafted by Deng Zihui. Its main thrust was to rectify the increasingly rash and impetuous tendency and protect the interests of private farmers.

March 19

Mao drafted an inner-party directive criticizing the "five excesses" of too many assignments, meetings, documents, etc., which warned against excessive interference in the small peasant economy that was "vastly different from the mechanized collective farming of the Soviet Union."

April 3

The party center compiled and distributed throughout the country a *Guide to Present Rural Work* that included the cautious directives of the previous months. Mao prepared a circular calling for conscientious study of the book.

April 3–23

The Rural Work Department convened the First National Rural Work Conference. In his concluding report, Deng stated that the impetuosity and rash advance that had spread nationwide was the principal deviation and hence the main danger to rural work. In order to rectify the situation, Deng advocated steady advance and, with considerable qualification, called for the protection of private property including the freedom to rent land, hire labor, loan money, and engage in private trade.

Spring

In the course of combating rash advance, more than 2,100 of 5,800 APCs in Hebei Province were disbanded. In the same period a considerably smaller number of "spontaneous" cooperatives in Zhejiang were banned. By the end of 1953 Deng was held responsible for such "mistakes."

June 15

On the eve of the National Financial and Economic Conference, Mao put forward the general line for the transition period that set out to achieve the three big socialist transformations of agriculture, handicrafts, and capitalist industry and commerce within ten to fifteen years or an even longer period of time. He was critical of both leftist and rightist deviations that departed from the general line, but stressed that the party's central task in the agricultural sphere was to develop the mutual aid and cooperativization movement.

July 2

In a speech to the Second Congress of the Youth League, Deng reflected Mao's formulation of the general line by arguing the need to limit development of the small peasant economy and place restrictions on rich peasants, while at the same time continuing to warn against adventurism.

August 12

During his harsh criticism of Minister of Finance Bo Yibo's "bourgeois ideology" concerning tax policy at the close of the National Finance and Economic Conference, Mao also attacked Bo's June 1951 argument that achieving full collectivization through mutual aid and cooperativization was "pure illusion," an attack that by implication touched Liu Shaoqi given Liu's comments on the Shanxi cooperatives in the same period.

September 26

The Central Rural Work Department approved and circulated an investigative report on villages in central Suiyuan made during the summer by the Rural Work Department of Gao Gang's Northeast Bureau. The report declared the struggle between the spontaneous capitalism of private peasant producers and the mutual aid and cooperativization movement was the main rural contradiction.

October 4

A party center notice transmitting a July 3 report by the North China Bureau affirmed that the policy of eliminating rash advance that had been pushed by Deng Zihui was important and timely. It commented, however, that rightist thinking emerged in some places during the campaign against leftism with the result that some APCs were unnecessarily "blown away."

October 15–November 4

Before and during the Third National Mutual Aid and Cooperation Conference convened by the party center from October 26 to November 5, Mao talked to leading members of the Rural Work Department emphasizing that mutual aid and cooperativization was a matter of vital importance and if socialism did not occupy rural positions capitalism inevitably would. On October 15, during a talk with Deputy Director Liao Luyan and other departmental leaders, he criticized the policies of the "four big freedoms" of renting land, hiring labor, etc., and "sustaining private property" that had been emphasized in the immediate post-1949 period and were now somewhat disingenuously linked to Deng's early 1953 program. Deng was outside Beijing at this time and he remained away from the capital during the conference on cooperativization, altogether spending two months in the October-December period carrying out rural investigations.

In a second talk on November 4, Mao once again demonstrated his displeasure with Deng's department that assertedly was not working for socialism but only interested in giving small favors to the peasants. He stated that "Rash advance is wrong, failure to set up cooperatives where they can be set up is also wrong, and forcible dissolution of cooperatives is even worse." Mao thus urged quickening the pace of cooperativization by demanding a target of 32,000 APCs by fall 1954, an increase from the existing 14,000, and also a target of 700,000 by the end of the First Five-Year Plan. The conference took heed of Mao's view by passing the "Resolution on the Development of APCs" that set an even higher target: 35,000 APCs by fall 1954 and 800,000 by the end of the First Five-Year Plan.

Later

With inner-party criticism launched as a result of Mao's displeasure, Deng made a careful self-criticism presumably in late 1953 or possibly early 1954, but he reportedly felt that he had not made any serious mistakes.

December 16

The above-mentioned "Resolution on the Development of APCs" together with the new target was formally approved by the Politburo.

1954

February 12

The Central Rural Work Department reported to the center, which endorsed and distributed the report a month later, on two problems in cooperativization: (1) overestimation of mass enthusiasm and rash approval of new APCs; and (2) overemphasis on control figures in original plans that resulted in the failure to approve APCs where sufficient conditions existed.

March 20

The Central Rural Work Department issued a circular declaring that after the expansion since winter 1953 the most important task of mutual aid and cooperativization was to consolidate the movement and shift work to production during spring plowing.

April 2–18

The Central Rural Work Department convened the Second National Rural Work Conference. The conference considered the expansion of cooperatives from 14,000 to 90,000 in winter 1953 and spring 1954 a great achievement and revised targets upward to 300,000 to 350,000 for 1955 and 1.3 to 1.5 million for 1957. At the conference Deng affirmed the correctness of rectifying rash advance in spring 1953. On the eve of the conference and presumably during the conference itself, however, he admitted that in some areas an overzealous implementation had produced rash retreat. Now both left and right deviations required rectification.

June 3

The party center approved the "Report of the Second National Rural Work

Conference" that called for "relying on the greater development of cooperatives," a step regarded as integral to "increasing agricultural production in order to keep in step with industrial development."

July 15

In a speech to a rural work conference convened by the Youth League, Deng reported that local plans indicated even higher targets of 600,000-plus APCs by spring 1955, 1.5 million by 1956, and 3 million by 1957.

September 15-28

At the first session of the First National People's Congress, Deng was appointed vice premier and head of the Seventh Office under the State Council responsible for agriculture.

October 10-31

The Central Rural Work Department convened the Fourth National Mutual Aid and Cooperation Conference that agreed on the target of basically completing the transition to lower stage APCs (i.e., incorporating 70–80 percent of the rural population) by the end of the First Five-Year Plan; higher stage cooperativization would only be pursued during the Second Five-Year Plan. The immediate target by spring 1955 was confirmed as 600,000 APCs.

December

A Ministry of Commerce circular called attention to the massive sale of livestock by peasants apparently unnerved by the rapid expansion of APCs and excessive grain purchases by the state. In the same period local reports pointed to the same phenomenon and the large scale killing of farm animals.

December 30

The party center approved and distributed the report and targets of the Fourth National Mutual Aid and Cooperation Conference. In its comment the center proposed the class line of "relying on the poor peasants and firmly uniting with the middle peasants so as to limit step by step and eventually eliminate exploitation."

Mao gave attention to middle peasant interests in personally revising this document.

1955

Ca. January 1

Deng reported to Liu Shaoqi concerning the tense rural situation and the grievances of the rural population.

January 4

Deng wrote to Zhou Enlai expressing great doubt about the approved target. Accordingly he proposed that the cooperativization movement should now shift to a stage of consolidation and controlled development. Deng's proposal was quickly accepted by the Politburo.

January 10

The party center issued a "Circular on Overhauling and Consolidating APCs" signed by Liu Shaoqi that adopted proposals drafted by Deng. These included calling on areas that had overfulfilled their targets to stop development, and areas where preparations had been inadequate such as Zhejiang and Hebei to reduce the number of cooperatives.

January 15

The party center issued an "Urgent Directive on Making Great Efforts to Protect Farm Animals."

February 8

In his concluding remarks at the Second National Planning Conference (January 6–February 8) State Planning Commission Chairman Li Fuchun lowered the target for APCs to 2.05 million by the end of the First Five-Year Plan, i.e., 50 percent of all peasant households in contrast to the former 70–80 percent target, while achieving the target of 600,000 APCs was to be delayed to the end of the year.

February 9

The Shanghai Bureau of the Central Committee headed by Ke Qingshi reported on the serious situation in Zhejiang and recommended that Zhejiang should stop advancing for a while in order to do a good job of consolidating and overhauling cooperatives.

However, in subsequent weeks APC expansion was even more rapid in Zhejiang.

February 25

The party center issued a "Directive Concerning the Problem of Implementing the Socialist Transformation of Agriculture in Minority Nationality Regions." It stipulated "taking more time and adopting a prudent and gradual approach" while criticizing the rash practice of "keeping abreast with the Han areas."

February 28

A *People's Daily* editorial, "Why Should We Pay Great Attention to APC Consolidation Work?," called for overcoming the prevailing view of "emphasizing development while ignoring consolidation."

March 3

The party center and State Council jointly issued an "Urgent Directive on Prompt Assignment of Grain Purchase Work and Stabilizing the Peasants' Production Spirit" that was signed by Mao. This instruction was based on the recommendations of the National Planning Conference to (1) implement a three fix policy of fixed quotas for the production, purchasing, and marketing of grain; and (2) set the moderate grain target of 90 billion jin for the financial year's unified purchase. It also called for slowing down the pace of cooperativization.

Same day

The State Council agreed with Liao Luyan's "Report on the State of Affairs in Agricultural Production in 1954 and Present Measures for Boosting Agricultural Production." Liao pointed out the lack of comprehensive planning and the lack of precision in previous agricultural planning.

About the same time

Mao sought out Deng individually for a talk concerning the pace of agricultural cooperativization in which he proposed that [only] 33 percent of peasant households be organized into APCs by the end of the First Five-Year Plan. This seemingly caught Deng by surprise and he reaffirmed the target of 50 percent set the previous month. Mao immediately disagreed by commenting that the target of 90 billion jin of grain for unified purchase was already "reaching to the limit," an apparent comment on the tense situation caused by the grain shortage. Mao insisted on the 33 percent target by the end of the plan period, a view Deng would hail in early May as an example of "Chairman Mao's foresight."

Afterward

Liu Shaoqi held a talk with Deng and proposed increasing the proportion of peasant households in cooperatives to one-third during the First Five-Year Plan, then adding another third in the Second Five-Year Plan and the final third in the Third Five-Year Plan.

March 5

Mao wrote to the Hebei Provincial Committee expressing concern about coercion and commandism in the cooperativization movement.

Mid-March

After listening to a work report by Rural Work Department leaders Deng Zihui, Chen Boda, Liao Luyan, and Du Runsheng, Mao gave an instruction, namely the famous three-word policy of "stop, shrink, develop" that placed the emphasis on consolidation, and observed that tensions in the countryside reflected rebellion of the productive forces that should be accommodated. Then or soon after Mao agreed to the contraction of APCs in Zhejiang and Hebei.

Shortly afterward

Sometime before the end of March Mao told Tan Zhenlin, head of the Second Office of the Central Secretariat responsible for agriculture, "to stop developing cooperatives until October 1956."

March 21–31

The National Party Representative Conference was held in Beijing. Mao gave the opening speech reasserting that it would take three five-year plans to achieve the step-by-step socialist transformation of agriculture, while Liu Shaoqi called in responsible delegates to emphasize that consolidation was the key issue. Deng's address to the conference stressed the policy of fewer but better cooperatives. He also declared the following targets that were presumably adjusted in light of Mao's most recent instruction: 800,000 APCs in 1955–56 that meant 21 percent of all peasant households; 1.2 million in 1956–57 that meant 35 percent of peasant households roughly by the end of the First Five-Year Plan; and to achieve the basic completion of semi-socialist cooperation by 1960, i.e., 70–80 percent of households.

March 22

The Central Rural Work Department issued a "Circular on Consolidating Existing Cooperatives" that stipulated that no new APCs should be set up regardless of locality and all efforts should focus on consolidation and spring plowing.

March 24–25

On the basis of a study meeting on the Zhejiang issue convened jointly with Tan Zhenlin to which provincial First Secretary Jiang Hua, who was then in Beijing, was invited, Deng recommended cutting down the number of APCs in Zhejiang presumably reflecting his understanding of Mao's position. To make sure of Mao's stand Deng further sought his approval through Chen Boda, concurrently Mao's secretary. Mao's agreement came through Chen's telephone message, and on March 25 Deng's instruction was issued in the form of a telegram to the Zhejiang Provincial Committee. The indirectness of this procedure seemingly left room for Mao's subsequent denial that the center had sanctioned the move. Apparently for this reason both the party center and the Zhejiang Provincial Committee were later spared blame.

April 1

Deng led a delegation to celebrations of the tenth anniversary of Hungary's liberation. During his absence Tan Zhenlin was put in charge of dealing with the Zhejiang issue. In a joint meeting of the Second Office of the Secretariat and the Central Rural work Department, Tan decided to send Du Runsheng and Yuan Chenglong to Zhejiang to make sure the policy of contraction was properly absorbed. Tan also suggested dissolving 17,000 APCs which was 2,000 more than the eventual contraction in Zhejiang.

April 4

The Fifth Plenary Session of the Seventh Central Committee entrusted the Politburo with appropriately revising the target set in the First Five-Year Plan. This resulted in Li Fuchun's July report that set the lower target of 33 percent of peasant households in cooperatives by the end of the plan period, obviously in line with Mao's March demand.

April 8

During a meeting called by Zhejiang Party Secretary Huo Shilian to "carry out thoroughly the instruction of the higher level," Du Runsheng reported on the policy of "all efforts to consolidation and resolute contraction" and exhorted the local cadres "to get off the horse quickly."

April 11

Du Runsheng and Yuan Chenglong telegraphed the Secretariat and Central Rural Work Department on the Zhejiang question calling for "resolute contraction" and "getting off the horse." Afterwards the Zhejiang Provincial Committee "unanimously" agreed and convened a cadre conference to assign the necessary work, Du returned to Beijing to obtain Tan Zhenlin's approval for contraction, and Jiang Hua phoned his Zhejiang subordinates from Beijing urging them to curb rash advance.

April 12

The party center approved Li Fuchun's February report on the First Five-Year Plan that contained the 50 percent target for peasant households in cooperatives by the end of the plan period.

April and May

Mao made several inspection tours particularly in the south to examine the cooperative movement. In view of the enthusiastic sentiments expressed by local officials, Mao began to have a more positive view of cooperativization than that reflected in current policy.

Shanghai Bureau Secretary Ko Qingshi, presumably during one of these southern tours, made the allegation to Mao that 30 percent of party cadres including senior officials were unwilling to pursue socialism and took the stand of middle peasants.

April 19

In a meeting with Deng, Liu Shaoqi indicated the need to dissolve 100,000 APCs on a nationwide basis.

April 20

Liu chaired a Secretariat meeting at which he pointed out that the general principle for the period from now on up to one year was to "stop the development of cooperatives and devote all efforts to consolidation." He stated that "Except in some individual districts, all expansion should come to a halt. After the fall we will review the situation again." Liu also remarked that "it would be the greatest victory if 500,000 APCs of the existing 670,000 were consolidated" and "it would be all right to have less than 400,000," thus implying that he would allow 170,000 or even 270,000 cooperatives to be dissolved on a national scale.

Same evening

Deng personally reported to Mao and made the assessment that the unhealthy development of the cooperativization movement was the fundamental cause of the tense situation in the countryside, a statement that Mao refuted the following month.

April 21–May 7

The Central Rural Work Department convened the Third National Rural Work Conference that emphasized all-out efforts to consolidate APCs pending further decisions in the fall.

In his opening speech Deng made a self-criticism for the overambitious target of 600,000 APCs made in the previous year and also claimed to have misinterpreted Mao's view on the role of the middle peasants to their disadvantage—an interpretation Mao later treated dismissively. At the close of the conference Deng's concluding report again articulated the cautious approach.

During the conference, Deng also relayed Liu Shaoqi's message that consolidating 500,000 APCs would be the greatest victory, yet he proposed a more modest target of only 50,000 to 100,000 APCs for reduction.

April 23

Liu Shaoqi called in provincial leaders telling them that "the pace of cooperativization simply can't be pushed any quicker; to maintain last year's pace is most dangerous."

Late April

On the basis of reports concerning cases where grain shortages were due to false claims by well-to-do peasants, Mao and the party center took several measures including an April 28 "Directive on Grasping Firmly Monopoly Grain Sale Work" to overhaul grain work. Such reports, together with the results of his own investigation trips and the dramatic decline in grain sales following overhauling, led Mao to believe Deng's estimation of tensions in the countryside had been overstated.

In this same general period various nonparty figures expressed concern about the bitter life of the peasants, a development that sat poorly with Mao.

Late April or early May

Mao, referring to the Zhejiang situation, warned Deng "not to repeat the 1953 mistake of dissolving a large number of cooperatives."

May 1

Both Mao and Deng attended the May Day parade at Tiananmen along with other leaders. On this occasion Tan Zhenlin repeated or foreshadowed Mao's warning not to repeat the mistake of dissolving cooperatives.

May 5 evening

Mao met with Deng. This is possibly the occasion when he warned Deng not to repeat the mistake of dissolving cooperatives.

May 6

In his summing-up to the Third National Rural Work Conference, Deng continued to urge guarding against rash advance, particularly among party cadres. He again emphasized consolidation and bolstered his argument by citing Mao's statement that expansion could stop now and stay stopped for one and one-half years.

May 8

Zhejiang Secretary Huo Shilian reported to the Central Rural Work Department by telephone on successes in consolidation work over the previous month that dispelled various leftist deviations. Huo affirmed the beneficial effect on peasant morale of the dissolution of 15,000 poorly run APCs in Zhejiang.

May 9

Mao called in Deng, Liao Luyan, Minister of Finance Li Xiannian, and Vice Minister of Grain Chen Guodong. During the discussion where Zhou Enlai was also present, Mao deplored the idea that the peasants' enthusiasm was not very high saying, "I have seen that wheat has grown to a person's waist, how can we say the peasants are slack in production." More importantly, Mao rejected completely Deng's assessment that poorly managed APCs were the main cause of the tense situation in the countryside. Instead he considered that it was caused by the grain problem that was in turn caused by the outcry of a small portion of peasants. Therefore, he called for reducing the target of grain purchase from 90 to 87 billion jin that would be "a concession made in exchange for socialism."

Mao further explored the possibility of achieving 40 percent of peasant households in cooperatives by the end of the First Five-Year Plan. On this, Deng's answer was that "last time [presumably in late March] we said one-third. It is better to stick to one-third," and Mao reluctantly replied, "All right, one-third." Yet he also commented that "the peasants want freedom but we want socialism" and "some party cadres are unwilling to carry out socialism." In this connection Mao mentioned Ke Qingshi's allegation that 30 percent of party cadres at all levels disagreed with building socialism.

May

While the exact date is not clear, most likely in early May and almost certainly before Mao's May 17 speech the party center criticized the idea of "accomplishing cooperativization in three years" in order to eliminate the individual peasant economy. This was, the party center declared, "the leftist mistake of rash advance."

This view was sharply rebuked by Mao in his end of the year notes to *Socialist Upsurge in the Chinese Countryside,* although he did not designate the party center as the source of the opinion.

May 17

Mao convened a conference of party secretaries from 15 provinces and municipalities mainly from the East China and Central-South regions. Its main agenda was to criticize "negative sentiment on the cooperativization question."

In his speech to the gathering Mao warned that "big mistakes will be made if there is no change." Although reaffirming the "stop, shrink, develop" policy, Mao clearly shifted his emphasis to development as he called for new targets totaling 340,000 APCs in seven key provinces while the meeting as a whole proposed a target of 1 million nationwide for 1956. Some provincial leaders used this occasion to air their complaints about the Central Rural Work Department, a development that increased Mao's doubts concerning the advice he had been receiving from Deng's department.

May 28

As a result of Mao's criticism, the Central Rural Work Department indicated to the party center that it would accommodate his wishes and revise afresh central documents concerning cooperativization.

June 10

Mao wrote his secretary Hu Qiaomu asking him to prepare briefing materials from information collected on the development of cooperativization in Hebei and Shanxi Provinces.

June 14

A Politburo meeting chaired by Liu Shaoqi heard a report by Deng and accordingly approved the new target of 1 million APCs by fall 1956 submitted by his department. The meeting agreed that "a big expansion should be made in the coming year" while proceeding with the consolidation of cooperatives already in existence. Yet at the same time Liu instructed that "after the cooperatives reach 1 million by next spring, we can close the door for a while. If the cooperatives are run well, middle peasants will willingly come to knock on the door [to ask to join]."

June 21

Tan Zhenlin reported on his investigation trip to Zhejiang in which he emphasized the importance of consolidation. Tan, however, noted approvingly provincial plans to develop additional cooperatives after completion of three fix grain work. Tan subsequently made a similar report on the Zhejiang situation on July 6.

Late June

Mao returned to Beijing after further investigations of APCs and invited Deng in for a talk where he said the recently agreed target of 1 million APCs seemed too small and instead proposed a target of 1.3 million for 1955–56. Deng, however, insisted on the original target approved by the Politburo and presented detailed arguments for his preference.

Shortly afterward

Mao took a two-month retreat first in Beijing and then in Beidaihe. This probably took place from early July, i.e., after his meeting with Ho Chi Minh on July 7, to August 20. The purpose of this seclusion was to investigate and study the cooperativization issue.

July 1

The party center issued a directive launching a campaign against hidden counterrevolutionaries. As the campaign subsequently unfolded counter-revolutionaries in APCs became one of its main targets.

July 5–30

The Second Session of the First National People's Congress was held. In the first two days Li Fuchun submitted the report on the First Five-Year Plan in which the long-term target by the end of the plan was still 33 percent of peasant households in APCs, but no immediate target was mentioned. On July 21 Vice Premier Chen Yun repeated the same target while at the same time harshly attacking those who claimed that cooperatives and grain work had been done badly for either having counterrevolutionary motives or having been taken in by "the clamor of landlords and rich peasants."

July 6

The party center commented on and distributed a Hebei Province directive on issues involved in overhauling APCs. The comment did not call for any further development in Hebei, one of the areas where a reduction of cooperatives had been stipulated in January, but instead emphasized the need to deal with middle peasant dissatisfaction.

July 11

Mao held a five-hour meeting with Deng, Liao Luyan, Rural Work Department Deputy Director Liu Jianxun, Du Runsheng, Tan Zhenlin, and Chen Boda in which he reiterated his opinion on further speeding up cooperativization and severely criticized Deng and others. Deng, however, stood by his views. After this conversation Deng revealed its content to colleagues in the Rural Work Department who were astonished by Deng's boldness in "offending Chairman Mao merely over hundreds of thousands of cooperatives." Deng could only smile wryly and say, "This is not a question [of numbers], what is at issue is that he thinks that [preconditions] for running cooperatives are not necessary. How could I not make myself clear?" After the confrontation with Mao, Deng further demonstrated his independence by preparing a speech, probably for delivery at the July 31 conference of party secretaries, that argued the practicality of existing plans and the need for suitable conditions for expansion.

July 18

Mao wrote to Du Runsheng requesting archives and documents from the Rural Work Department on the cooperativization issue. Mao soon concluded that Deng and his department were "rightist and short of enthusiasm," and using these materials began to draft his report "On the Question of Agricultural Cooperativization."

July 20

Tan Zhenlin's Second Office of the Secretariat received Mao's new instruction to accomplish the target of 50 percent of peasant households in APCs by the end of the First Five-Year Plan.

July 22

Mao praised the draft of Liao Luyan's speech to the National People's Congress in which Liao emphasized the importance of cooperativization to agricultural production while acknowledging the need to correct excesses in the development of the movement. Liao, like Chen Yun, also forcefully rejected the view that cooperativization had been done so badly as to damage the production enthusiasm of the peasants.

July 28

Lin Hujia, member of the Standing Committee of the Zhejiang Provincial Committee, reported by telephone on the Zhejiang APC issue to the Shanghai Bureau. Although conceding shortcomings, the report held that the policy of "resolute contraction" was correct. Shanghai Bureau Secretary Ke Qingshi relayed this report to Mao after arriving in Beijing for the new cooperativization conference of provincial secretaries. Mao ordered its distribution together with his own note that "This estimation is not correct."

July 29

Mao commented on and ordered distributed to the new conference "A Summary of the Recent Situation in the Agricultural Cooperativization Movement" that had been compiled by the Central Rural Work Department three days earlier. In his comment, Mao advocated using the "objective possibilities" of the peasants' dissatisfaction with their poverty to push cooperativization forward.

July 31

Mao convened the conference of provincial, municipal, and autonomous region secretaries on the APC question in Beijing. In his famous keynote speech, "On the Question of Agricultural Cooperativization," Mao rebuked those people who "say that last year's plan for establishing 500,000 APCs was too big and rash and so is this year's plan to set up another 350,000." Although not mentioning him by name, Deng was compared to "a woman with bound feet" who failed to realize a high tide of cooperativization was imminent.

The Rural Work Department, also not named, assertedly could only offer leadership that lagged far behind the movement.

While impatient with this state of affairs, Mao was comparatively prudent in steering a middle course between rightist and leftist tendencies and set a target no more radical than the early 1955 target of the State Planning Commission. That is to say, Mao demanded a target of 50 percent of peasant households in APCs by spring 1958 compared to the same planning commission goal by fall 1957, although for the first time a time limit (i.e., by the end of 1960) was set for basically completing the semisocialist transformation of lower stage cooperativization.

Moreover, Mao's new 1.3 million target was not presented as a formal party center decision but simply as a "provisional control figure, yet to be confirmed."

He appealed to local leaders to pursue this target saying, "I hope that on their return the responsible comrades of the various provinces and autonomous regions will look into the matter [of doubling the number of cooperatives to 1.3 million], work out approximate plans in accord with concrete conditions, and report to party center within two months. We shall then discuss the matter again and make a final decision."

After Mao's speech, Deng expressed support for the Chairman's criticism and admitted his previous policy was relatively passive.

August 1

At the conclusion of the conference of secretaries Mao declared the debate with Deng resolved and everyone at the present conference had spoken well.

August-September

Following the above conference, provinces convened meetings to relay Mao's report, check up on right-deviationist thinking, and review targets in provincial cooperativization plans that were substantially revised upwards. From August 13 to October 2 the party center circulated reports from ten provinces on these meetings together with its own comments personally drafted by Mao.

During this same period a general atmosphere of antiright conservatism developed that extended well into 1956 and affected a wide variety of fields. According to Zhou Enlai in May 1956, "we have spent eight or nine months on opposing conservatism and rightism since August last year."

August 26

Mao instructed Deng Xiaoping and Yang Shangkun, who in their positions as party secretary-general and head of the center's General Office respectively were responsible for the flow of paper, to inform the Rural Work Department that for the coming months the center would write telegrams to the localities in response to their reports on cooperativization, thus bypassing the department. This was further indicated in the same instruction by Mao's order that people should not write "to be handled by the Rural Work Department" on such documents.

The department was not completely cut out of APC policy, however. On September 1 Mao directed that Deng should be asked to handle telegrams concerning appropriations for training cooperative cadres and for agricultural credit. Most significantly, Liao Luyan played a major role in drafting model regulations for APCs that Mao heartily endorsed on September 26.

Same day

Mao wrote a circular asking that the revised version of his July 31 report be distributed to lower levels. This version added substantial new sections that largely criticized "some comrades" who used the Soviet experience to justify their "crawling thought."

August 31

In a comment on the report of the Anhui Provincial Committee, Mao praised its criticism of "right-deviationist opportunist thought" concerning cooperativization. This was the first central document to propose criticism of such thinking.

September 4

The *People's Daily* published an article written by a district party secretary entitled "It is Entirely Possible to Have More and Better Cooperatives." This was probably the first signal of Mao's new policy on cooperativization to appear in the official press.

September 7

In response to Mao's initiative, the Politburo decided to convene the Sixth Plenary Session of the Seventh Central Committee as an enlarged plenum attended by local leaders with cooperativization as the top item on the agenda. Mao's secretary Chen Boda was responsible for drafting the resolution on cooperativization to be considered at the plenum.

Same day

In commenting on the report of the Fujian Provincial Committee Mao comprehensively expounded his views on class policy, especially policy toward middle peasants. This reportedly convinced many comrades to support the acceleration of cooperativization.

September 25

Mao wrote the preface for *How to Run APCs*, a work he personally edited. In the preface he condemned the antirash advance of 1953 as well as that of spring 1955, yet he claimed that "there is still a lack of unity of will [concerning cooperativization] within the party" thereby necessitating a Central Committee plenum to sort out differences.

September 26

Mao wrote a sharp comment on a draft self-criticism prepared by Deng Zihui for the coming plenum. Mao accused Deng of "serious capitalist thinking" and having "no respect for the opinions of the center."

October 4–11

Chen Boda made the key report on cooperativization at the Sixth Plenary Session of the Seventh Central Committee. Participants made sustained criticism of rightist deviations and Deng made a self-criticism emphasizing his lack of correct class analysis that failed to distinguish well-to-do middle peasants from other middle peasants. The resolution of the plenum dismissed Deng's policies as right opportunism, approved the 1.3 million APC target, and further speeded up cooperativization by advancing the basic completion of semisocialist APCs to spring 1958, i.e., two years earlier than Mao's July proposal.

In the closing speech to the plenum on October 11 Mao described the present session as "a great debate" concerning the correctness of the party's general line and singled out by name Deng and his department as responsible for the major mistakes in rural work, refuting their views in great detail. Mao referred to these erroneous views as if the party center had nothing to do with them at any time, thus obscuring the support he and other top leaders had given Deng to varying degrees. However, in an apparent effort to reduce the tension created by the criticism at the plenum, Mao declared: "Comrade Deng Zihui has made a self-criticism. Although some comrades at group meetings felt that it was not thorough enough, we of the Politburo and other comrades have talked it over and found it satisfactory on the whole."

October 13

Mao issued a circular to party leaders calling for opinions on a third revision of his July report on cooperativization that gave additional explanations of the worker-peasant alliance among other changes.

October-November

After the Central Committee plenum a new upsurge in developing APCs took place in the provinces. The result was a new escalation of targets that had the effect of advancing the date for basically achieving semisocialist cooperativization another year and a half to the end of 1956. Moreover, by the end of 1955 the actual number of APCs exceeded 1.9 million, 600,000 more than Mao's July target.

Mid-November

Mao convened a meeting in Hangzhou with fourteen regional and provincial leaders that drafted fourteen articles on agricultural development. Shortly thereafter at a similar meeting in Tianjin this was expanded to seventeen articles.

December 6

Mao gave a talk on opposing rightism and conservatism in which he stated that the main thrust of the seventeen articles was to counteract conservatism. He also advanced the idea of "more, faster, better" results in building socialism, a slogan that in slightly expanded form was to mark efforts to "leap forward" in both early 1956 and 1958-60. Two more points are notable in this speech. First, in contrast to his long-held idea of accomplishing the socialist transformation of agriculture in eighteen years, Mao (repeating a goal he had raised on November 24) now deemed that ten years would be long enough, which meant that by the end of 1959 cooperativization of a fully socialist nature could be basically achieved. Second, if Mao had refrained from criticizing the party center before and during the October plenum, this was no longer the case. For the first time Mao directed his criticism at the center for "neglecting its duty" to keep the antirash advance campaign in check.

While Mao clearly identified right conservatism as the main deviation in this period, in this and several other statements from November 1955 to January 1956 he also warned against excessive leftism.

December 21

Mao drafted a notice inviting opinions from local leaders on the seventeen articles. The notice echoed the new plan for cooperativizaton seen in the above speech, i.e., basically to achieve lower stage cooperativization by the latter half of 1956 and higher stage cooperativization by the end of 1960, if not by the end of 1959.

On the basis of consultations involving these local leaders and concerned central officials, the seventeen articles were expanded into an ambitious forty-article twelve-year program for agricultural development that was adopted by the Supreme State Conference on January 25, 1956.

December 27

Mao rewrote his preface for the book *How to Run APCs*, that was now retitled *Socialist Upsurge in the Chinese Countryside*. The preface repeated the above target. While claiming complete victory in the debate on the pace of cooperativization, Mao still urged criticism of rightist and conservative thinking "without stop" as he called for speeding up not only the socialist transformation of handicrafts and capitalist industry and commerce, but also industrialization and the development of science, culture, education, and other fields of work.

1956

Early January

Publication of *Socialist Upsurge* and statistics indicating that by the end of 1955 there were already 75 million peasant households or 63 percent of the entire rural population in APCs clearly delighted Mao. He revealed such feelings to his secretary Tian Jiaying saying that he had never been so happy and even the great victory of 1949 had not pleased him as much.

Part I: Reform Era
Party History Accounts

1

ZHU YONGHONG

Reflections on the Party's Policy Toward the Rural Individual Economy During the First Seven Years of the State*

During the first seven years of our state, the individual economy in the countryside basically was transformed into a single system of public ownership. Twenty years later, however, the party once again put forward the policy of "developing various economic forms under the predominance of the public ownership system." This unexpected change naturally leads to a rethinking of the policy of the party regarding the rural individual economy during the first seven years after the establishment of the state. After the victory of the new democratic revolution, it was correct for the party to implement, step by step, the socialist transformation of the individual economy in the countryside. This article aims to provide a preliminary analysis of the leftist mistakes committed during the process of transformation. Hopefully this will help us better understand agricultural policy for the preliminary stage of socialism.

I. The practical basis of policy toward the rural individual economy and the course of its development

There were several features of the rural situation at the time of the establishment of the PRC: (1) Except for the small portion making up the cooperative economy (there were 18 APCs in 1950), an individual economy that was "similar to the ancient, dispersed type" was the predominant form [of production]. (2) The level of productivity of this type of individual

*Zhu Yonghong, "Reflections on the party's policy toward the rural individual economy during the first seven years of the state," in *Zhonggong dangshi yanjiu* (Research on CCP history), no. 2 (1989), pp. 53–56.

economy was very low. At that time there were only 64 livestock, 9.7 waterwheels, and 6.6 carts for each 100 households, and 1 old-style plow for each 2 households; grain output was about 130 jin per mu [1 jin = 1/2 kilogram; 1 mu = 0.067 hectares—Eds.]. The total production of major agricultural products was much lower than the highest levels in history.[1] (3) To solve the difficulties caused by the shortage of the means of production and of labor and animal power, there arose the demand of the peasants themselves for mutual aid in labor. (4) On the one hand, the broad peasant [masses] displayed full gratitude and love to the party for obtaining land through land reform. On the other hand, as private laborers they also wished to recuperate, prosper, and build fortunes through the land.

These basic characteristics constitute the practical basis on which the party formulated its policy regarding the individual economy in the countryside at that time. Due to the predominance of the individual economy in the country it became imperative to lead the way to a cooperative system. It was inconceivable that a modernized socialist economy could be built on the basis of small-scale farming. Yet at the same time, because of a small cooperative economy and a massive individual economy and the dual character of individual farmers who were enthusiastic about both mutual aid in labor and the individual economy, the transformation of the individual economy would necessarily be a long-term process. To realize the socialist modernization of the individual economy that dominated in the countryside, it was imperative to create the necessary conditions. These included a good worker-peasant alliance, rapid national industrialization, the gradual technological transformation of agriculture, and the adoption of an economic form for the transition from the individual to cooperative systems that must be suitable for the broad rural situation in our country and based upon voluntary participation and mutual benefit, etc. A long transitional period was required to create these conditions. For this reason, within a relatively long period individual peasant production would continue to occupy an important position in the overall agricultural economy. It would be wrong to dampen the incentives of the individual peasant economy.

With respect to the basic characteristics of the countryside at the time of the establishment of the new China and the determining factors of the party's policy on the individual economy derived from these characteristics, the party made a scientific analysis and took strategic decisions on the eve of the PRC and during the initial period of the state. However, soon afterward the party neglected its cautious and scientific approach in analyzing the individual economy. As a result, the policy concerning the individual economy was derailed until the economy basically was transformed into a system consisting solely of public ownership. The development of the party's policy on the individual economy in the countryside could be summarized as "leaning toward the left." It can be divided into five stages.

The first stage: from the Second Plenary Session of the Seventh Central Committee [in March 1949] to the formulation of the center's "Resolution on Mutual Aid and Cooperation in Agriculture (Draft)" in December 1951.

As the Chinese countryside was entering a new era during the course of the history of Chinese revolution, the Second Plenary Session of the Seventh Central Committee conducted an analysis of the rural situation and came up with projections of major policies. The plenum pointed out the following important points: After the birth of the new China, individual agriculture and the handicraft economy constituted 90 percent of the national economy. Because of the abolition of the feudal land ownership system, "it is possible to lead the development of agriculture toward the direction of modernization and collectivization, while at the same time this process should be done cautiously, gradually and positively." But because of the weakness of the socialist state-owned economy and because of the "backwardness of the Chinese economy at the moment," "both at present and during a relatively long period of time in the future our agriculture and handicraft industry are and will remain dispersed and individualized in terms of their basic forms." Moreover, "during a relatively long period of time after the victory of the revolution, the enthusiasm for private capitalism in the cities and the countryside should be exploited, wherever possible, to facilitate the advance of the national economy."[2]

The plenum not only pointed out the necessity and feasibility of transforming the individual economy in the countryside, it also in clear-minded fashion recognized the long-term and arduous nature of this kind of transformation. On the one hand, it pointed out the direction of socialist development for individual agriculture. On the other hand, it fully affirmed the position and functions to be performed by the individual economy during a relatively long period after the establishment of the state. These views fit well the practical situation of the Chinese countryside at that time. After the establishment of the state, in villages of old [liberated] areas that had been in the forefront of land reform "new problems" of "middle peasantization" began to emerge, including demands for "individual farming" and the "right to hire labor" on the part of some peasants, the loosening of mutual aid and cooperative organizations, and the buying and selling of land. Faced with these "new problems" divisions emerged within the party regarding the understanding of the individual economy in the countryside. On April 17, 1951, the Shanxi Provincial Committee proposed "upgrading mutual aid and cooperative organization" in order to curb the "spontaneous tendency" of the individual peasants and further to destabilize and eliminate the private ownership system. During the small white villa meeting [sic] of the North China Bureau in late April 1951 and in his comment on the report of the Shanxi Provincial Committee on July 3, Liu Shaoqi twice criticized the thinking of the Shanxi Provincial Committee that attempted to build socialism on the basis of the strength of the peasants alone and blindly weakened and dismissed private ownership without taking objective conditions into consideration as "agrarian utopian socialism."[3] Yet the opinion of the Shanxi Provincial Committee had the support of Mao Zedong. Nevertheless, the view expressed in the "Resolution on Mutual Aid and Cooperation in Agriculture (Draft)" formulated by the center in December 1951 regarding the individual economy in the countryside was still correct. The resolution scientifically summarized the enthusiasm of the peasants after land reform as combining the two aspects of "individual economy and cooperative labor." It also maintained that the peasant's enthusiasm for these two aspects was "the basic factor leading to the rapid recovery and development of the national economy and facilitating the industrialization of the country." Once again it pointed out that "according to the present economic conditions of the country the individual peasant economy will continue to exist as a large proportion [of the whole] for a relatively long period of time." Hence "we should not neglect and harshly obstruct the peasants' enthusiasm for this type of individual economy."[4] In short, our party's understanding of the individual economy in the countryside during this stage was relatively correct.

The second stage: from early 1952 to the promulgation of "The Center's Comments while Transmitting the Report of the Northeast Rural Work Department."

Two major developments happened in the countryside during this stage. The first was that after the promulgation of the "Resolution on Mutual Aid and Cooperation in Agriculture (Draft)" the mutual aid and cooperation movement rapidly developed in those villages that had completed land reform. During the movement, the tendency of impetuosity and rash advance emerged in many districts. This tendency manifested itself as "one-sidedly going after high forms and looking down on mutual aid teams, discriminating and attacking households engaging in individual production, resorting to coercion and commandism, and turning over [to the collective] the means of production."[5] To correct this development, in spring 1953 the center criticized the mistakes of "infringing on the interests of individual peasants and blindly attacking the private ownership system" as manifested in the course of impetuosity and rash advance, and emphasized that [we must] "pay attention to not doing tomorrow's affairs today."[6] It also reiterated the legitimate right to engage in individual farming and reaffirmed the positive effects of the "individual economy," the "rich peasant economy," "hiring labor," "borrowing and lending, free trade, and free renting out of land." Finally, it pointed out, that it was essential to "protect the initiative of the individual peasants." The goal was to "develop mutual aid and cooperation while at the same time stabilizing the initiative of individual households."[7] These understandings and policies of the center completely conformed to the spirit of the policy on individual farmers formulated at the Second Plenary Session of the Seventh Central Committee [in early 1949].

The second development to emerge in the countryside during this stage was as follows. After land reform and the criticism of impetuosity and rash advance, the incentive to become rich was once again mobilized among the individual peasants. Phenomena such as hiring labor, borrowing and lending money, buying and selling land, and engaging in trade and individual production developed in different regions with different levels of intensity. In view of this situation, in May 1952 the Northeast Bureau took the lead in arguing that "the incentives provided by the individual peasant economy will lead to the old path," [and] "the spontaneous development of capitalist elements" "will lead to a capitalist future."[8] This point of view received the approval of the center. In summer 1953 the Rural Work Department of the Northeast Bureau reiterated this viewpoint in its "Investigation Report concerning Wubaoshan and Xinlin Villages of the Ninth District in Suizhong." At the same time it believed that "the struggle between the spontaneous tendency of the individual peasants taking the old road of capitalism and the movement toward mutual aid and cooperation led by the party" "has become the main contradiction among the various contradictions existing in the countryside."[9] On September 26 of the same year the Central Rural Work Department distributed this report to various regional rural work departments. In a comment on the report it affirmed that "the report is very good" and reminded various regions "of the need to conduct an ideological struggle between the two lines."[10] This implied that: (1) the party in effect accepted the formulation that the individual economy in the countryside was a force for capitalism; (2) it began to guard against the "negative effect" of individual peasants pursuing prosperity on [the development of] mutual aid and cooperation; (3) it raised the "contradiction" of the mutual aid and cooperation movement with the development of the individual economy to the high level of a struggle between two lines and two futures. It became the major contradiction in the countryside.

The third stage: from Mao Zedong's "Two Talks on Mutual Aid and Cooperation in Agriculture" in October 1953 to the time preceding the publication of Mao Zedong's speech "On the Question of Agricultural Cooperativization" in July 1955.

In July 1953 Mao Zedong comprehensively explained the general line of the party during the transition period. After that the party's understanding and policy on the individual economy in the countryside underwent a major change of direction. The party now regarded the individual economy as "isolated, dispersed, antiquated, and backward." [It reckoned that] "the increase in production by individual peasants would be limited," that "there is no future for individual farming," and that "productive relations based on individual ownership and large-scale supply were diametrically opposed."[11] [It further considered that] "the four big freedoms benefited the rich peasants and well-to-do middle peasants" and therefore was "a bourgeois concept." [The party] clearly pointed out that the individual initiative of the peasants [could not help but] produce the spontaneous tendency toward capitalism.[12] The relationship between individual ownership and collective ownership was raised to the level of a life-or-death struggle between capitalism and socialism.[13] Based on this understanding it was natural for the party to put forward the strategy of "working out a solution for [curbing] the individual ownership system" and the policies of "limiting the freedom of the middle peasants" and "prohibiting the buying and selling of land."[14] It was true that at the time the party still emphasized "nondiscrimination and no harsh measures toward individual peasants," and also emphasized that "with respect to those go-it-alone households that do not want to participate in mutual aid and cooperation at this moment, [we] must adopt the attitudes of protection, assistance, and patient education." It was also true that the party acknowledged that "peasants engaging in individual farming still had a certain potential in production." However, under the premise of a fundamentally dismissive attitude toward the individual economy at this stage, the above policies emphasized by the party could hardly be put into effect during the movement. Consequently the following phenomena became widespread at this stage: "attacking, mocking, and restricting households engaging in individual farming," "struggling against well-to-do middle peasants," communizing the property of middle peasants, and forcing individual peasants to join the cooperatives. In addition there was the excessive purchase of grain by the state during the period. As a result, in different regions there were incidents of peasants selling and killing livestock, destroying the means of production, and withdrawing cattle from the cooperatives. All of this suddenly intensified the volatile situation, so much so that by spring 1955 it became necessary to introduce the policy of "stop, shrink, develop." In May the center criticized the leftist mistake of rash advance [as revealed in] the idea of "accomplishing cooperativization in three years" and impatience to eliminate the individual economy.[15] It also pointed out that [the policy of] "contraction" implied "giving a bit of space to the individual economy."[16]

The fourth stage: from the publication of Mao Zedong's "On the Question of Agricultural Cooperativization" in July 1955 to the time preceding Mao Zedong's "Talks at a Conference of Secretaries of Provincial, Municipal, and Autonomous Region Party Committees" in January 1957.

The implementation of the policy of "resolute contraction" and the overhaul of APCs led to an easing of tension in the countryside. Yet soon afterwards Mao Zedong criticized [the so-called] "woman with bound feet." He condemned the policy of "resolute contraction" for being "a right opportunist policy."[17] This was followed by the struggle against the rightist tendency within the party. The party's policy on the individual economy in the countryside made a rapid turn toward an even more leftist direction. In October of the same year Mao Zedong further advanced the view that the goal of agricultural cooperativization was to eliminate the roots of capitalism from the vast territory of our countryside. Not only was capitalism to be exterminated, but small-scale production was to be eliminated as well.[18] In treating the individual peasants (at that time individual peasants consisted mainly of well-to-do middle peasants who had not joined the cooperatives), Mao Zedong believed that "in the Chinese countryside a major aspect of the struggle between the two lines is the peaceful competition between the poor and the lower middle peasants on the one hand and the well-to-do middle peasants on the other."[19] Thus individual peasants were put on the opposite side of the poor and lower middle peasants and of socialism. With regard to the period [necessary] for completing the transformation of the individual economy, by September 1955 Mao Zedong still agreed that it would take eighteen years. [But] three months later Mao Zedong advanced the timetable by nine years which meant that the transformation should be completed by 1959.[20] The extraordinary pace of the development of the agricultural cooperativization movement and the implementation of the leftist policy on the individual economy once again provided the dynamic of instability in the countryside—including coercion and commandism in the course of precipitating [cooperativization], the tense relationship between the poor peasants and middle peasants, well-to-do middle peasants and individual peasants being publicly denounced, the prohibition of the peasants' legitimate sideline production, confused management of the cooperatives, excessive accumulation, a decrease in the income of APC members, etc. After fall 1956 the strained situation in the countryside again intensified resulting in another effort by the center to correct these deviations. At the end of 1956, in a comment on a report on disturbances in various regions, the center approved the proposal from below that it was necessary "to make concessions and give consideration" in the party's policies toward upper middle peasants, those with special income, and households experiencing difficulties. It also instructed that [we may] resolutely allow some people to withdraw from the cooperatives; that [we should] appropriately relax restrictions on the proportion of profits; allow cooperative members to retain some private fruit trees, woods, ponds and family plots; and allow subsidiary production by households experiencing great difficulties due to labor shortage.[21]

The fifth stage: from January 1957 to the end of the same year. If it can be said that during the previous stages the party still left some room for temporarily preserving the individual economy in the countryside, then [we have to say] basically such room no longer existed during this stage. The view and attitude toward the well-to-do middle peasants who best represented the individual peasants became essentially confrontational. In January 1957 Mao Zedong defined the well-to-do middle peasants as "a wavering stratum."[22] He further said that "the ideological struggle against the petty bourgeoisie, especially the well-to-do middle peasants, is a struggle that will occur again and again over many years. The well-to-do middle peasants are quite influential and extremely formidable so we must be watchful."[23] In October of the same year during the Third Plenary Session of the Eighth Central Committee, Mao Zedong once again pointed out that "the targets of the socialist revolution are the bourgeoisie, the bourgeois intellectuals, and the upper-petty bourgeoisie (this means the well-to-do middle peasants in the countryside)."[24] In terms of policy, there were no more "concessions" to disturbances in the countryside. And with the unfolding of the large-scale antirightist struggle in the cities "a large-scale socialist education movement" was launched in the countryside in August 1957. Using the form of "carrying out a two-road debate on socialism and capitalism," the movement effectively criticized the capitalist thinking of the well-to-do middle peasants. [Urged on by] the fine horse of the cooperativization movement and the whip of socialist education, the original plan of transforming the individual economy in eighteen years was completed fourteen years ahead of schedule. At the end of 1957 the remaining individual peasants accounted for only 3 percent of the total rural population. The aim of establishing a single public ownership system was thus achieved with great success.

[In the remainder of the article the author analyzes the causes of the rapid elimination of rural individual economy with attention to Marxist-Leninist theoretical influences, errors in the estimation of peasant enthusiasm after land reform, and the influence of traditional values.]

Notes

[The notes that are numbered page by page in the Chinese text have been renumbered consecutively throughout this translation.]

1. *Zhongguo nongye hezuo shiliao* (Materials on the history of Chinese agricultural cooperation), 1986 trial edition, p. 2.
2. *Nongye jitihua zhongyao wenjian huibian* (A collection of important documents on agricultural collectivization), vol. 1, pp. 1–2.
3. Ibid., pp. 32–33.
4. Ibid., p. 37.
5. Ibid., p. 76.
6. Ibid., p. 127.
7. Ibid., pp. 136–39.
8. Ibid., pp. 63–65.
9. Ibid., p. 181.
10. Ibid.
11. Ibid., pp. 198–218.

12. Ibid., pp. 209–16.

13. See Mao Zedong, "Two talks on mutual aid and cooperation in agriculture," and "Speech and remarks at the rural work conference," October 1953.

14. *Nongye jitihua*, vol. 1, p. 197; [and] Mao Zedong, "Speech and remarks at the rural work conference."

15. *Nongye jitihua*, vol. 1, p. 334.

16. Ibid., p. 320.

17. Ibid., p. 451.

18. Ibid., pp. 434–35.

19. Ibid., p. 511.

20. Ibid., p. 522.

21. Ibid., pp. 648–53.

22. Ibid., p. 666.

23. Mao Zedong, "Remarks at a conference of secretaries of provincial and municipal committees."

24. Mao Zedong, "Speech at the Third Plenary Session of the Eighth Central Committee."

2

Gao Huamin

Rectifying the Problem of Impetuosity and Rash Advance in the Agricultural Mutual Aid and Cooperativization Movement in 1953*

In the past, people's understanding of the question of rectifying the tendency of rash advance in the agricultural mutual aid and cooperation movement in the first half of 1953 was not identical. Some comrades believed that correcting the rash advance tendency on this occasion was engineered by the Central Rural Work Department of the Central Committee without authorization. Others even believed that it was a "sinister wind" blown by "Liu Shaoqi behind the back of Chairman Mao and the party center" [which sought] "to oppose the agricultural cooperativization movement in a fundamental way and to uproot all cooperatives."[1] In this article, I would like to express my own understanding of this issue.

I. The tendency of impetuosity and rash advance in the agricultural mutual aid and cooperation movement

To examine the issue one should first of all make clear whether the tendency of rash advance did exist at that time.

By fall 1952, the number of peasant households participating in mutual aid teams and cooperatives amounted to 45.42 million, or 40 percent of total households. Among these there were 8.03 million mutual aid teams and 4,000 lower stage APCs, with 57,000 households having joined the cooperatives. In spring 1953, the mutual aid and cooperation movement developed further resulting in the emergence of the tendency of impetuosity and rash advance in many regions. Its concrete manifestations were as follows:

(1) Publicly owned assets were blindly expanded in the course of

*Gao Huamin, "Rectifying the problem of impetuosity and rash advance in the agricultural mutual aid and cooperativization movement in 1953," in *Dangshi yanjiu* (Research on party history), no. 3 (1981), pp. 18–24.

developing APCs by infringing on the interests of the middle peasants. According to reports by various places in North China, this had become a very serious phenomenon. For example, through monetary payment to individual owners some cooperatives had collectivized all livestock and farming tools. This unchecked increase of public assets put the lower stage cooperatives in deep debt. Some APCs had a debt of more than 200 million yuan (old currency). This amounted to 69.5 percent of their total annual income. Many cooperatives [also] engaged in large capital construction. These cooperatives forced their members to sell their carts and horses for public use. Even old farm tools and old furniture were uniformly bought for the cooperatives at discounted prices regardless of whether there was any need for them. This greatly increased the financial burden of the cooperatives.[2] There also emerged the phenomenon of eating from a big pot in some isolated cases. For instance, in the western part of Guangdong Province some mutual aid teams collectivized the main property of the peasants whose houses were occupied and remodeled into large dining halls. Immediately after the establishment of the collective farms (that is, higher stage APCs—Author) set up under the direct leadership of the Heilongjiang Provincial Committee, members of the farm dined together. Although these were individual cases, their effects were far reaching. "The peasant masses criticize the approach of these cadres as 'proceeding too fast, taking one step when in fact two steps should be taken.' They also describe some APCs as being 'big stalls with little stock but deep debt, high production yet low profit.' " ("Directive of the Center to Party Committees at All Levels on Spring Plowing and Production.")

In addition, there emerged the phenomenon of infringing on the interests of the middle peasants in some mutual aid teams. This problem existed in many places in the Southwest. "Some mutual aid teams simply use the farm cattle of the middle peasants at no cost. Some even collectivize farm cattle for public feeding and public use at a very low price, and such payment is not made to the owners for a long period of time." "Some regions have no basis at all for mutual aid. Nevertheless, they proceed with collectivizing the cattle. At the same time, the burden of cattle feeding and labor is not divided reasonably. This results in the phenomenon of 'fat cattle becoming skinny and skinny cattle dying of poor feeding.' The same thing also happens in East China and Central-South China."[3] As pointed out by the party center: in many places in new [liberated] areas and regions with a weak basis for mutual aid, some local cadres "[over-]emphasize the interests of poor peasants and farm laborers within the mutual aid teams at the expense of those of middle peasants. This greatly damages incentives for production on the part of individual [i.e., private] peasants who constitute the overwhelming majority of the village population in the new [liberated] areas."[4]

(2) In guiding the mutual aid and cooperation movement, emphasis was placed on the cooperatives with little regard to the mutual aid teams. This was because of the one-sided emphasis on enlarging the scale [of rural organizations]. This phenomenon of emphasizing the cooperatives at the expense of mutual aid teams was particularly evident in old [liberated] areas and well-organized regions such as the Northeast and North China. Some regions blindly went after higher forms. They advocated that "small teams should join together to form large ones," that "those with less than five households are not counted as teams," and that "it is glorious to join larger teams," etc. Other regions blindly merged small cooperatives into large ones. In Daming County in Hebei Province, the 180 cooperatives established in 1952 were merged to form 82 [larger] cooperatives.[5] At that time, in North China "many localities have the erroneous idea that 'it is better to have more than less, to have larger than smaller' [and] 'the more the better, the bigger the better' in the course of establishing cooperatives. This wrong idea was pushed even further in some individual districts."[6]

(3) In terms of work methods, some regions adopted the method of coercion and commandism that contradicted the principle of voluntariness. According to a report by the *People's Daily* on April 2, 1953, many village party members in Shanxi Province used coercion and commandism in dealing with the peasants. For example, a secretary of a village branch announced the following in a mass meeting: "Now I command that everyone should join the mutual aid teams. Those who do not join are not patriotic." In Daming County in Hebei Province some villages used the method of forced registration to compel the masses to join the cooperatives. Those who refused were sent on official errands or forbidden to use farming tools. This caused [great] ideological confusion. Lower stage cooperatives in some regions also adopted the method of coercion and commandism to accumulate public property. A village in the Changzhe District in Shanxi Province advocated the slogan: "Encircle at all levels, attack from both within and without, set task forces, succeed in one night." By the next morning, this village had seized 160 sheep initially owned by members of the cooperatives. [As a result] the masses outside the APCs immediately sold their 70 sheep after sensing that something was wrong.[7]

From the above we can understand that the tendency of rash advance was not an isolated phenomenon. [Quite the contrary,] it was manifested with different levels of intensity in many regions. On October 4, 1953, the center's comment on the "Report" by the North China Bureau on July 3 also said that "there has emerged from last winter to this spring the tendency of rash advance during the course of developing and upgrading the organization of mutual aid and cooperation in many regions."

Because of this tendency, there was widespread misunderstanding of what socialism is among the basic-level cadres and masses in new and old [liberated] areas. They looked at socialism with the idea of egalitarianism found in the small peasant economy and regarded socialism as synonymous with "eating from a big pot." In villages of the new [liberated] areas there was a general fear among the middle peasants of showing their riches. They believed that "the poor live a much easier life while the rich live a troubled life." Some poor peasants and farm laborers even believed that "it is glorious to be poor." In villages of the old [liberated] areas, opinions based on a misunderstanding of [our] party's policy became popular. According to a report in the *People's Daily* on May 13, 1953, in Heilongjiang Province ideas such as "getting organized and putting everything into common stock," "leveling the rich and the poor in order to achieve common prosperity," and "letting the rich wait [while] promoting the poor to reach the same level in socialism" were in vogue. Many rich households were [therefore] afraid to mention the word "rich." Others were afraid to be called middle peasants. There was "the negative sentiment of eating more, dressing more, enjoying more; raising fewer horses, working less in the fields, bearing fewer burdens." These types of thinking and sentiments were detrimental to the development of production. Hence it became necessary to rectify the tendency of rash advance in the mutual aid and cooperation movement. The center pointed out following in its "Directive to Party Committees at All Levels on Spring Plowing and Production": "In order to lead and organize correctly the peasants and mobilize their incentives for production, it is necessary to rectify earnestly the tendency of impetuosity and rash advance which has emerged in the mutual aid and cooperation movement in agricultural production."

II. Rectification of the tendency of impetuosity and rash advance

Concerning the tendency of rash advance in the mutual aid and cooperation movement, on January 31, 1953, Comrade Liu Lantao, the chief leader of the North China region, pointed out in "A Reply to All County Committee Secretaries on the Question of [How to] Lead Agricultural Production" that "right now in many localities [our comrades] are neglecting the work of leading and promoting the mutual aid teams that commonly exist in large numbers and that should serve as the basis for APCs. In terms of guiding the cooperatives, there is the tendency of rash advance as manifested in striving for more and larger cooperatives." On questions such as how to run and manage a mutual aid team or a cooperative, how to handle profit sharing, how to pay for the utilization of privately owned means of production, etc., there existed the tendency of "blindly going after higher forms, blindly expanding elements of socialism, and creating common property both excessively and impatiently. This tendency much be checked and rectified."[8]

On March 2, 1953, the North China Bureau issued a directive on "Rectifying the Tendency of Blind and Rash Advance in the Development of APCs." It demanded that "party committees at all levels must pay great attention to the serious consequences produced by the mistakes of leftist adventurism." They should adopt immediate measures "to stop and rectify" the tendency. On March 26 the *People's Daily* published the party center's "Resolution on Mutual Aid and Cooperation in Agriculture," [the center's] "Directive to Party Committees at All Levels on Spring Plowing and Production," and its editorial "The Key to Leading Agricultural Production." These three documents were collectively named *Guide to Present Rural Work* by the center and published by the People's Publishing House. These three documents elucidated the basic principles, policies, and work methods that must be grasped by our party in guiding rural work at that time. On April 3 the center issued a special instruction calling for party committees at various levels to organize cadres to study the three documents [in the hope of] raising the standard of their thinking and their understanding of policy to a higher level. [Afterwards] party committees at various levels used these documents as a weapon to examine and rectify the tendency of impetuosity and rash advance that had already emerged in rural work.

On April 3 the Central Rural Work Department convened the First Rural Work Conference. On the twenty-third Comrade Deng Zihui made a summary report. He talked about two tendencies existing in various places in the mutual aid and cooperation movement at the time. One was a laissez-faire and wait and see attitude. The other was impetuosity and rash advance. He considered that "generally speaking the new [liberated] areas are more likely to have the laissez-faire and wait and see attitude while the old [liberated] areas are more likely to commit impetuosity and rash advance. But if impetuosity and rash advance are rectified in the old [liberated] areas, the opposite rightist deviation might emerge [in the same areas]. In any case, as far as the present nationwide tendency is concerned, impetuosity and rash advance is clearly the major deviation as well as the primary danger."

He further analyzed the ideological source of impetuosity and rash advance as lying primarily in the misrepresentation of the nature of the mutual aid teams and cooperatives as well as in the failure to understand the process of [and relation between] industrialization and agricultural collectivization. He argued that "eating from a big pot in the cooperatives must be rejected. Common production and consumption happen only in communism. They cannot be achieved today. If we insist on achieving common production and consumption today the result would be disastrous." He emphasized that we had to pay attention to household sidelines at the same time we were trying to establish a good collective economy. He thought some distinction should be made concerning the slogan "mutual aid should be implemented all the time and on every occasion" put forth by some localities. He suggested that it was better to have individual farming rather than mutual aid in jobs such as raising chickens and pigs, growing vegetables, and other household sidelines. He advocated that newly established cooperatives should not be too large in scale. "The most appropriate form should consist of no more than thirty households." On the question of leadership style he proposed that it "should be based on the real situation of a particular time and place. Policies should be formulated according to local conditions and seeking truth from facts." [We should] oppose a work style that tries to curry favor with higher authorities, finds out their mood and pleases them, and that reports only the good things but not the bad things or vice versa," etc. These ideas were indeed based upon the objective situation and have been proven correct in practice. On June 4 the *People's Daily* published a report entitled "The Mutual Aid and Cooperative Movement Advances Steadily after Rectifying the Deviation of Rash Advance in Our Rural Work Across the Country." It pointed out that "the deviation of rash advance in various areas has basically been rectified for the time being."

From the above account we can say that the move to rectify the tendency of rash advance was not engineered by the Rural Work Department without authorization. Nor was it a sinister wind blown by Liu Shaoqi. Furthermore, the accusation that its goals were "to oppose the agricultural cooperativization movement in a fundamental way and to uproot all cooperatives" was totally groundless. In fact, the move to rectify the tendency of rash advance was implemented by the Central Rural Work Department in accord with the spirit of the party center's directives. We should affirm the successes that were achieved.

From an overall perspective the tendency of rash advance "was rectified in time before serious damage was done."[9] During the course of rectification, the incentives for mutual aid and cooperation on the part of the masses were protected and mutual aid and cooperative organizations were consolidated. On the other hand, production was at no time obstructed. Especially after the publication of the center's two documents and the *People's Daily* editorial, great results were achieved in implementing the principles and policies of agricultural mutual aid and cooperation on the part of party committees at various levels as well as in leading cadres' thinking onto the right track. Corresponding measures were adopted by all regions in dealing with the tendency of blind and rash advance. The result was positive and achievements were the main thing. These were manifested in the following:

(1) The nature of mutual aid teams and lower stage cooperatives was made clear. The phenomenon of blindly expanding public property was basically overcome. The mood of the peasants for production was stabilized. The misunderstanding with respect to socialism on the part of the basic-

level cadres and masses was cleared up. The phenomenon of infringing upon the private property of the peasants was rectified. Psychological burdens were lifted. Incentives for production were boosted. [The author continues with examples from particular areas and production statistics.]

(2) In terms of the scale of organization, the phenomenon of emphasizing cooperatives at the expense of mutual aid teams was rectified and the thinking that "it is better to be large than small" was overcome. Basic level cadres in North China and the Northeast rectified their wrong approaches in leading mutual aid and cooperation by strengthening their leadership over the mutual aid teams. For instance, through correcting the tendency of rash advance in North China cadres came to realize that the mutual aid teams must be taken as the core [of the cooperativization movement] under the conditions at the time. Simultaneously APCs should be developed in a steady and controlled manner. "The misunderstanding of emphasizing cooperatives at the expense of mutual aid teams is beginning to change. Mutual aid teams that have been neglected for quite a while become active once again and enjoy further development."[10]

[The author then provides statistics on reductions in the number of peasant households in APCs as a result of rectification.]

(3) The work style of coercion and commandism was overcome relatively well. The phenomenon of establishing an excessive number of cooperatives that attacked individual farmers due to impetuosity and rash advance gradually changed. According to the "Report to the Center on the Situation in Thoroughly Implementing the Center's Three Documents, [i.e.,] the Directive on Spring Plowing and Production, etc." prepared by the Southwest Bureau on June 6, 1953, "the thinking of the leading cadres at the county level and above has been substantially changed." Many leading cadres engaged in rural work began to realize that the socialist transformation of small-scale farming could not be achieved by mere administrative means. Consequently this enabled the mutual aid and cooperation movement to find the right track.

In terms of the speed of development of the mutual aid and cooperation movement, progress was still made in 1953 compared to 1952. In 1953 the number of peasant households joining the mutual aid and cooperative organizations amounted to 45.91 million households, or 39.5 percent of all peasant households. This meant an increase of 490,000 households from the year before. Why was there an increase in the number of households, while the percentage of total peasant households [in cooperatives] decreased by 0.5 percent? This was because of the increase in the peasant population. In 1953 the number of peasant households was 116.325 million. There was an increase of 2.642 million over the 113.683 million households of the previous year. In 1953 there were 7.45 million mutual aid teams. Compared with the year before, the total number of households increased while the number of teams decreased. This was because the average number of households in each team increased from 5.7 households in 1952 to 6.1 households in 1953. In 1953 there were 15,000 lower stage cooperatives whose members numbered 273,000 households, or 0.2 percent of all peasant households. Compared to the year before, there was an increase of 11,000 cooperatives. The number of households also increased by 216,000.[11]

By mid-December 1953 the number of peasant households joining the mutual aid teams and cooperatives numbered about 47.9 million, or 43 percent of the total number of households in the countryside. Of these there were about 14,000 APCs consisting of more than 273,000 peasant households.[12] From the above account one can see that there was an increase in the number of households joining both mutual aid teams and cooperatives in 1953, that indeed marked a step forward. Although the development of mutual aid teams slowed down during the first half of the year and the number of cooperatives decreased a bit in the second half, there was no decrease in the number of households. Thus, there was no basis for some comrades to argue that "between 1952 and October 1953 the agricultural cooperativization movement was almost completely halted in the whole countryside" and that "the number of cooperatives decreased by 0.5 percent."[13]

The effort to rectify the tendency of rash advance clarified people's understanding of the nature of the mutual aid teams and lower stage cooperatives. It also provided preliminary experience on to how to bring about a healthy mutual aid and cooperation movement. On this point the center showed its approval. In October 1953 the center issued a directive while transmitting the July 3 report of the North China Bureau to party committees at all levels. In it the center commented that "in rectifying the tendency of rash advance that emerged during the agricultural mutual aid and cooperation movement from last winter to this spring, party committees at all levels have paid attention both to overcoming mistakes and protecting achievements while encouraging activists among the masses to advance forward. In general, they have done a good job." In its "Report for Approval concerning the Question of the Rehabilitation of Comrade Deng Zihui" of December 8, 1980, the party group of the State Agricultural Commission also talked about this issue: "In light of either the situation at the time or what happened later, it was both prudent for Comrade Deng Zihui, in view of the impetuosity and rash advance that had already emerged in some places, to have proposed in 1953 that such a tendency must be curbed."

Everything can be divided into two aspects. This move to rectify the tendency of rash advance was quite right. However, there were also some shortcomings in concrete work.

(1) Some cooperatives that should not have been dissolved were dissolved. In the course of rectifying the tendency of rash advance there

appeared to be a lack of systematic criticism of the leftist thinking of rash advance and [equally of] rightist thinking that resulted from the antileftist campaign in some places. In its comment of October 1953 on the report of July 3, 1953, by the North China Bureau, the center pointed to this problem as follows: "The analysis and criticism of the leftist thinking of rash advance and certain right-deviationist thinking that grew under the cover of the antileftist struggle are neither systematic nor profound." Due to the short time and urgent tasks the overhauling of some cooperatives in some places was done in a very rough manner. [As a result,] "some APCs that should not have been blown away were blown away."[14] There were 9,283 cooperatives in the North China region, among which 7,100 were individually inspected and overhauled, and 2,621 APCs, accounting for 36 percent of the total number, were changed back into mutual aid teams. In the process of overhauling there were actually some cooperatives that should have been shut down but were not, whereas some that should not have been were. In addition, although some cooperatives were closed down, their farm cattle, farm tools and some other items were not disposed of in time, and so on so forth.

(2) Some cooperatives that could have been developed were not. Generally speaking, at that time the crop yields of the mutual aid teams were higher than those of private farmers, while those of the lower stage cooperatives were higher than those of the mutual aid teams. This fact appeared attractive to the poor peasants in terms of joining the teams or cooperatives. The lower stage cooperatives set up on the basis of land shares and unified management entailed socialist elements on the one hand, and were founded on private ownership on the other. Such a semipublic, semi-private form of organization was comparatively easily accepted by the poverty-stricken peasants. This was shown by the spontaneous establishment of cooperatives in some areas. For example, among the 7,300-odd cooperatives, about 3,000 were set up by the masses spontaneously or without formal approval. By spring 1953 there were 849 cooperatives in Zhejiang Province, among which 602 were spontaneous ones. However, in some places they were treated as [signs of] rash advance and thus were forbidden without exception. For example, in Daming County, Hebei Province, it was stipulated: "The development of cooperatives should be halted immediately. Setting up spontaneous cooperatives without approval will not be allowed, nor will the merger of cooperatives be allowed, nor will any increase in the number of households in the cooperatives through forcible means be permitted. Those who disobey will be punished for violating discipline."[15] This thus prevented the movement from being further developed in those areas where the movement could have been developed.

The problems described above indicate that the [real] situation in a big country such as ours was very mixed and complicated. From the perspective of the whole country the situation varied from place to place. Although rash advance happened in many regions, the laissez-faire tendency also existed in some other regions. Meanwhile, the degree of rash advance also varied from region to region. As Comrade Deng Zihui pointed out in his concluding speech of April 17, 1954, at the Second National Rural Work Conference: It is true that "impetuosity and rash advance took place in every big region" last year. However, "rash advance was not equally serious in all places. In some places it was not [serious]." Therefore, in rectifying a tendency we should proceed from the practical situation. Wherever there is leftism, we should rectify it accordingly; wherever there is rightism, we should also rectify it. In dealing with the main deviation we should not neglect the minor one either. "We should carry out our struggle on two fronts by rejecting both leftism and rightism."[16] [This] avoided allowing the other [opposite] tendency to evolve when attempting to get rid of the main deviation. These experiences were highly valuable not only for the growth of agricultural production, but also for work in any other field.

III. An analysis of several different views

There have been a number of views in assessing the above rectification of the tendency of rash advance. In the following paragraphs I would like to present them and my [criticisms] in the hope of clarifying the issue and distinguishing between right and wrong.

The first view thinks that the pace of development in the First Five-Year Plan set by the Rural Work Conference convened by the Central Rural Work Department in 1953 was right-deviationist, [namely] it "deviated from the party's general line for the transition period." I think that the real issue is not whether or not it deviated from the general line for the transition period, but concerns how to implement [the general line]. At that time, Comrade Mao Zedong proposed that the basic task for rural work was to accomplish basically socialist transformation of the countryside on a nationwide basis within ten to fifteen years or a bit longer. Comrade Deng Zihui actually passed on [Mao's message] word for word at the First National Rural Work Conference. It was also in accord with the spirit [of Mao's message that Deng] made the plan for the development of the mutual aid and cooperation movement during the First Five-Year Plan. The original plan set the target that the households to be organized should account for 80 percent of all peasant households. It was later reduced to about 70 to 80 percent in the old [liberated] areas and to 50 to 60 percent in the new [liberated] areas. In the original plan APC membership should account for 45 percent of peasant households in the old [liberated] areas. This was later reduced to 30 to 40 percent. The original figure for the new [liberated] areas was 12 percent and it was later reduced to 6 to 10 percent. All these targets were in accord with the demands of the center at the time.

In the case of the APCs, the gist of the "Resolution on Mutual Aid and Cooperation in Agriculture" concerning the expansion of cooperatives approved by the center on February 15, 1953, was as follows: "In areas where the masses have relatively rich experience in mutual aid and the key members of the leadership are relatively strong, a third form of organization, that is, [lower stage] APCs [that the peasants join] by contributing their shares of land, should be established with some priority and good leadership." Since at that time the lower stage cooperatives were still at the stage of trial experiments at key points, "the party center's policy [on these APCs] is one of steady advance according to necessary and possible conditions for the development of production." Not until December 1953 did the center propose the idea in its "Resolution on the Development of APCs" that the APCs "are to become increasingly the key link to continuous progress in our leadership of the mutual aid and cooperation movement." The Resolution made the following stipulations. We were to "strive to have about 20 percent" of peasant households join the cooperatives during the First Five-Year Plan. "Upon completing the First Five-Year Plan, in some areas APCs are likely to become or come very close to becoming the major form of agricultural production whereas in some other areas they can only have limited development to a certain extent." Therefore, it cannot be said that [the Rural Work Department's plan] deviated from the general line for the transition period, still less that it was a right-deviationist approach.

The second view is that it was wrong for Comrade Deng Zihui to advocate the "four big freedoms" at the First Central Rural Work Conference. In his concluding report at the First Central Rural Work Conference Comrade Deng Zihui said: "It is inappropriate to propose the slogan 'four big freedoms' in sweeping terms," but we should correctly handle the four issues of hiring labor, borrowing and lending money, renting land, and engaging in [private] trade. In other words, "We should relate these issues to current policy and the direction for [further] development, yet at the same time we should also distinguish them [from current policy] so that the peasants' enthusiasm can be maintained while progress can also be made in line with the general direction." Under the guidance of the above thinking he made the following remarks regarding these four issues. Regarding hiring labor, in light of the fact that no one dared to hire labor he said: "We should allow raising the slogan of the freedom to hire labor." Nevertheless, "we do not grant people the sort of freedom found in capitalist countries concerning questions such as hired laborers' wages and their various kinds of remuneration, and therefore such freedom is conditional." Regarding borrowing and lending money, he said: "Today we should advocate freedom in borrowing and lending simply because the peasants need money and the state does not have enough money to help them solve all their problems and difficulties, so they have to borrow money." However, [Deng continued,] "does this mean that we will allow the rampant development of usurious loans? No! We will implement cooperation in credit and offer low-interest loans so as to defeat usurious loans gradually through economic struggle."

Regarding renting land, he said: "The land law permits freedom in buying and selling land and renting out the land. Therefore, we cannot prohibit [such behavior] today. However, the above freedom is very limited. As a matter of fact, only widowers, widows, orphans, the childless, relatives of martyrs, soldiers, and workers as well as the disabled are allowed to rent out their land." "Since at present the purchase and sale of land is permitted, can we allow it to happen freely? No. We simply wish to do our best to help the impoverished peasants overcome their difficulties through other means such as giving loans and providing mutual aid and cooperation so they do not come to the point of selling their land." Regarding [private] trade, he said: "The freedom of engaging in commercial transactions is not outlawed. But this must be put under the leadership and control of state-run trade. In this case leadership means control" that does "not allow [private trade] to flourish." This formulation hardly contradicted our party's basic policy at the time. Indeed, under the special historical conditions [our party's policy] should and could have been applied flexibly. At that time, our country's economy was composed of five elements among which the small scale production sector, like the boundless ocean, was found everywhere. Under these conditions it was unrealistic to wipe out these types of bourgeois freedoms. In light of our party's policy at the time "the rights of all landowners freely to manage, buy, sell, and rent their land are recognized"[17]; "the rich peasant economy is still allowed to develop"[18]; borrowing and lending money was also allowed and in fact the "free borrowing and lending of money should be encouraged" among people in disaster areas;[19] [and] according to the center's documents the freedoms to hire labor and to trade were allowed under specific conditions. If we compare our party's policies at that time with Comrade Deng Zihui's remarks, they were on the whole identical except that the scope of "freedom in borrowing and lending money" proposed by him was somewhat different from the formulation of the Government Administration Council. Correctly carrying out measures that embodied such a spirit [as done by Deng Zihui] was advantageous to economic development and fitted in well with the situation of the time.

The third view considers that Comrade Deng Zihui one-sidedly emphasized that we should "proceed from the current situation of the small peasant economy." This question deserves investigation. What was the composition of the ranks of agricultural producers after the completion of land reform? "They were mainly composed of 100 million households of individual farmers on the basis of small-scale production and small-scale private ownership. Mutual aid teams were merely a collective form of labor organization [loosely] founded on the basis of the individual farming economy while semisocialist APCs comprised no more than 0.2 percent of all peasant households. The cultivated area of the state farms (including all provincial and county farms not using tractors in plowing) fell short of 0.3 percent of the total cultivated area. As far as the rich peasant economy is concerned, its proportion of the economy in both old liberated areas and areas liberated later is quite minimal."[20] Under such circumstances the comrades working in the countryside should have taken into account the above features of economy. Rather than marking time by staying at the stage of the small peasant economy, this approach of proceeding from the actual situation of the small peasant economy actually meant that when we launched the mutual aid and cooperation movement we "should not forget the level of the masses' consciousness, we should [instead] proceed with our down-to-earth experience from the masses' actual needs, and with the current production situation of the small peasant economy."[21]

The "Directive of the CCP Center on Rural Work by Taking into Account the Characteristics of the Small Peasant Economy" of March 3, 1953, pointed out that a large number of cadres should be educated to "remember always and take into consideration the characteristics of the small peasant economy in assigning tasks in the countryside, in working in the villages, and in directing agricultural production." Neglecting this point will easily lead to leftist or rightist mistakes when guiding the mutual aid and cooperation movement. In the light of the above directive there is no reason to dismiss Comrade Deng Zihui's emphasis on "proceeding from the current situation of the small peasant economy."

As the above analysis shows, Comrade Deng Zihui and the Central Rural Work Department under his leadership adhered to the socialist direction, were enthusiastic about developing the collective economy, and rectified the tendency of impetuosity and rash advance in the agricultural mutual aid and cooperation movement in 1953. All this was done in accord with the spirit of the center's instructions. History has proven that his opinion was correct and he made achievements in his work. We should respect history and restore historical truth.

Notes

[The notes that are numbered page by page in the Chinese text have been renumbered consecutively throughout this translation.]

1. *Woguo nongye de shehuizhuyi gaizao* (Our country's socialist transformation of agriculture), 1st edition, Shanghai renmin chubanshe, September 1977, pp. 55, 57.

2. *Xinhua yuebao* (New China monthly), no. 6 (1953), p. 146.

3. *Renmin ribao* (People's daily), March 28, 1953.

4. "Directive of the CCP Central Committee to party committees at all levels on spring plowing and production."

5. North China Bureau [of the party center], *Jianshe* (Construction), no. 207.

6. North China Bureau, "Rectifying the deviation of blind and rash advance in the development of APCs." See North China Bureau, *Jianshe*, combined vol., no. 8.

7. *Renmin ribao*, March 30, 1953.

8. North China Bureau, *Jianshe*, no. 202.

9. "Directive of the CCP center while transmitting to party committees at all levels the 'Report of the North China Bureau to the center concerning the situation after the rectification of the tendency of impetuosity and rash advance in the mutual aid and cooperation movement in agricultural production and present work tasks,' " October 4, 1953, in North China Bureau, *Douzheng* (Struggle), no. 234.

10. "Report of the North China Bureau concerning the situation after the rectification of the tendency of impetuosity and rash advance in the mutual aid and cooperation movement in agricultural production and present work tasks," July 3, 1953, in North China Bureau, *Douzheng*.

11. The data on the expansion of cooperatives in 1952 and 1953 were collected in the middle of the year. Another interpretation is that they were the statistics at the time of income distribution after the fall harvest.

12. "Resolution on the development of APCs," passed by the center on December 16, 1953.

13. *Woguo nongye de shehuizhuyi gaizao*, p. 57.

14. *Mao Zedong xuanji* (Selected works of Mao Zedong), vol. 5, p. 120.

15. North China Bureau, *Douzheng*, no. 207.

16. *Mao xuanji*, vol. 5, p. 152.

17. *Land reform law of the People's Republic of China*.

18. "Resolution of the CCP center on mutual aid and cooperation in agriculture."

19. "Directive of the Government Administration Council of the Central People's Government concerning stepping up the work of increasing crop output and providing disaster relief," *Renmin ribao*, May 17, 1953.

20. *Renmin ribao* editorial, "The key to leading agricultural production," March 26, 1953.

21. "Directive to party committees at all levels concerning production during spring plowing" by the center.

3

JIANG BOYING

Selection from *Biography of Deng Zihui**

Chapter 12: In charge of the
Central Rural Work Department (1953–1962)

[This chapter has been heavily excerpted to focus on events before 1955, as well as to give some attention to Deng's activities in 1956 after the "high tide." The first section of the chapter is entitled "Rectify the Tendency of Impetuosity and Rash Advance."]

Upon arriving in Beijing, Deng Zihui settled in a lodge in Zhongnanhai very close to Chairman Mao Zedong's residence. Mao Zedong called Deng Zihui in for a talk in which he briefed Deng on the task of establishing the Rural Work Department and its mission in the period ahead.

Deng Zihui felt deeply that his appointment as the director of the Central Rural Work Department by the party center indicated the party's trust and hopes in him. He realized on the one hand that it was quite a huge responsibility to take part in leading the 400 million Chinese peasants out of the backwardness caused by thousands of years of feudal rule and onto the broad road of socialism. At the same time he was fully confident that such a historical task could be accomplished under the leadership of the Chinese Communist Party and Mao Zedong, together with the intense revolutionary fervor expressed by the peasants of the whole country.

Deng Zihui always kept in mind Mao Zedong's teaching concerning following the mass line [that Mao had given] in 1929 in Sujiapo in western Fujian. This teaching taught him always to make investigations and studies of the masses' views as the primary source for policy making. Soon after he assumed office at the Rural Work Department, he pointed out to the cadres at a departmental meeting that investigation and research and seeking truth from facts were the preconditions for doing rural work well and that they should become a rule for the Rural Work Department. He asked all working personnel, except those who were old, weak, and sick, to go to countryside in order to maintain close contact with the peasants, and to oppose and overcome bureaucratism.

---

*Jiang Boying, *Deng Zihui zhuan* (Biography of Deng Zihui) (Shanghai: Shanghai renmin chubanshe, 1986), pp. 293–94, 304–308, 310, 312–14, 328–29.

On February 9, 1953, Deng Zihui convened a Rural Work Department cadres conference at which he explicitly expounded his views on the socialist transformation of agriculture in our country in light of the party's general line for the transition period and Mao Zedong's directive. He maintained that after the completion of land reform [the Chinese people] would be faced with two roads. The first one was to allow rampant development of private money lending and allow the rich peasants to purchase peasants' land and labor at low prices. The end result of this would be that the rich peasants would snatch the fruits of land reform and the villages would become bankrupt again. "This is a capitalist road" and "a painful one. We won't travel on such a road." The other was a new road, "that is, the road of getting organized as instructed by Chairman Mao."

[The author continues with an extensive discussion of the rash advance tendency and the efforts of Deng Zihui, the party center and Mao to bring it under control in the first half of 1953. See Document 2 for a detailed analysis of these developments.]

Deng Zihui was a [pragmatic] person who laid stress on investigation and research. He carefully read and examined over and over again materials and reports sent in from various places. Despite this he was not content with these materials that after all were secondhand information and hence unable to satisfy his need to lead rural work well. He decided to pay personal visits to the countryside to conduct some on-the-spot investigations. From October to December 1953, with some working personnel, he did two months of investigation and study successively in Wuhan, Nanjing, Shanghai, Hangzhou, Shangrao, Fuzhou, Longyan, Ruijin, Ganzhou, and Nanchang. Throughout his journey he held discussions with comrades responsible for rural work in various places [in order to] understand the situation of mutual aid and cooperation, and especially to investigate the circumstances of the work of rectifying impetuosity and rash advance since the spring. During this fact-finding trip he presented a dozen or so reports that were heard by more than 20,000 people in total. He conveyed the center's plan to complete the socialist transformation of agriculture in a ten to fifteen year period, [and] carried out propaganda on the party's general line for the transition period, its general tasks and the policy of state monopoly purchase and marketing of grain. He gave instructions on advancing further the rectification of the leftist rash advance mood, overcoming the rightist tendency of biding one's time and letting things drift, and enthusiastically guiding the agricultural cooperativization movement.

Before this trip the center was pleased with Deng Zihui's and the Rural Work Department's work and fully affirmed their proposals, especially those regarding the rectification of impetuosity and rash advance. On October 4, 1953, it also issued a notice to the whole party instructing that "in order to exploit the political achievements of the rectification effort and to prepare the ideological ground for a healthier and greater development of the mutual aid and cooperation movement, another review of the movement should be made and the reeducation of the cadres should be carried out."[1] Without doubt this notice by the center was very important and timely for taking further steps in exposing and eradicating the ideological sources of impetuosity and rash advance.

In reality, however, this directive by the center was not actually implemented because divergent opinions emerged within the party over the issue of "opposing rash advance" soon after it was dispatched. At the same time the Central Rural Work Department received criticism for its efforts to rectify the leftist tendency since spring 1953. The critics maintained that the campaign to oppose impetuosity and rash advance had become a gust of wind that blew away some APCs that should not have been blown away. It had committed the mistake of forcing the dissolution of cooperatives, hence it was merely "marking time" without advancing.

Such being the state of affairs Deng Zihui was also criticized and reproached not only for his so-called right-deviationist error concerning the pace of cooperativization but also for his alleged error of one-sidedly emphasizing "making something of the small peasant economy" instead of relying on socialism.

In response to this inner-party criticism Deng Zihui conducted a serious and careful self-examination. After reflecting conscientiously on his own work during the previous year, however, he did not think that he had made any serious mistakes on these issues. He insisted that he had been unswerving regarding the socialist direction for Chinese agriculture, namely from mutual aid to collectivization. He also maintained that the theoretical viewpoints he held concerning the role of agriculture during the period of socialist transformation were fully in line with the center's policy as well as the reality of the Chinese countryside. For this reason he hardly felt pessimistic or the need to alter his convictions despite the criticism. On the contrary, he had a more positive attitude and greater enthusiasm in assuming leadership over the even larger agricultural cooperativization movement through summing up experiences, drawing lessons, and attempting to explore ways to consolidate cooperativization in the course of the movement.

[The author now begins a new section entitled "Exploring the Way of Consolidating and Further Developing Agricultural Cooperativization." The first two plus paragraphs note the speedup of cooperativization after the criticism of rectifying rash advance and Deng's awareness of the problems involved.]

On March 20, 1954, in view of the fact that spring plowing was about to start and in view of the pretentious and superficial progress of cooperativization in some regions, the Central Rural Work Department issued a

"Directive on Contracting the Development of APCs and Shifting Our Efforts to Production." In it [Deng Zihui] in timely fashion pointed out to the whole party that doubling the number of the cooperatives "is a great victory. However, the victory is not stable. At present the most important task in the mutual aid and cooperation movement is to consolidate the victory in earnest, to do all we can to ensure the indispensable quality of every newly established cooperative, and to run well all the new and old cooperatives so as to lay a firm foundation for greater development in the future."

[The following paragraph gave further details of this directive.]

An important matter after the establishment of cooperatives was the need to do collective management well in order to enable cooperatives to increase production and their members' income. Whether we could give full play to the superiority of cooperatives was the key to attracting more individual [i.e., private] peasants to join the cooperatives and ensuring their consolidation and development. At that time Deng Zihui had already started summing up experience on this matter. Between April 2 and 18, 1954, the Central Rural Work Department convened the Second National Rural Work Conference. In his concluding report at the conference, Deng Zihui preliminarily expounded his understanding of how to consolidate and further develop the APCs.

In summing up the experience of the mutual aid and cooperation movement Deng Zihui [again] affirmed the positive significance of rectifying the tendency of impetuosity and rash advance in 1953. He pointed out bluntly and unambiguously: "Last spring the center rectified impetuosity and rash advance in rural work and subsequently succeeded in overcoming the phenomenon of the 'five excesses' [of too many assignments, meetings and training courses, documents and reports, organizations, and side jobs for activists]. These efforts had a tremendous impact on this year's mutual aid and cooperation movement." "The view that there had been no impetuosity and rash advance in the past year and that opposing rash advance and the 'five excesses' was taking the position of the small peasant economy is simply wrong." He also remarked [without reservation] that denying the existence of rash advance last year and gainsaying the positive role of opposing rash advance "is not taking the attitude of seeking truth from facts."[2]

[The author continues with several pages of discussion concerning Deng's concluding report and the department's report on the conference, a discussion including Deng's proposal of an agricultural production responsibility system. For a summary of this conference, see Document 4, pp. 83–84. For a translation of Deng's views as published on the eve of the April conference, see *Current Background*, no. 305 (1954).]

In September 1954, Deng Zihui attended the First Session of the First

National People's Congress where he was appointed Vice Premier of the State Council and concurrently Director of the Seventh Office of the State Council in charge of the Ministries of Agriculture, Forestry, Water Conservancy, and Meteorology. [The author continues by summarizing Deng's speech to the Congress.]

By fall 1954 the number of APCs in the whole country had increased from 14,000 in 1953 to 220,000 while cooperative membership accounted for 4 percent of all peasant households. In view of the healthy and rapid development of the movement the center approved the plan proposed by the Fourth National Mutual Aid and Cooperation Conference. That is to say, prior to the 1955 spring plowing the number of APCs was to reach 600,000. Lower stage cooperativization was to be basically completed nationwide by 1957. Therefore, during the Second Five-Year Plan (1958–62) the movement was to shift gradually to achieving higher stage cooperativization.

Deng Zihui held that to be able to implement this plan smoothly within the following three years, the year 1955 would be crucial for turning the movement into an upsurge of cooperativization. Facing this crucial stage in the socialist transformation of Chinese agriculture, Deng Zihui repeatedly emphasized this point in his concluding report to the Fourth National Mutual Aid and Cooperation Conference [in October 1954]: "Next year is the year when the foundation for the greater development of cooperativization in the future will be laid. If the 600,000 APCs are really run well, if the foundation is well laid and a good example is set, then a massive development of cooperatives can be expected and it will be much easier to run them well.[3] If not, then the situation will be quite different and we may end up rewriting the whole plan despite our reluctance [to do so]." "Therefore, the whole party must be cautious and conscientious in running the cooperatives well. We cannot afford to be careless or act hastily." "We are only allowed to do it well. We are neither allowed to spoil it nor allowed to come up with any waste [i.e., poorly run cooperatives] to make up the numbers." He further said that if we run 600,000 APCs well, this batch of rural socialist strongholds will be a basic position for drawing the middle peasants and poor peasants toward triumphing over village capitalism. If we consolidate this position and build well this foundation, and afterwards again advance steadily, then we can obtain twice the result for half the effort.

Deng Zihui earnestly warned the participants at the conference [against undue optimism]: "Now there is some blind optimism. Deceived by shouts of bravo from the lower ranks, people think that everything is going wonderfully and therefore develop an appetite for big plans. Accordingly they raise [the target] at each level. This [sentiment] tends to lead to acting impetuously, committing coercion and commandism, and disrupting the course of the movement. On this point everyone should pay full attention. I ask comrades from all places to keep a sober mind so as to handle development plans realistically, to avoid increasing the target at each level, and to strive for advancing prudently and running the cooperatives well. In any case we won't backtrack."[4] Meanwhile, he advised that they should not care only about establishing, to the neglect of consolidating, cooperatives. The goal of setting up cooperatives is after all to run them well and get them consolidated. He emphasized that cadres must become experts on [cooperative] production and constantly draw lessons from the experience of consolidating cooperatives.

The above basic points that Deng Zihui made at this conference received the support of the center. In December 1954 the CCP center approved and distributed the "Report on the Fourth National Mutual Aid and Cooperation Conference" drafted by the Rural Work Department. The center pointed out in its comment: "The center approves the report by the Central Rural Work Department on the Fourth National Mutual Aid and Cooperation Conference. Since the agricultural cooperativization movement in the whole country is at the stage of preparing the ground, the foundation must be laid well."

Unfortunately, due to blind optimism and the sentiment for rash advance that emerged from the preliminary success of agricultural cooperativization, the above valuable opinions of the center and Deng Zihui were not adequately recognized or taken seriously by the whole party. Instead the increasingly evident differences within the party over the pace of cooperativization touched off a debate in 1955.

[A lengthy section entitled "The Debate on Agricultural Cooperativization" follows concerning the events of 1955 that are more richly detailed in Documents 4 and 5. The author next began a section entitled "Bringing Up Again the Responsibility System for Agricultural Production.]

After the great debate of 1955 over the course of agricultural cooperativization that led to the erroneous criticism of so-called "right-deviationist opportunism," the rural work front within the party was overwhelmed by "the fear of rightism" that in turn engendered the sentiment for more blind and rash advance. From then on the development of agricultural cooperativization deviated from the correct policy on mutual aid and cooperation formulated by the center and also from Mao Zedong's correct stipulations and planning regarding agricultural cooperativization. In March 1956 agricultural cooperativization in its elementary form was basically completed throughout the country. By the end of 1956 higher stage agricultural cooperativization was miraculously accomplished in the whole countryside. It was announced that now the socialist transformation of agriculture in our country had finished ahead of time. If we estimate that the movement started in 1953, [then it is clear that] the historical process [of cooperativization] was achieved within four years instead of the ten to fifteen years as originally planned.

While on the one hand encouraged by the rising upsurge of cooperativization, Deng Zihui on the other hand expressed great concern over the problems of coarse work and mismanagement during the hasty move from lower to higher stage APCs and from semisocialist to full socialist cooperatives. He insisted that we ought to have a great development of agricultural cooperativization yet at the same time the work of consolidation should not be overlooked. He also insisted that we should bravely welcome the new upsurge of the movement but this movement must be put under more vigorous leadership and more prudent policies. Amidst the songs of eulogy celebrating the success of cooperativization, he soberly saw the remaining problems in the movement and felt that a stable consolidation period for the collective rural economy was desperately required so that the remaining problems could be dealt with and solved with great efforts and the great success already achieved could be consolidated.

In 1956 at the National Conference of Rural Work Department Heads, the National Advanced Producers' Representative Conference, and the Third Session of the First National People's Congress, he honestly analyzed the problems existing during the upsurge of agricultural cooperativization. He went on to expound the view that after accomplishing agricultural cooperativization throughout the country it was necessary to overhaul and consolidate the cooperatives in order to improve their quality. Meanwhile, following his previous attempt in 1954 he once again stressed the importance of establishing the agricultural production responsibility system for the consolidation of cooperativization.

Deng Zihui considered that since fall 1955 the agricultural cooperativization movement "has been carried out on an unprecedentedly large scale and at an unusually fast pace." "This was not only an unprecedented victory for the Chinese socialist revolution, but also a splendid undertaking with great historical significance for the world." "However, can we therefore think that there are no shortcomings and mistakes in our cooperativization movement? This would obviously be wrong. [To be sure] there are many shortcomings and mistakes in the movement [including] even some very serious ones. To conceal and overlook these shortcomings and mistakes will only have disadvantages and won't do us any good. Therefore, we should thoroughly expose and quickly rectify them."[5] In Deng Zihui's analysis, problems in the [then] current agricultural cooperativization mainly had five aspects: First, cooperatives in many places were run in an extravagant and wasteful way that resulted in their members' dissatisfaction. Second, there was a lack of overall planning of production, sideline production was neglected, and cooperative members' household sideline production was restricted. Third, the principle of voluntariness and mutual benefit was not implemented in establishing cooperatives. Fourth, there was chaos in management and the blind pursuit of high targets that resulted in difficulties in implementing the production responsibility system's work and output contracts. Fifth, the conditions of place and time were overlooked and uniformity was enforced in spreading the reform of farming techniques.

Deng Zihui held that these problems of course had objective causes, but "they were mainly caused by overly large plans and too urgent demands made by the concerned higher-level departments. An even more important cause of mistakes, shortcomings and the difficulties in rectifying them was that many cadres lacked the realistic spirit of seeking truth from facts and implementing policies according to local conditions as well as lacking the democratic style of consulting their subordinates and the masses in making decisions."[6] Deng Zihui's sober understanding and courage in talking honestly at that time were difficult to achieve and thus worthy of our esteem.

[The remainder of the chapter examined Deng's subsequent career until the Rural Work Department was abolished on Mao's demand in 1962.]

Notes

[The notes that are numbered page by page in the Chinese text have been renumbered consecutively throughout this translation.]

1. "The CCP center's comments while transmitting the 'Report of the North China Bureau to the center concerning the situation after the rectification of the tendency of impetuosity and rash advance in the mutual aid and cooperation movement in agricultural production and present work tasks,' " October 4, 1953.

2. Deng Zihui, "Summary report at the Second National Rural Work Conference," April 1954.

3. "Comrade Deng Zihui's summary report at the Fourth National Mutual Aid and Cooperation Conference," October 29, 1954.

4. Ibid.

5. Deng Zihui, "The situation of the agricultural cooperativization movement in the past year and future work," June 19, 1956.

6. Ibid.

4

LIN YUNHUI, FAN SHOUXIN, and ZHANG GONG

Selection from *China 1949–1989: The Period of Triumph and Advance**

Chapter 9: The rebellion of the productive forces and the policy of "stop, shrink, develop"

From winter 1952 to spring 1953 an upsurge in the agricultural mutual aid and cooperation movement resulted in the first rash advance. In 1954 the expansion of APCs, characterized by shareholding one's land with dividends on the land and labor, caused another upsurge. In early 1955, the CCP center decided to rectify rash advance for the second time.

I. Overpurchasing grain

1. The plan for expanding [cooperatives] became increasingly ambitious

Due to wide publicity for the "Outline for Propaganda about the General Line for the Transition Period," the task, which was set by the party center in the [December 1953] "Resolution on the Development of APCs," of raising the number of agricultural cooperatives to 35,300 in 1954 and to 800,000 in 1957, soon led to overfulfillment of the plan. In spring 1954 there were already 90,000 cooperatives.

On February 12, 1954, the Rural Work Department reported to the center on the current situation and problems regarding the establishment of APCs. It pointed out that attention should be paid to two problems in current work. The first problem was the lack of a sober analysis of the masses' enthusiasm and consequent rash approval of establishing cooperatives. The second problem was overemphasis of the control figures in the original plans and the failure to give approval [for establishing cooper-

---

*Lin Yunhui, Fan Shouxin, and Zhang Gong, *1949–1989 nian de Zhongguo: kaige xingjin de shiqi* (China 1949–1989: The period of triumph and advance) (Henan: Henan renmin chubanshe, 1989), pp. 532–77.

atives] where the conditions were satisfied. The report emphasized the following points: The leading bodies of some prefectures, counties, and districts lacked a sober analysis of the masses' enthusiasm. Neither did they understand that although some of the masses were highly enthusiastic because of their considerable understanding of APCs and decided, after consideration, to participate in the cooperative movement, a fairly large portion of the masses were only temporarily enthusiastic and might change their attitude when dealing with specific problems concerning the establishment of cooperatives. Some wanted to join cooperatives thinking that "it is better to take the socialist path earlier rather than later." Others were outwardly enthusiastic but their hearts were full of worries. Only seeing the masses' outward enthusiasm in a sweeping and superficial manner while failing to see the misgivings in the minds of the masses who took a wait-and-see attitude or lagged behind [the movement], the above leaders approved easily and hastily the establishment of cooperatives. APCs were set up prematurely when [the leaders] were satisfied with the masses' enthusiasm that had been stimulated by the propaganda on the general line during grain purchase work, took it for granted that casual approval could lead to the establishment of APCs, and underestimated or neglected the necessarily profound and detailed work of propaganda, education, and organization concerning the general policies and specific practices of APCs. With respect to these problems, the report suggested some measures for improvement. On March 12 the party center approved this report and distributed it to party committees in all places.

At the Second National Rural Work Conference in April [1954] the following conclusions were reached: With the progress of national socialist industrialization, a continuously increasing population in urban industries and mining, the continuous rise in urban and rural living standards, and natural population growth (increasing by 10 million annually), and in order to meet the needs of industrial construction for the export of agricultural products, it was necessary to increase by large amounts the annual production of grain, cotton, oil crops, and other crops for industrial raw materials. That is to say, with developing industries, agriculture should be developed proportionally. If agricultural development fell behind the needs of industrial development, a balance between industrial and agricultural production could not be kept, the whole construction plan of the country would be consequently upset and the needs created by the people's continuously rising living standards would not be met. It would arouse popular discontent and cause severe difficulties. According to data collected from various areas, the existing APCs could raise production by 20 to 30 percent within the first or second year after their establishment and maintain a certain growth rate in production during the coming years. These growth rates were higher than those of mutual aid teams and much higher than those of the private peasant economy. Therefore, the cooperativization movement should be the focus of not only rural work, but also of the production movement. The boost in agricultural production and the development of mutual aid and cooperation should be seen as integrated and should not be separated from each other. The view and the practice of separating production from cooperativization and setting them against each other are mistaken. On the basis of the above conclusions, the original plan in the resolution regarding the development of APCs was revised at the conference. It was decided that in 1955, 300,000 or 350,000 APCs should be established. By the end of 1957, the planned number of the APCs was raised from 800,000 in the original plan to 1.3 or 1.5 million, cooperative membership as a percentage of peasant households was also raised from 20 percent in the original plan to about 35 percent, and the cultivated land in APCs should cover more than 40 percent of the total cultivated land of the country. In particular, in the Northeast, Shanxi, Hebei, Shandong, Henan, and other old liberated areas more than 50 percent of cultivated land should be owned by the cooperatives. Moreover, cooperativization should be carried out first in the plains, high yield and cash crop areas, and in suburban districts. During the period of the Second Five-Year Plan (by around 1960), cooperativization should be basically completed in most areas of the country.[1] On June 3 the party center approved and distributed a report by the Central Rural Work Department regarding the Second National Rural Work Conference. It pointed out that this report was approved at a central conference on May 18 and it was hoped that various places would actively exert efforts to run the existing 90,000 APCs throughout the country really well so as to prepare for the imminent great development of cooperatives.

Under the guidance of the spirit of the Second Rural Work Conference that was approved by the center, another 120,000 APCs were established in summer 1954. There were altogether 220,000 APCs, including the original 90,000 APCs. At the Fourth National Conference on Mutual Aid and Cooperation of October of the same year, the plan for the expansion of agricultural cooperatives was again revised and the target of 300 or 350,000 APCs for 1955 proposed in April was raised to 600,000 before the 1955 spring plowing. The conference considered that the above plan was on the whole appropriate and suggested that the center approve it. The conference also proposed the following basic steps for the progress of socialist transformation of agriculture in our country. The first step was initially to accomplish basically elementary cooperativization around 1957. These APCs were to be successively changed into higher stage cooperatives during the Second Five-Year Plan in different places at different times. During this stage, only elementary technological improvement and partially mechanized cultivation would be implemented. During the second step, large scale agricultural mechanization would be implemented over roughly the Third and Fourth Five-Year Plans by equipping agriculture on the basis of the development of industry.[2]

The party center approved the development plan for APCs proposed at the Fourth Conference on Mutual Aid and Cooperation. It required that in addition to the prefecture and county [party] committees, which would devote most of their efforts to the central task of the mutual aid and cooperation movement, the provincial committees should appoint a secretary or deputy secretary to be in charge of concrete affairs regarding agricultural mutual aid and cooperation. Moreover, the first secretaries should be responsible for overall leadership and guidance to ensure the rapid and healthy development of the movement and to consolidate the worker-peasant alliance.

Under the guiding thought of welcoming a big expansion of APCs, cadres in many places blindly made ambitious plans, concentrated on percentage figures alone, excessively emphasized, and even competed with each other in, setting up big and higher stage APCs, for they only saw the initiative of a small number of core members. As a result they used simple and crude methods to force the peasants to join cooperatives by erroneously publicizing [the following slogans]: "working by oneself is against the law"; [and] failing to join cooperatives is [pursuing] capitalism." To give an example that happened in Zhejiang Province, at a conference where rich peasants were publicly denounced in Shanlian District, Wuxin County, the head of the propaganda department of the county committee said: "Whoever wants to take the socialist path should set up cooperatives. Whoever does not join the cooperatives will be like [the rich peasants]!" In some places, when grain was purchased according to the state plan, peasants working by themselves were made to suffer losses by being assigned output [targets] higher than those in the cooperatives. For fear that they would be reclassified as rich peasants and landlords and as a consequence would live a tough life, many peasants cried bitterly and begged to join the cooperatives.[3]

Also, since some existing cooperatives offered too low prices for the means of production and livestock of the peasants who joined the cooperatives, or although offering fair prices could not pay them, the actual interests of the peasants were damaged. The peasants could not help but feel panicky and fear "nationalization."

By the end of December 1954 the number of APCs surged to 480,000 and the momentum for expanding cooperatives grew stronger and stronger.

2. Overpurchasing 10 billion jin of grain[4]

While an upsurge of expanding APCs was being set off, the state monopoly purchase of grain unfolded in the countryside nationwide during November and December [1954].

In summer 1954 the worst flood of the past few decades swept the Yangtze and Huai River regions and Hebei Province. The irrigation works constructed during the past few years, such as the Jin River flood diversion project, the Huai River irrigation works, and other projects, had a notable effect on storing and diverting the floodwater. They safeguarded the cities along the Yangtze River and the embankment along the Jin River, and reduced the losses caused by the flood throughout the countryside. In the whole country 16.13 million qing [1 qing=6.67 hectares—Eds.] of cultivated land were flooded. After draining floodwater, rescuing seedlings, and reseeding, 11.31 million qing of cultivated land and 60 million people were affected by the flood. The flood seriously hindered the accomplishment of the agricultural production plan. In 1954, grain output was 339 billion jin, an increase of 5.3 billion jin from the previous year, and accounted for 94.2 percent of the planned target. Cotton output was 21.3 million dan [a unit of weight equivalent to 50 kilograms—Eds.], a decrease of 220,000 dan from the previous year, and accounted for only 77.5 percent of the planned target.

Although crop output failed to reach the planned target, the planned quotas for grain purchase were not reduced. In order to ensure the accomplishment of this task, the planned quotas were in fact increased to some extent when they were transmitted to lower levels. As a result, by the end of 1954, 103.6 billion jin of grain was purchased and 110 percent of the original plan was achieved. In the whole country, 10 billion jin of grain was purchased beyond the original plan and serious phenomena of coercion and commandism appeared. The South China Subbureau of the party center pointed out the following in its report to the center: While publicizing the grain policy to the peasants, the cadres only emphasized that the peasants should sell their surplus grain to the state in accordance with the notice and arbitrarily imposed on peasants who failed to do so the labels of violating the law, capitalist spontaneous forces, and so on. The commandist style of work was thus widespread and developing. In some areas serious commandism and even worse activities occurred to the extent of violating the law and [party] discipline, leading to vicious cases. For example, under the instruction of the responsible comrade of the county party committee, the party branch of Lianxi Township, Xinhui County, tied up eight to nine peasants in the whole township, among whom was the head of the production team of the cooperative. After that, the county cadres carried lever scales and weighed the household grain of each household. If a peasant did not sell, they tied him up right away (two people were tied up). They publicly denounced a middle peasant who used part of his grain to feed his ducks and confiscated the land certificate of peasants who did not sell their surplus grain (the certificates of three households were confiscated). In the ninth district in Gaoyao County, fifty-three people were tied up and beaten during the purchase of grain. Meanwhile, in Yikeng Township of this district thirty-six households were searched. In Dongwei Township of the tenth district, a rich peasant's house was sealed. An old woman was also sealed within the house and hung herself eventually. Since some cadres thought erroneously that publicly denouncing a large number of rich peasants meant a "high tide," severe beatings took place in every district in the county. As a result, the masses made it known: "The Communist Party is fiercer than the Guomindang." Throughout the province 111 persons committed suicide over the question of grain purchasing. The causes of the above problems were that the branches and the party committees of each district did not extensively and properly explain the policy regarding grain purchase. They failed to discover in time and resolutely stop the spreading commandism and various unlawful and undisciplined activities on the part of some cadres. In addition, the heavy tasks to be completed within a short period of time made cadres try to meet the target by any means.[5] It is worth pointing out that these phenomena of serious coercion and commandism, unlawfulness, and indiscipline existed in not a few areas of the country.

II. The productive forces rebel

Too rapid and too rash expansion of the agricultural cooperatives and oversimple and crude work [methods] infringed on the peasants' interests. Coercion and commandism during grain purchasing, which also resulted in the purchase of the peasants' grain ration, seriously disturbed the peasants. As a result, the productive forces suffered damage and rural relations were strained in every aspect.

1. The massive sale and slaughtering of livestock

In the December 1954 "Circular on the Present Situation of the Market for Cattle and Sheep and the Problem of the Production of Pork," the Central Ministry of Commerce pointed out: Since the fourth quarter, in many areas the numbers of cattle and sheep on the market increased instantly and purchase plans were overfulfilled. Moreover, the prices of cows, milch cows, lambs, small pigs, and baby pigs dropped correspondingly. Such a situation existed in almost every major market throughout the country. For example, farm cattle were killed in large numbers in Rehe Province, the livestock in north Shanxi flowed back into Suiyuan, and the number of small pigs raised by the peasants in Sichuan Province decreased sharply.

According to a December 1954 report by the Rehe Provincial Committee, since the fall something extremely abnormal happened on the cattle market: the prices of the livestock dropped in general from one-third to about one-half and a large number of cattle flooded the market. In the third quarter, state enterprises bought 15,877 oxen, overfulfilling the plan by 199.1 percent, and the number was six and a half times more than that of the same period of last year; [they also] took in 114,842 sheep, overfulfilling the plan by 99.4 percent, 10.2 times more than that of the previous third quarter. According to the statistics of two months and ten days of the fourth quarter, 171,442 oxen and 168,276 sheep were bought, some of which were farm animals and dams. Farm animals were killed in some areas. According to the report by Ningcheng County, 149 donkeys were killed throughout the county; 21 donkeys were killed in seven villages of the tenth district of Lingyuan; among the villages, 10 donkeys were killed in the one village of Yandayingzi alone. Donkey killings were also found in Kalaqing Banner, Pingquan, Zhaoyang, Chifeng, and other places. Since the government prohibited killing farm animals, some peasants went so far as to break the legs of the donkeys intentionally and then request to kill them. In Kalaqing Banner, it was found that some households owning farm animals, upon finding out that the state enterprises did not purchase farm animals, knocked out the teeth of their oxen and then dragged them to the market for sale, or did some other things of this sort.[6]

The report by the South China Subbureau of the party center also said that during the latter period of the grain purchasing movement (late December 1954), peasants everywhere slaughtered a large number of pigs and ducks and the prices for pigs thus dropped dramatically. In Zhang-jiabian Township, Zhongshan County, alone, more than 70 sows were killed and the prices for baby pigs dropped sharply from the normal price of 600,000 to 1,000,000 yuan (old *renminbi*) to 140,000 yuan per dan. In east Guangdong, in the ninth district of Chao'an County, more than 40 sows were found dead in only one day. In Taishan County, a peasant household killed each of the 10 baby pigs that were just born.[7]

The sale and slaughter of large numbers of livestock tremendously decreased the number of farm animals and doubtlessly [led to] an extremely severe destruction of the productive forces in the countryside.

2. The overall tense situation in rural relations[8]

Another critical symptom of the damage to rural productive forces was that the peasants were not enthusiastic about production. The means of production for spring plowing were poorly prepared, the number of farm cattle in general decreased, few new farm tools were added, little repair work was done to existing farm tools, and the most important fertilizer—barnyard manure, decreased because of the reduction in the number of pigs, oxen, and sheep. Water conservancy and pest elimination plans, as well as other plans, were not completed. The rate of attendance in many APCs dropped dramatically. This was because the assignment of work and workpoints in the cooperatives was unfair and mainly because the cooperative members reported that they did not eat enough and, therefore, could not do heavy work and did not show up for work. In some areas members of the Youth League also reported that they were hungry, felt cold, and had sore legs and that, as a result, they could not even attend the branch meeting of the Youth League.

Peasants had severe worries over the grain issue. Peasants around Gangkou Town, Zhongshan County, Guangdong Province, covertly sent someone at night to see whether the grain in the granaries had been shipped away or not. Upon seeing the ships transporting the grain sail away, they burst into tears on the bank of the river. In many areas households short of grain that had not received grain purchase certificates went to the houses of the rural cadres and cried, weeping and wailing endlessly out of great anxiety.

Discontent with the party and the people's government was widespread among peasants (including many township and village cadres). The peasants in Xinhui and Gaoyao Counties let their complaints be known: "We have nothing to eat after one year of hard work"; "The Communist party is good, however, it is now punishing people to death"; "We don't know what is going on with the government because the party is pushing us to death"; "The Communist party has changed its face"; "Grain is purchased every year and we don't know how to live from now on."

After the purchase of grain, relations changed between the district cadres and township and village cadres on the one hand, and between township cadres and the masses on the other. Many township and village cadres reported that the masses walked away upon seeing them whereas the district cadres did not trust them and frequently criticized them and stuck bad labels on them so that they themselves did not dare to report to the true situation to higher levels.

This demonstrated that because of hastiness and rash advance in the expansion of APCs and the "excessive" grain purchase by the state, relations between the peasants on the one hand and the party, government, and township and village cadres on the other, between township and village cadres and cadres at higher levels, and between the countryside and the cities, all became strained.

3. A scientific judgment

Mao Zedong made an extremely profound scientific judgment on the sale and slaughter of large numbers of farm animals and the decline in peasants' production initiative at that time. He said:

> "Relations of production should suit the demands for the development of productive forces. Otherwise, productive forces will rise up and rebel. The

present slaughter of pigs and oxen by the peasants is the uprising and rebellion of the productive forces."[9]

III. The three-word policy of "stop, shrink, develop"

1. Two proposals[10]

Regarding the rural situation, soon after the Central Ministry of Commerce issued a circular on the market situation for oxen and sheep, on January 4, 1955, Deng Zihui reported to the Premier and the party center on the situation of agricultural cooperativization and put forward two proposals in the form of a Work Bulletin (no. 1) of the Seventh Office of the State Council. The bulletin said:

[The authors quote extensively from the bulletin that is translated in full in the original documents section of this volume, pp. 155–56. The sections quoted here are the second, third, and (bulk of the) fourth paragraphs. These sections note the high rate of APC expansion since fall 1954 with local targets totalling 700,000 APCs, and the nature of and reasons for shortcomings in the new cooperatives. They also raise two proposals: (1) that a charter specifying the semisocialist nature of cooperatives be made; and (2) that the overall movement shift to controlled development and enter a stage of consolidation. The second proposal is highlighted in the text here, although apparently not in the original. The excerpt also noted that it would be "the greatest victory" even if only 500,000 APCs were established.]

2. Four urgent directives[11]

Accepting Deng Zihui's proposals and taking into account the overall situation, the party center issued four urgent directives from January to March. They were: "Circular on Overhauling and Consolidating APCs" of January 10, "Urgent Directive on Making Great Efforts to Protect Farm Animals" of January 15, "Directive concerning the Problem of Implementing the Socialist Transformation of Agriculture in Minority Nationality Regions" of February 25, and "Urgent Directive by the CCP Central Committee and State Council on Prompt Assignment of Grain Purchase Work and Stabilizing the Peasants' Production Spirit" of March 3.

These directives suggested it was naturally a good thing to have such a rapid development of cooperatives within a brief few months, but a comprehensive estimate of the favorable situation was needed. Neither should we applaud blindly nor should we look at the work of cooperativization in an oversimplified manner and neglect the likely serious doubts and worries of the peasants, especially middle peasants, during the change in the relations of production and the likely consequent shocks in the countryside. In view of the state of the peasants' actual thinking, ideological education should be conducted repeatedly, organizational work carried out painstakingly, critical economic problems in cooperatives solved carefully, and present production activities organized well. Otherwise, immature outcomes would occur, the cooperativization movement would be prevented from advancing continuously, and severe consequences unfavorable for production might follow. It should not be taken for granted that no deviations would occur because the party enjoyed high respect from the peasants and the present semisocialist policy of cooperativization received the support of the peasants. In the period when the cooperativization movement developed rapidly, if we did not do our work well and let deviations occur, we would encounter various phenomena unfavorable to production. However limited and short-lived these phenomena might be, they would cause great losses. For this reason, we should make every cautious and conscientious effort to avoid them.

These instructions comprehensively analyzed the causes of the severely strained state of rural relations. They pointed out that we should notice that in many places a serious situation developed where the peasants slaughtered a large number of pigs and oxen, failed to collect fertilizers eagerly or prepare for spring plowing actively, and displayed a low mood for production. This might partially result from the resistance and sabotage of a small number of rich peasants and other unhealthy elements. However, on the whole, it was essentially a warning given by the masses of middle peasants because of their discontent with some party and government policies. This situation could be attributed to many things. They included roughness and hastiness in the mutual aid and cooperativization movement in some areas, too early and too hasty incorporation of livestock into the cooperatives at too low market prices that were not, moreover, paid out as scheduled, shortcomings in rural supply work, and so on. However, the main cause of peasant discontent was as follows. The peasants did not know where the state monopoly purchase and marketing work stood. They felt that no matter how much they increased production the state would correspondingly increase the purchase of grain. They also felt that the amount of grain purchased was too large whereas the grain left for their own use was too small (the grain ration was a bit tight and there was no grain or inadequate grain for livestock), and that their actual needs were not met. Finally, they had complaints about the supply of many materials and goods that was ample in cities and tight in the countryside.

The directives emphatically pointed out that the fundamental reason for the shortage of grain lay in insufficient production. The development of production was the decisive link in solving the grain problem. However, the peasants were realistic. If they did not benefit from the increase in output they would not be enthusiastic about it. Therefore, all measures of rural work should center on the development of production. They should be favorable for production and for promoting peasant initiative in production. And [these measures] should avoid any damage to their initiative.

On the basis of the above analysis, the directives drew up concrete plans for the overhaul and consolidation of APCs, vigorous protection of farm animals, and grain purchase work in the countryside.

Regarding the question of the consolidation of APCs, the center decided several things.

First, the cooperativization movement at present should basically shift to a stage in which development is controlled and consolidation is emphasized. The following policies should be respectively implemented depending on the circumstances in different regions: stop development and concentrate on consolidation; appropriate contraction; and further expansion while proceeding with consolidation. A few examples follow.

In the provinces of the Northeast, North China, and East China where the original plan for development had been basically achieved or overfulfilled, [development] should be halted and all efforts should be devoted to consolidation.

In Shandong, Henan, Hebei, Zhejiang, and other provinces where the original plans were too big or where the movement unfolded hurriedly without adequate preparation, the movement should contract appropriately. Excessively high targets in the original plans should be reduced. Under the principles of no damage to the enthusiasm of activists and guaranteeing the quality of newly established cooperatives, the number of cooperatives and that of peasant households in cooperatives should be reasonably reduced.

In the provinces in the Central-South, Southwest, and Northwest where there was still a long way to go before the plan was fulfilled, already established cooperatives should be carefully consolidated and during consolidation preparations for continuing development should be made.

Second, during the work of consolidating cooperatives emphasis should be placed on publicizing the principle of voluntary participation, the broad masses of cooperative members should be allowed to speak about the doubts and worries in their minds, and education work should be conducted in the light of their thinking that had been exposed. We should not fear even if a small number of people wished to withdraw from the cooperatives because the voluntary union of all the cooperative members is the most fundamental guarantee of well-run cooperatives. For the nominal cooperatives that existed in name but not reality, if they still could not be run after receiving help, they should be allowed to change back into mutual aid teams and [hopefully] become cooperatives again in the future.

Third, as far as the agricultural cooperativization movement in the minority nationality regions was concerned, only after national characteristics and political, economic, and cultural backwardness were fully taken into account, and only when we were determined to take a longer time and follow a cautious and gradually progressive policy to realize socialist transformation, could the mutual aid and cooperativization movement in these regions be pushed forward healthily and smoothly. If, without considering local particularities, attempts were made to push forward the movement at the same pace as that in Han nationality regions, inevitably the mistakes of impatience and rash advance would be made. They would cause losses and difficulties in our work, affect the healthy development of the mutual aid and cooperativization movement, and even give rise to mass disturbances.

Regarding the issue of vigorous protection of farm animals, the center instructed: The protection of farm animals should be taken as one important work [duty] at present, and the policy of protecting farm animals should be implemented conscientiously.

First, in the agricultural cooperativization movement, the problem of incorporating farm animals into the cooperatives should be handled appropriately and impatient and careless sentiments should be overcome. It should be understood that the problem of incorporating farm animals into the cooperatives had a direct bearing on the interests of the households owning the animals and on the unity between the middle and poor peasants. The class policy of relying on poor peasants and firmly uniting with middle peasants should be correctly implemented. It should also be understood that in accordance with the principle of mutual benefit and through democratic appraisal, fair and reasonable monetary compensation should be paid by installment within not too long a period, and payment should not be delayed except in the case of rare disasters. In the newly established cooperatives, farm animals need not be hastily turned over to the cooperatives for monetary compensation. Instead, in accordance with the principles of unity and mutual benefit between the poor and middle peasants, the method of private ownership for public use could be adopted in order to prevent livestock owners from suffering losses and to stabilize their mood concerning livestock breeding.

Second, earnestly help the masses resolve fodder difficulties in order to ensure a safe winter for their livestock.

Regarding the purchase and sale of grain in the countryside, the center decided:

1. The targets for purchase and sale of grain set by the state should be realistic and practical. The measure of fixed targets for production, purchase, and sale should be further adopted. That is, prior to spring plowing each year, in every township that was treated as the basic unit, the general output target should be decided. The purchase and sale targets would be announced to the peasants in the township to let them know how much grain they need to produce, how much grain the state would purchase, how much grain they could keep for themselves, and how much grain would

be given to households short of grain. This measure would enable the peasants to have a good idea about the plan, stabilize their mood, and ease the tense situation in the countryside. Only under such circumstances could the peasants make their production plans and arrange their household affairs, and the development of agricultural production and state control of the purchase and sale of grain in a planned manner be facilitated.

2. In accordance with the principle of taking care of both the state's needs and the peasants' capacities, the target for the purchase of grain for this year (July 1955 to June 1956) was set at 90 billion jin.

The party center thought that while slowing down the pace of agricultural cooperativization, accomplishing well the above tasks concerning the protection of farm animals and the purchase of grain would be of great significance for easing the tense situation in the countryside and stabilizing the peasants' mood.

3. "The policy was a three-word scripture"[12]

Although the CCP center's above instructions were quickly passed on to every province and district, the expansionary momentum of the cooperativization movement did not decrease. In early February there were 580,000 cooperatives throughout the country. In April the number of cooperatives increased to 670,000 plus. In addition, there were many "spontaneous cooperatives."

In early March, upon returning from his trip outside Beijing, Mao Zedong asked the responsible persons of the Central Rural Work Department, Deng Zihui, Chen Boda, Liao Luyan, and Du Runsheng, to make a work report. Mao Zedong affirmed the measures adopted in rural work during this period and made a summary. He said: "The policy is a three-word scripture—first stop, second shrink, third develop." It was decided among them right at that occasion that the movement should contract a bit in Zhejiang and Hebei Provinces, that in general the movement should stop in the Northeast and North China, and that it should expand appropriately in other areas (mainly new [liberated] areas).

On April 20 the CCP Central Secretariat called a report-back conference attended by the responsible persons of the Central Rural Work Department. The conference pointed out: "The general policy from now on is to stop expansion and devote all efforts to consolidation." The conference also held: "There are already 670,000 cooperatives. Some provinces exceed their targets by 20,000 or 30,000 cooperatives. Since our subjective strength can not control it, the movement should contract a bit." Later at the conference of secretaries of provincial and municipal party committees, Mao Zedong reemphasized his opinion of "stop, shrink, develop."

The three-word policy of "stop, shrink, develop" summarized by Mao

Zedong indicates that in spring 1955, regarding the basic policy of overhauling and consolidating APCs, there was a unanimous view among the party center, the Central Rural Work Department, and Mao Zedong himself.

IV. Overhauling cooperatives throughout the country

1. Positive achievements

Under the concrete guidance of the party center and Mao Zedong, the Central Rural Work Department and the Second Office of the Central Secretariat immediately adopted resolute and effective measures to unfold the consolidation of APCs in order to alleviate the tense situation in the countryside.

On March 22 the Central Rural Work Department issued a "Circular on Consolidating Existing Cooperatives"[13] in which it put forward the following explicit principles and measures to deal with a common problem in the newly established cooperatives of some cooperative members who joined the cooperatives unwillingly or not very willingly. [Here the authors quote a substantial section of the "Circular" concerning three principles for dealing with the problem; see the text below, pp. 161–64. In brief, the measures called for educating the peasants, analyzing the causes of peasant unhappiness with the cooperatives and devising methods to deal with the problems revealed, and allowing peasants in APCs that existed in name only to engage in private production. Emphasis was placed on respecting the will of the peasants including permitting them to withdraw from the cooperatives, and on the need to reduce reasonably the number of APCs and the proportion of peasant households in cooperatives.]

At that time, the problem was most serious in Zhejiang Province where the development of agricultural cooperatives was the fastest and where activities occurred that seriously damaged the interests of middle peasants. The report of February 9 by the Shanghai Bureau of the CCP center said: By mid-January [1955] the number of cooperatives in Zhejiang increased from last fall's 2,016 to 41,883, a rise of more than 20 times. Since the scale of the movement was massive and there were very many problems, a "marking time" period was needed so as to concentrate all efforts on consolidating APCs. However, since then the cooperativization movement in Zhejiang did not "mark time" to consolidate. On the contrary, it advanced more rapidly and consequently the number of cooperatives rose to 53,000; besides this there were "another nearly 10,000 spontaneous cooperatives." The percentage of peasant households with cooperative membership was approaching 30 percent in the province. In a few places the number of cooperatives increased by 50 times. Such rapid development was largely due to the blind pursuit of numbers by some cadres that led to commandism and serious infringement of middle peasant interests. In encouraging the peasants to join cooperatives, some cadres working on establishing cooperatives publicly announced that those who joined APCs would be assigned a lighter quota for state grain purchase whereas those who did not would have a heavier one. In many places various pieces of land were joined together into a single piece in order to set up cooperatives. In doing so, the peasants who did not join the cooperatives were forced to exchange their land with those who did. This practice infringed on individual peasant interests, even more seriously. Propaganda even went so far as to use slogans such as "To join or not to join the cooperatives is like taking Mao Zedong's or Chiang Kai-shek's path" to blackmail the peasants and force many of them to join the cooperatives. Some peasants remarked: "Even if cooperatives are a death trap, I will still join them."[14] This situation intertwined with the shortage of grain contributed to even more instability in the countryside. At that time, not only did the Central Rural Work Department send someone directly to investigate, but also the Central Financial and Economic Committee, the Central Discipline-Inspection Committee, and the Central Political and Legal Small Group one after another handed in to the center numerous materials regarding the "tense situation" and asked it to help the Zhejiang Provincial Committee adopt measures to ease and stabilize quickly the situation.

To resolve quickly the severe problems in Zhejiang Province, on March 24 responsible persons of the Second Office of the Central Secretariat and the Central Rural Work Department invited the current First Secretary of the Zhejiang Provincial Committee, Jiang Hua, to a joint study [of the question] chaired by Tan Zhenlin and Deng Zihui. In accordance with the spirit that the agricultural cooperatives in Zhejiang should contract that was affirmed by Mao Zedong, a recommendation was drafted for a telegram to be sent to the Zhejiang Provincial Rural Work Department. The thrust of the telegram was: Stop development, contract appropriately, consolidate with all strength, and eliminate negative consequences caused by rash development and the violation of the principle of voluntary participation and mutual benefit. The telegram emphasized: "The correct policy can only be: Make every effort to run well those cooperatives with appropriate conditions. Make no rash retreat. Concerning those lacking adequate conditions for being run well, we should straighten out the thinking of the basic level backbone and cooperative activist elements, unite with them, and with them jointly lead the masses to reorganize [the cooperatives]. We also need their leadership [in helping] the peasants who withdraw from the cooperatives to engage in production. Regardless of whether these peasants decide to go back to the mutual aid teams or to individual production, we should help them to do well in production. We should not in any case hurt their feelings, so that we can continue striving to run the cooperatives well in the future." The telegram also suggested that "if 30,000 APCs can be consolidated, it could still be regarded as a great achievement." Meanwhile, it was pointed out that the above target for contraction should be known to members of the provincial committee and should not be passed on to lower levels. The telegram was written in the name of the Central Rural Work Department. After it was drafted, Deng Zihui entrusted Chen Boda to give it personally to Mao Zedong for approval. Soon afterwards Chen told Deng Zihui on the phone that "the center agrees." The telegram was thus sent out on March 25. After it was sent out, Deng Zihui went on an overseas tour. Tan Zhenlin then called in the responsible people of the Second Office [of the Central Secretariat] and the Central Rural Work Department for a meeting attended by Jiang Hua at which it was decided to follow up [the telegram] by sending Du Runsheng and Yuan Chenglong to the Zhejiang Provincial Committee to pass on further oral messages. Besides, Tan Zhenlin and Jiang Hua respectively and personally informed the Zhejiang Provincial Committee about the conclusions of the study [carried out at the conference]. Chaired by Huo Shilian, the provincial standing committee engaged in serious discussion and unanimously agreed [with the center's assessment]. Accordingly, at a four-level cadre conference called by the provincial committee assignments were made. The work of consolidation with all-out efforts and resolute contraction was immediately launched.[15]

After more than one month of work, the following preliminary achievements were made in Zhejiang Province by early May: those cooperatives that could be consolidated were more consolidated; members of hopeless cooperatives retreated to either mutual aid teams or to individual farming; [and] of those members caught in a dilemma, some chose to withdraw and others to remain. Consequently 15,000 APCs were disbanded in the whole province during contraction, while 40,000 cooperatives were preserved after consolidation. On the issue of joining cooperatives, errors infringing on middle peasant interests were rectified once tense contradictions between middle and poor peasants were removed, and tension caused by the shortage of grain was eased. As a result, the peasants recovered their enthusiasm for production while the cadres enhanced their understanding of policy. On May 8, in his report by telephone to the Central Rural Work Department, Huo Shilian of the Zhejiang Provincial Committee said: In many townships of every prefecture there were good results from publicizing the policy of mutual benefit and voluntary participation and carrying out cooperative consolidation. In well-run cooperatives the members were satisfied, their confidence was enhanced rather than shaken, and as a result we had more favorable conditions to help them run their cooperatives well. In the cooperatives with major problems, those problems were quickly solved. After peasants from the cooperatives shifted to mutual aid teams or individual farming, they were free of their worries and thus increased [the use of] fertilizers and the number of seedlings transplanted. There were three major effects of the all-around publicizing of the policy: (1) The cadres were enlightened. Before that, the cadres did not realize the harm caused by the left deviations in the previous policy that infringed on the interests of middle peasants. After they listened to the masses' opinions they came to realize this. (2) The masses came to understand the party's policy. Some poor peasants had thought of cooperation as dividing output equally among the partners while some middle peasants perceived it as a second land reform. (Last year in some old cooperatives dividends were given out on the basis of the number of mouths. And this year the practice of first dividing up the middle peasants' investment and then state loans gradually spread.) To remove such misunderstandings would have great benefits for social productivity and cooperativization. (3) The cooperation policy was back on track and beneficial to grain production. Earlier, in order to conceal their wealth, middle peasants spent all their savings on the purchase of grain. After the worries in their minds toward cooperation policy were removed, the situation improved. All of the above circumstances proved that this make-up effort in terms of the policy itself and in publicizing the policy had positive significance in Zhejiang. This was necessary not only for cooperatives that should be dissolved, but also for cooperatives that should be consolidated, and even more so for the broad masses.[16]

According to statistics in "A Summary of the Recent Situation of the Agricultural Cooperativization Movement" of July 26, 1955, compiled by the Second Office of the Central Rural Work Department, the outcome of the nationwide overhaul and consolidation of APCs was as follows. After the implementation of the "stop, shrink, develop" policy, among the original 670,000 cooperatives, 650,000 plus survived after consolidation. The areas of contraction were: 15,000 cooperatives [were dissolved] in Zhejiang, 7,000 in Hebei, [and] 4,000 in Shandong. There was no significant change in other provinces; in fact the number increased in some provinces. Thus with rises in the number of cooperatives in some provinces and decreases in some other provinces, the number of cooperatives in the entire country was reduced by 20,000 plus.

2. The so-called cutting down of 200,000 cooperatives

During the Cultural Revolution the above correct policy and measures for consolidating APCs and their positive achievements were depicted in another way. It was alleged that Liu Shaoqi, "using the opportunity" of Mao Zedong's "absence from Beijing," "produced the reactionary policy of 'stop, shrink, overhaul' and personally approved the plan to cut down cooperatives extravagantly. Within a bit more than two months 200,000 cooperatives were chopped down throughout the country."[17] This was an entirely ground-less and false accusation.

As stated above, the three-word policy of stop, shrink, develop was Mao Zedong's concise and clear-cut summary of the gist of the principle [initially] raised in the January 10 circular of the CCP center in which three policies were proposed for adoption respectively in different regions: stop development and concentrate on consolidation with full strength; appropriate contraction; [and] develop further during the course of consolidation.

While the policy of stop, shrink, develop was carried out in Zhejiang and other provinces, to check up on and guide the implementation of the policy, on April 20 the Central Secretariat called a report-back meeting attended by the responsible persons of the Central Rural Work Department to examine and guide the movement. At the meeting Liu Shaoqi pointed out that the general policy for work concerning agricultural cooperatives in the coming year was to "stop development and consolidate with full strength." He said: "The movement should stop now on all fronts and we shall review the situation again after the fall. In certain counties, districts, and townships where no cooperatives have been set up, cooperatives can be established on a trial basis as long as long as conditions are ripe. In the Southwest and Central-South where the tasks for grain purchase are not heavy, cooperatives can be developed yet they should not be developed too fast." The meeting affirmed the work of contraction in some provinces. Liu Shaoqi pointed out: "670,000 cooperatives have already been established throughout the country. Among those provinces where the number of cooperatives exceeds the target, some even exceed it by 20,000 to 30,000. Since our subjective strength cannot handle that many APCs, we should contract a bit." He held that "It will be the greatest victory if we can consolidate 500,000 and some additional ten thousands of cooperatives." He said: "Wherever the conditions are ripe for consolidation, full effort should be devoted to consolidation. During the course of consolidation [we must make sure that our] policy links up with the masses, and [we must respect the masses'] free will. Consolidation will be false unless our policy links up with the masses. It was accepted at the meeting that "no fixed number needs to be observed during contraction and it will be all right to have less than 400,000 cooperatives." Before this meeting Liu Shaoqi mentioned in a talk with Deng Zihui the necessity of cutting 100,000 cooperatives in order to stabilize the situation and asked for his opinion. In accordance with the spirit of the instruction of the center, at the Third National Rural Work conference held between April 21 and May 7 Deng Zihui summarized the work of agricultural cooperativization in the country, and in view of the experience of handling the cooperativization issue in Zhejiang Province and Liu Shaoqi's opinion, Deng proposed to the provinces the tentative idea of cutting 50,000 to 100,000 cooperatives. Afterward, since the summer harvest was about to start, consulting with the provinces [about this] was no longer thought necessary and his idea was abandoned.[18] Therefore, [the number] actually reduced was 20,000-odd cooperatives.

At the Tenth Plenary Session of the Eighth Central Committee in 1962, Mao Zedong brought up again the theme of class struggle and criticized the so-called sinister dark wind, the wind of going it alone [i.e., individual farming], and the wind of reversing verdicts. He criticized Deng Zihui for "being almost entirely pessimistic about the situation" and for "vigorously advocating assigning [farm] output to the individual peasant household." Mao claimed: "These are related to his consistent unwillingness to develop cooperatives and his giving orders to cut down unsparingly hundreds of thousands of cooperatives before the summer 1955 conference, and to his energetic advocacy of the four big freedoms and his 'frequent favor giving without commitment to righteousness.' "[19]

Thus it can be seen that the charge of "cutting down 200,000 cooperatives" was [wrongly] deduced from the opinion formed at the Central Secretariat meeting of April 20, 1955, that "no number needs to be set during contraction" and that "it would be all right to have less than 400,000 APCs." It was also deduced from Liu Shaoqi's talk with Deng Zihui about the necessity of cutting down 100,000 cooperatives in order to stabilize the situation, from Deng Zihui's tentative idea about reducing 50,000 to 100,000 cooperatives that he proposed to the provinces, and from Mao Zedong's criticism about "cutting down hundreds of thousands" of cooperatives. It was not a historical fact.

Chapter 10: Antiright-deviationism and the socialist high tide

According to the general line for the transition period, the task of socialist industrialization and transformation would be accomplished within three Five-Year Plans, that is, fifteen years or a somewhat longer time. However, since summer 1955 the agricultural cooperativization movement speeded up so drastically that the entire socialist transformation was basically completed in a hurried manner by 1956. As far as the general line for the transition period is concerned, we must acknowledge a strategic shift from planning to finish socialist transformation in fifteen years to accelerating the transformation. The change in guiding thinking was first of all reflected in the pace of the development of cooperativization.

I. A debate over "getting on or off the horse"

1. The resolution in the spring

The program for agricultural cooperativization proposed at the Fourth

National Conference on Mutual Aid and Cooperation and approved by the CCP center required "organizing more than 50 percent of the total peasant households into cooperatives by 1957 and making APCs in the existing form the major form of production for the main rural areas throughout the country."[20]

In March 1955, after proposing the three-word policy of stop, shrink, develop, Mao Zedong met with Deng Zihui alone. Mao Zedong suggested having one-third of peasant households in the country join APCs within each of the three Five-Year Plans. Deng Zihui, however, suggested having 50 percent of the total peasant households join cooperatives in the First Five-Year Plan. Mao Zedong disagreed immediately, arguing that grain production had already reached its limit, that the target for grain purchase was 90 billion jin and no more, and that within the First Five-Year Plan the APCs should incorporate one-third, instead of 50 percent of total peasant households. Afterward Mao Zedong told Tan Zhenlin that until the next October (October 1956—Authors) the development of the cooperativization movement should stop. Based on this spirit, during the National Party Conference [of March 1955] Liu Shaoqi called in the responsible persons of all provinces for a talk in which he emphasized that the central issue of the present agricultural cooperativization was to consolidate and run well the group of cooperatives that had been set up. He said: "To have further development, consolidation should be done for it is not possible to proceed faster, for the cadres have not been trained and our experience is not yet mature. It will be risky to develop the movement at the same pace as last year."[21]

Entrusted by the CCP center, the Central Rural Work Department convened the Third National Rural Work Conference between April 21 and May 7.[22] At the conference Deng Zihui passed on Mao Zedong's opinion about incorporating one-third of the total peasant households into cooperatives in the First Five-Year Plan. In his opening speech and concluding remarks at the conference, he comprehensively analyzed the situation and problems concerning the development of agricultural cooperativization and set forth the policy for future work.

Deng Zihui pointed out that it should be affirmed that our achievements were the main aspect, for we had set up hundreds of thousands of socialist strongholds in the countryside and initially established the position for agricultural cooperativization, both of which were important support for our future cooperativization.

He said tensions varied in extent in different regions of the countryside. The tensions were essentially those in the relationship between workers and peasants and in that between middle and poor peasants. The following three causes resulted in tensions: (1) most obvious was the state monopoly purchase and marketing of grain; (2) the transformation of private business in the cities and countryside was so fast that the circulation of goods between the two areas was "obstructed in small respects although open on the whole"; (3) even more fundamentally there was something wrong with the socialist transformation of agriculture (mainly in terms of cooperation in production). Under the category of socialist transformation all three above factors were basic causes creating tensions. However, the social transformation of the countryside—including cooperation in production, in supplies and sales, in credit, and in state monopoly purchase and marketing of grain with cooperation in production as the pivot and the primary link in changing the relations of production, was the most basic cause. The reasons were as follows. The peasants could engage in production and solve living problems for their families when they were farming individually as long as they owned their land, draft animals, and farm tools. A fundamental change happened when they joined cooperatives. Although they still owned the means of production and could get payment for them, they could not freely control them. The right of control went to the APC. This was a fundamental change. The peasants naturally would be very concerned with the means of production they owned after they handed them over to the cooperatives. The above change was the most profound revolution that would have a huge impact on the peasants as a whole despite the fact that at the time not many peasants had joined the APCs. For example, it was reported that in the Northeast livestock generally lost weight after they were incorporated into cooperatives and some of them laid down with sickness while a few even died. Upon seeing this, how could the peasants not get scared and worried? This was materialism. At least the peasants who were the heads of their households would not sleep well. How could they not worry when they saw that there was little hope of an increase in production?

He further pointed out that there were three defects in the work of cooperativization. The first was that last year's plan for establishing 600,000 APCs was a little too big and a little too rash. The main causes for this were that our estimate of our own subjective strength was too high, that the development of cooperatives went beyond the cadres' subjective expectations and capacity for leadership, and that we overestimated the peasants' socialist consciousness. As peasants judged things by their eyes and not by their ears, their socialist consciousness was based on what they saw and not on what they heard. Since "it is better to see once than hear a hundred times," we ought to let the peasants see in order to have them believe. While it was easy for poor peasants and relatively easy for lower-middle peasants among the middle peasants to accept cooperatives, it was difficult for the majority of old middle peasants and well-to-do middle peasants, and for upper-middle peasants including new middle peasants, to do so, for the newly established cooperatives might not produce higher yields than they did. Some comrades tend to be a bit idealist in making high estimates and in failing to judge the rise in peasants' socialist consciousness on a materialist basis (in terms of the poor or good performance of cooperatives). They take lightly [the task of] running cooperatives well, and their understanding of the arduous nature of increasing production is insufficient. The second mistake was, as far as the policy was concerned, to have violated the principle of voluntary participation and mutual benefit. The third mistake was increasingly to have simply used administrative orders in conducting work rather than following the mass line.

In accordance with the spirit and determination of the instructions by the CCP center and Mao Zedong, Deng Zihui stressed four policies for future agricultural cooperativization: "(1) In general we must halt development. Originally we said that [expansion] should stop in the coming fall. Later the chairman (indicating Mao Zedong—Authors) said that we could simply stop it and wait until the fall of next year, [in other words] we would stop for one and one-half years. (2) We shall work on production right away and consolidate it with all our strength. (3) In a small number of provinces the movement should be contracted appropriately. (4) Mutual aid teams should be run well and consolidated well in order to take good care of individual farmers."

2. The change in May

At the end of April the responsible comrades of the center returned to Beijing to participate in the celebrations for May Day. On the evening of May 9 Mao Zedong met Li Xiannian, Deng Zihui, Liao Luyan, and Chen Guodong one after another in Yinian Hall of Zhongnanhai. He told them that the center thought that the original 90 billion jin (of grain) could be reduced to 87 billion and that this was a concession through which the reduction in grain purchase could be exchanged for socialism. He also said that since the coming two to three years would be a crucial period for agricultural cooperativization, the foundation for cooperativization should be laid down during these three years. He also asked them whether we could have 40 percent [of all peasant households] join cooperatives. Deng Zihui replied: "Last time we said one-third. It is better to stay around one-third." Mao Zedong responded: "All right, one-third." However, he held that peasants had contradictory attitudes toward socialist transformation and that they wanted freedom. He said that some cadres represented such feelings of the peasants and did not want to build socialism. He also referred to the words of Ke Qingshi of the Shanghai Bureau[23] that 30 percent of party cadres at high, middle and low levels represented middle peasants' feelings and disagreed with building socialism.[24]

On May 17 the CCP center convened a conference of the secretaries of fifteen provincial and municipal party committees from the East China and

Central-South regions and from Hebei, Tianjin, Beijing, etc., to discuss again agricultural cooperativization. At the conference, Mao Zedong gave a speech[25] that, although reemphasizing the policy of stop, shrink, develop, was mainly devoted to criticizing so-called passive feelings on the issue of agricultural cooperativization.

[Here the authors quote in full the first and third paragraphs of the available sections of Mao's speech; see the original 1955 documents section, pp. 195–96, for the complete available text. In addition, cf. Bo Yibo's discussion, below, pp. 148–49. The sections quoted first stated that a serious mistake would be committed if the passive feelings were not changed. The authors then commented that "In interpreting the three-word policy of stop, shrink, develop, [Mao] stressed development and raised specific targets for the APCs to be set up in various provinces." The quotation continued with the observation that one-sided contraction would damage the initiative of the cadres and masses, and with both general guidelines for different areas and specific provincial targets.]

3. Where the differences lay

On June 14 the Central Politburo heard a report by the Rural Work Department and approved a plan to develop up to 1 million APCs in 1956 on the basis of the existing 650,000 cooperatives. Liu Shaoqi said: "After the cooperatives reach 1 million by next spring, we can close the door for a while. If the cooperatives are run well, middle peasants will willingly come to knock on the door [to ask to join cooperatives]. The key is to ensure that middle peasants voluntarily join cooperatives."[26]

After the June Politburo conference, Mao Zedong had a talk with Deng Zihui in which Mao Zedong proposed that the target for the development of cooperatives between 1955 and 1956 should double the number of the existing 650,000 APCs to 1.3 million. However, Deng Zihui insisted on increasing the number by 50 percent. At that time his opinion favoring slower development was based on the following reasons. First, the cooperativization movement as a whole should keep in step with the pace of industrialization. The First Five-Year Plan was a period for building the basis for industrialization, a period when progress in the technological transformation of agriculture might be very slow, and cooperativization could only rely on manual labor. Under such conditions we must bring about a comparatively outstanding development of agricultural production, surpassing the normal level of well-to-do middle peasants.

The first step in demonstrating the superiority of the socialist collective economy is to set an excellent example to peasants outside the cooperatives. [To do this] it is imperative to make a good job of management, especially in distribution according to work and labor organization. During the early stage of the development of cooperatives when conditions in all fields were poor, it was unsuitable for the accomplishment of the above required tasks to establish too many cooperatives too abruptly.

Second, in view of reports about the actual situation in various places, there were many problems with and a very heavy task of consolidating the existing 650,000 APCs. If we set up more cooperatives, consolidation and development would have to be undertaken at the same time. This would go beyond the level of the masses' consciousness and the cadres' capacity for leadership. It would make both aspects of work difficult to accomplish and negatively affect the development of production.

Third, the year from 1955 to 1956 was a time for laying the foundation. Its success would be extremely important for the accomplishment of full cooperativization later on. In the past few years in the old [liberated] areas, the leaders had been mainly committed to the work of developing cooperatives and little consolidation had been done. Although 20 to 30 percent of all households joined cooperatives there, the foundation was not solid and thus the movement should be slowed down in order to make a good job of consolidation and again advance on the basis of consolidation. In the new [liberated] areas where there were no habits and tradition of cooperation, the main task should be to continue to set up key points for cooperatives on the basis of the experience and lessons of the old [liberated] areas, suitably again expand a little, establish a certain number of cooperatives so that there could be several cooperatives in each township, devote all efforts to running them well so that cadres could be trained, set up models, and build a foundation for development from the key points to wider areas.

As far as outlying districts and minority nationality regions were concerned, land reform had not been carried out in some of these areas while in some others production was extremely backward using slash and burn methods and accountants could not be found. In the above areas cooperatives were difficult to set up and a longer time was to be allowed for preparation. In short, the work method that Mao Zedong had been teaching should be adhered to: actively and steadily unfold the movement from key points to all areas in groups and by stages. In doing things this way, from the viewpoint of the present specific aspect the movement might seem slow. Yet it would seem faster and better in terms of cooperativization as a whole.[27]

On July 26 the Second Section of the Rural Work Department put in order "A Summary of the Recent Situation in the Agricultural Cooperativization Movement" that reported that, according to the data in available materials, the plan for the expansion of cooperatives from 1955 to 1956 was for an increase from the existing 650,000 to 1.03 million APCs (the data on development in Shanxi, Zhejiang, and Rehe Provinces, the Inner Mongolian Autonomous Region, and Beijing and Tianjin municipalities was not available) and from more than 16.9 million to about 29.2 million households in cooperatives (increases in the number of households in cooperatives in Inner Mongolia and in Beijing and Tianjin municipalities were not available). On July 29 Mao Zedong distributed copies of this summary, on which he commented, to the comrades at the conference of secretaries of provincial, municipal, and autonomous region party committees convened by the center. His comments were:

We must oppose mistaken rightist and leftist viewpoints:

1. There are two problems, that is, "no advance" and "rash advance" concerning the development [of cooperatives]. The problem now is not that of having to criticize rash advance and "going beyond objective possibilities," but that of having to criticize failing to realize and make use of "objective possibilities," that is, failing to see and make use of the broad peasant masses' enthusiasm for the socialist road due to insufficient land, poverty, or their not-well-off lives. However, some of us fail to realize and utilize such existing objective possibilities [for the development of the movement]. What aspect of the peasants' dual character, that is, which aspect of the contradiction in their thinking between collective and individual farming, dominates? With propaganda and the demonstration effect of cooperatives, the thinking of collective farming will come to dominate a group of peasants, then a second group of them, later a third group of them, then the majority of them, and eventually all of them. We shall gradually (within fifteen years) create such domination.

2. The issue concerning changing ownership is a question of correcting the policy. The problem of some people taking petty advantage at the expense of others has already occurred. Peasants should be educated not to take petty advantage. All policies in question should be corrected and loans should be made to support the poor peasants. On the other hand, however, middle peasants should be educated to take the interest of the whole into consideration and not to mind the minor injustices that happened when they joined the cooperatives as long as production increases and as long as their output and income are higher than the previous year. Instead of making a "full compromise," both poor and middle peasants should be taught to take into consideration the interests of the whole cooperative. Full compromise will deprive us of socialism. Our policy is both to unite and struggle [with middle peasants].

3. We must follow a fixed direction and not waver. To have other people not waver, we have to be firm first. To avoid wavering, we should see the essence and the dominant or the main aspect of things. We shall not neglect the nonessential and secondary aspects of things and shall solve all existing problems. However, we shall not treat these aspects as the main aspect of the things and lose our direction.[28]

Mao Zedong's above comments clearly show that his debate with Deng Zihui was concerned with not only hundreds of thousands of cooperatives but also the issue of guiding thought. He suggested taking advantage of the broad peasants' attitude toward change arising from their poverty and lack of land or their not-well-off lives and guiding them toward socialism. In Deng Zihui's opinion, however, certain conditions were needed to run cooperatives well and, while running the existing cooperatives well, with preparations actively being made, the cooperativization movement should proceed gradually in a cautious and conventional manner. This is where their differences lay. At that time, some comrades at the Central Rural Work Department were surprised that Deng Zihui [dared to] debate with Mao Zedong merely over hundreds of thousands of cooperatives and thought that there was no need to "bring disaster." Deng Zihui explained to them with a wry smile: "This is not a question of several hundred thousand more cooperatives. What is critical is that he thinks that even those conditions for running cooperatives are not necessary. How could I not make myself clear?"[29]

4. Criticism of "a woman with bound feet"

On July 31, 1955, at a conference of secretaries of provincial, municipal, and autonomous region party committees convened by the CCP center, Mao Zedong gave a report entitled "On the Question of Agricultural Cooperativization."[30] In this report, he brought the debate on agricultural cooperativization to a climax and criticized Deng Zihui for his right-deviationist mistake. At the very beginning of the report, he made the following points categorically:

> A high tide in the new socialist mass movement is imminent throughout the countryside. But some of our comrades, tottering along like a woman with bound feet, are complaining all the time, "You're going too fast, much too fast." Too much carping, unwarranted complaints, boundless worries, and countless taboos—all this they take as the right policy to guide the socialist mass movement in the rural areas.
>
> No, this is not the right policy. This is wrong.
>
> The high tide of social transformation in the form of rural cooperativization has already arrived in a number of places and will soon sweep the whole country. It is a vast socialist revolutionary movement involving a rural population of more than 500 million, and it has tremendous world-wide significance. We should lead this movement actively, enthusiastically, and in a planned manner, instead of dragging it back by whatever means.

This report charged that "Opinions of the Central Rural Work Department about Current Cooperativization Work in Zhejiang Province" was the result of "being scared and panic-stricken by success." The report said:

> "With the adoption of a policy that was called "resolute contraction" in Zhejiang (not by the decision of the Zhejiang Provincial Committee), out of

the 53,000 cooperatives in the province 15,000, comprising 400,000 peasant households, were dissolved at a single stroke. This caused great dissatisfaction among the masses and cadres, and it was altogether the wrong thing to do. This policy of "resolute contraction" was decided on in of state of panic. To take such a major step without the approval of the center was wrong too.

It seems to me that there are two tendencies in the face of success: (1) To become dizzy with success, which leads to swelled heads and left-deviationist mistakes. Of course, that's bad. (2) To be scared of success, which leads to "resolute contraction" and right-deviationist mistakes. That's just as bad. The trouble now is of the latter kind, for some comrades have become scared of the several hundred thousand small cooperatives.

The report regarded the nature of the debate as "the difference between two lines." It claimed that Deng Zihui's opinion was based on the "stand of the bourgeoisie, rich peasants, or well-to-do middle peasants with their spontaneous tendencies towards capitalism to the neglect of the whole country and people from the standpoint of the working class." It said:

> Some comrades take a wrong approach to the vital question of the worker-peasant alliance, proceeding from the stand of the bourgeoisie, rich peasants, or well-to-do middle peasants with their spontaneous tendencies towards capitalism. They think that the present situation in the cooperative movement is very dangerous, and they persuaded us to "get off the horse quickly" in our present advance toward cooperativization. They warn us: "If you don't, we will run the danger of breaking up the worker-peasant alliance." We think exactly the opposite. If we don't get on the horse quickly, there will be the danger of breaking the worker-peasant alliance. There is a difference of only a single word here—one says off while the other says on—yet it demonstrates the difference between the two lines. As everybody knows, we already have a worker-peasant alliance built on the basis of the bourgeois-democratic revolution against imperialism and feudalism, a revolution that took the land from the landlords and distributed it to the peasants in order to free them from the bondage of feudal ownership. But this revolution is over, and feudal ownership has been abolished. What exists in the countryside today is capitalist ownership by the rich peasants and a vast sea of ownership by individual peasants. [Mao continued by arguing that the worker-peasant alliance would not hold firm if spontaneous capitalism in the countryside was allowed to grow unchecked, thus resulting in the polarization of new rich peasants and well-to-do middle peasants on the one hand and poor peasants on the other; see *Selected Works of Mao Tsetung*, vol. V (Peking: Foreign Languages Press, 1977), pp. 201–202.]

As a consequence, Deng Zihui's correct opinion was refuted and the "antiright-deviationist" struggle in the form of criticizing "a woman with bound feet" on the issue of agricultural cooperativization began from this point.

5. "Exterminate capitalism"

Between October 4 and 10, 1955, the Enlarged Sixth Plenary Session of the Seventh Central Committee was held by the CCP Central Committee. At the session, on the behalf of the Central Politburo, Chen Boda gave a report entitled "An Explanation of the Draft Resolution on the Question of Agricultural Cooperativization," and Deng Xiaoping gave a report entitled "An Explanation of the Draft Resolution on the Convening of the Eighth National Party Congress." Liu Shaoqi, Zhou Enlai, Zhu De, Chen Yun, Peng Dehuai, Peng Zhen, Deng Xiaoping, and others also gave speeches at the session. Finally, Mao Zedong made concluding remarks at the session entitled "The Debate on Agricultural Cooperativization and the Current Class Struggle."[31] The conference adopted a "Resolution on Agricultural Cooperativizaton"[32] and other resolutions.

In his concluding remarks, Mao Zedong further expounded his strategic guiding thinking and for the first time clarified his strategic attempts to facilitate work in all fields and to exterminate capitalism and small scale production. He said:

> Our present session has been a great debate. This debate concerns the question of whether our party's general line for the transition period from capitalism to socialism is entirely correct or not. This party-wide debate was triggered by the question of our policy on agricultural cooperativization, on which your discussion has also centered. However, the debate covers a wide range of subjects, bearing on the work of the departments of agriculture, industry, communications, transport, finance, monetary affairs, trade, culture, education, science, public health, etc., on the transformation of handicrafts and capitalist industry and commerce, the suppression of counterrevolutionaries, the armed forces, and foreign affairs; in short, it touches on the whole range of our work, the work of the party, government, armed forces, and people's organizations. There should be a great debate of this kind, for nothing like it has been conducted in our party since the promulgation of the general line. We must unfold the debate in the countryside and in the cities as well so that our work in every sphere and its tempo and quality will fit the tasks set by the general line and be covered by a comprehensive plan.
>
> [Mao went on to argue that only with the socialist transformation of agriculture would it be possible to isolate the urban bourgeoisie and facilitate the transformation of capitalist industry and commerce; see *Selected Works of Mao Tsetung*, V, 212, 213–14.]
>
> Agricultural cooperativization will enable us to consolidate our alliance with the peasants on the basis of proletarian socialism and not of bourgeois democracy. This will isolate the bourgeoisie once and for all and facilitate the final elimination of capitalism. On this matter we are quite heartless! On this issue Marxism is indeed cruel and has little mercy, for it is determined to exterminate imperialism, feudalism, capitalism, and small production to boot. In this respect, it is better not to have much mercy. Some of our comrades are

too kind, they are not tough enough, in other words, they are not so Marxist. It is a very good thing, and a significant one too, to exterminate the bourgeoisie and capitalism in China, a country with a population of 600 million. Our goal is to exterminate capitalism, obliterate it from the face of the earth, and make it a thing of the past.

[The long quotation from Mao concluded with a brief paragraph where he reviewed the measures taken in internal class struggle over the past year including handling the grain question and tackling cooperativization; see *Selected Works of Mao Tsetung*, V, 215.]

The resolution passed by the session elevated Deng Zihui's opinion on agricultural cooperativization to a mistake of "right-deviationist opportunism." The criticism of the so-called right deviation and right-deviationist opportunism at the July conference of secretaries of provincial, municipal, and autonomous region party committees and the Seventh Plenary Session of the Seventh Central Committee infringed on the tradition of democratic discussion within the party and "seeking truth from facts" and promoted the development of left-deviationist thought within the party.

II. Changes of the plan with each passing day

1. The July Plan

In his report "On the Question of Agricultural Cooperativization," Mao Zedong held that a high tide of social transformation in the form of agricultural cooperativization had already swept through some places and was going to sweep through the whole country. Under this premise, he raised a number of suggestions regarding the number of the cooperatives to be developed in the country between 1955–56 and the overall planning for social and technological transformation of the countryside. He said:

In spring 1955 our party center decided that the number of APCs should be increased to 1 million. This means an increase of only 350,000 over the existing 650,000, or a little more than 50 percent. It seems to me that this may be a bit too small. Probably the figure of 650,000 ought to be roughly doubled, that is, to rise to something like 1.3 million, so that, except in some of the border areas, there will be one or more small APCs of a semisocialist nature to serve as models in each of the country's 200,000-odd townships. In a year or two these cooperatives will gain experience and become old ones, and people will learn from them. There are still fourteen months to go between now and the fall harvest of October 1956, and it should be possible to complete this plan for establishing cooperatives. I hope that upon their return the responsible comrades of the various provinces and autonomous regions will look into this matter, work out appropriate plans according to the concrete situation, and report to the center within two months. We shall then discuss the matter again and make a final decision.

We must now realize that there will soon be a nationwide high tide of socialist transformation in the countryside. This is inevitable. By spring 1958, at the end of the final year of the First Five-Year Plan and the beginning of the first year of the Second Five-Year Plan, cooperatives of semisocialist nature will embrace some 250 million people in the whole country, about 55 million peasant households (averaging four and one-half persons each), which will mean half the rural population."[33] [Mao then further elaborated on future developments, stating that by 1960 semisocialist cooperativization would be basically achieved. He also noted that during the Third Five-Year Plan (1963–67) the development of fully socialist collectives would proceed simultaneously with technical transformation including mechanization. See *Selected Works of Mao Tsetung*, V, 202–203.]

2. Enlarging the plan one [province] after another[34]

After the conclusion of the conference of secretaries of provincial, municipal, and autonomous region party committees at the end of July, in August each province one after another held enlarged meetings of provincial committees or meetings of prefecture secretaries and municipal committees to relay and study Mao Zedong's report, check up on right-deviationist thinking and revise provincial plans for the development of agricultural cooperativization. From the reports to the CCP center by various provinces, we can see not only the state of thinking within the party after Mao Zedong criticized so-called right-deviationism, but also the sincerity, innocence, and naïveté regarding the issue of socialism within the party. Some examples are provided below:

[The authors quote excerpts from the reports of the Hubei, Liaoning, Anhui, Shanxi, Henan, Zhejiang, Kansu, Fujian, and Yunnan Provincial Committees that express support for Mao, criticize past right-deviationist mistakes, and lay down new and significantly increased targets for cooperativization. As the reports of Hubei, Liaoning, Anhui, Zhejiang, and Fujian are reproduced either in full or in more extensive excerpts, together with Mao's comments on them, in the original 1955 documents section of this volume, pp. 203–207, the sections from these reports included here are not translated. In addition, a very brief excerpt from the Kansu report concerned almost solely with new APC targets is also deleted. What follows are the excerpts from the remaining three provinces.]

The report of the Shanxi Provincial Committee said:

"We carried out self-criticism at the meeting. Everybody thought that Chairman Mao's remarks were quite right. The main reason why we had right-deviationist conservative sentiments was because 'our approach to the problem was wrong.' We only saw one-sidedly that there were many problems not only in the backward cooperatives, but also in many advanced and long established cooperatives. For this reason, we believed the wrong view that 'it was easy to develop yet difficult to consolidate.' At the same time, since we thought that both the strength and experience of cadres could not catch up with the development of the cooperative movement, and since we did not realize that 'cadres and peasants would transform themselves through their own struggle,' we had plenty of unnecessary worries. During the discussions the secretaries of prefecture committees also conducted self-criticism."

"The meeting decided the speed of developing cooperatives as follows: In 1955 the number of APCs would increase from 31,786 to 42,000 or 44,000, and the percentage of peasant households with cooperative membership would be raised from 41 percent to 51–55 percent. In 1956 the number of cooperatives would increase to 52,000–54,000, and the percentage should reach 67–70 percent. In 1957 the number of cooperatives would increase to 56,000–58,000 (reaching a state of saturation), and the percentage should be 75–80 percent. After the basic completion of semisocialist transformation of the countryside in our province in 1957, rich peasants will be eliminated and the rural class configuration will experience fundamental change."

The report of the Henan Provincial Committee said:

"After we heard Chairman Mao's relayed instruction on the question of agricultural cooperativization, everyone enthusiastically supported it and was elated with joy. We also carried out careful studies and discussion, criticism, and self-criticism, and criticized erroneous thinking. Particularly since we examined the provincial and prefecture committees' guiding thinking concerning the cooperativization movement last fall, we clarified our class stand and mass viewpoint, and our courage for and confidence in socialist revolution were significantly enhanced. . . . The meeting approved the following targets. By the end of 1957 there should be 180,000 APCs and cooperative membership should account for no less than 60 percent of peasant households. By the end of this winter and the beginning of the coming spring there should be 100,000 cooperatives and APC membership as a percentage of peasant households should reach 30 percent."

The report of the Yunnan Provincial Committee said:

"Everyone unanimously supports the chairman's instruction and says that they will firmly carry it out. In the past we vacillated in both our thinking and our work regarding the socialist transformation of agriculture. The chairman's unambiguous instruction regarding this strategic problem not only makes us to stop this vacillation but also greatly encourages the enthusiasm and creativity of the whole party and broad masses."

"Through our discussion, the plan for the development of APCs in our province is as follows: Before the fall harvest this year the number of APCs will increase from the existing 7,100 to 30,000. Before spring plowing next year the number will increase by 5,000–10,000, and cooperative membership will cover 23 percent of peasant households. In the fall and winter of the next year it will increase by 21,000 and 40 percent of peasant households will have cooperative membership. By 1957 the number of APCs will increase to 73,000. With the enlargement or merger of cooperatives, among the 3.48 million peasant households there will be 1.94 million households in cooperatives and they will account for about 55 percent of peasant households."

Regarding the demand proposed by Mao Zedong in July that 50 percent of peasant households join semisocialist cooperatives by spring 1958, with the exception of Anhui, Fujian, and Gansu that did not specify their plans, the other six provinces all proposed that they would complete and overfulfill their plans before winter 1957.

3. The October resolution[35]

Since many provinces promised that by spring 1958 the plan of having 50 percent of total peasant households join cooperatives would be overfulfilled ahead of time, with the intensifying criticism of right-deviationist opportunism at the Sixth Plenary Session of the Seventh Central Committee, the sentiment for blind rash advance and anxiety for quick success further developed in the party. The resolution at the Sixth Plenary Session of the Seventh Central Committee proposed even more radical demands. It said:

"In order to lead the agricultural cooperativization movement actively and in a planned manner, we need to have plans for stage-by-stage implementation of cooperativization in the whole country and in each province (or autonomous region), prefecture (autonomous prefecture), county (autonomous county), district, township (minority nationality township), or village. These plans should take into account not only the common features but also the concrete differences of the cooperativization movement in various areas. In view of the different conditions in different areas and the speed of development of the cooperativization movement in various places, there will be the following three main situations:

First, in areas where the mutual aid and cooperative movement is fairly advanced, where up to 30–40 percent of total peasant households joined the cooperatives by summer 1955, APCs should be developed to cover up to 70–80 percent of all peasant households by spring 1957 and agricultural cooperativization of a semisocialist nature can be basically realized. These areas mainly include the provinces in North and Northeast China and parts or large parts of some other provinces.

Second, the majority of provinces throughout the country are areas where the degree of cooperativization in summer 1955 already covered about 10 or 20 percent of all peasant households. In these areas cooperativization of semisocialist nature basically can on the whole be accomplished by spring 1958.

Third, in areas where the foundation for the mutual aid movement is fairly weak and where there are only a few APCs, it will take a longer time to accomplish cooperativization. These areas include mainly remote or border regions. In some of these areas there has been neither land reform nor mutual aid organizations. In these areas very gradual policies or even waiting for a long period should be adopted.

When the provincial, municipal, and autonomous region party committees formulate their plans for cooperativization, they should pay attention to establishing higher stage APCs (of a full socialist nature) on a trial basis in places with [suitable] conditions. In some places where agricultural cooperativization of a semisocialist nature basically has been achieved, plans can be made to change elementary APCs into higher stage APCs in accordance with the needs of the development of production, the level of mass understanding of the matter, and local economic conditions."

The requirement in the resolution to adopt distinct guiding methods toward cooperativization work in different areas is of course correct. However, in the resolution the original plan to raise the cooperative membership to 50 percent of all peasant households by spring 1958 was changed into a new plan to accomplish semisocialist cooperativization by spring 1957 in relatively advanced areas and by spring 1958 in most areas throughout the country. The resolution also unambiguously raised the issue of transforming the APCs from lower to higher stage. This is doubtlessly likened to adding a pile of wood to an already burning fire, making the fire stronger and stronger, and raising the temperature higher and higher.

4. Fulfilling [the plans] ahead of time

After the Sixth Plenary Session of the Seventh Central Committee, propelled forward by the criticism of right-deviationist opportunism, various places one by one set off great mass fervor in the agricultural cooperativization movement. In October 1955 the five provincial committees of Shanxi, Zhejiang, Guangxi, Sichuan, and Guangdong made reports to the CCP center.[36]

The report of the Shanxi Provincial Committee said: "Encouraged by Chairman Mao's report, 14,821 new cooperatives have been preliminarily established throughout the province within less than two months in addition to the existing old cooperatives. There are altogether 46,607 cooperatives in the whole province. Recently 600,000 peasant households have joined the cooperatives (including those who recently joined old cooperatives). There are altogether 1.94 million peasant households in APCs. The above 1.94 million, accounting for 60 percent of peasant households in the whole province, have already fulfilled our original plan for the end of this winter and the beginning of next spring." "Comrades from various places estimate that by the next spring plowing there will be 2.1 million plus households taking part in the cooperatives, accounting for 66 percent of peasant households in the whole province. By that time 40 counties (there were altogether 95 counties and five cities in the province—Authors) will have basically accomplished semisocialist cooperativization."

The report of the Zhejiang Provincial Committee said: "There are already 25,700-plus newly established cooperatives throughout the province and more than 750,000 peasant households joining the new cooperatives or enlarged old cooperatives. Including households already in old cooperatives, there are altogether 1.63 million households in APCs covering up to 33 percent of peasant households in the whole province. Most of the townships that have fulfilled their control figures actually surpass the initial target. In those townships with a good basis for cooperativization, cooperative membership has accounted for 70–80 percent of peasant households. In those townships with an average basis for cooperation, about 50–60 percent [have joined the cooperatives]. In those townships where basis for cooperation is relatively poor, 30–40 percent [have joined]. . . . After two months' work the negative impact caused by the wrong policy of resolute contraction has been basically eliminated. A high tide in the cooperativization has already swept most areas throughout the province."

The report of the Guangxi Provincial Committee said: After meetings of cadres from the three levels, "people's enthusiasm for socialism is unprecedentedly high." "Right now the work of establishing cooperatives is entering an intense stage. The 20,850 cooperatives that are already under way (mainly those in two crop areas) have reached the second or third stage of development. In one crop areas there will be 16,851 cooperatives under way around the end of this month or early next month. Taken together, the first group of cooperatives will number 37,701 reaching the target of 70 percent [of households in APCs] between the end of this winter and the beginning of next spring." The report also introduced the experience in mobilizing the masses, pointing out that from the very beginning of efforts to establish cooperatives two crucial measures were adopted everywhere. The first was to mobilize the masses' thinking. A comparison between the two lines in production, living conditions, sale of surplus grain, resistance to calamities, and future prospects were made in educating the masses of peasants. Through the comparison they realized the superiority of cooperatives and the backwardness of the private economy.

A number of activities were extensively conducted such as visits to old cooperatives and inviting cadres from old cooperatives to give reports and answer questions. These measures produced significant results. For example, in Wuming County and other areas, activists took the lead in criticizing old thinking. They used the example of two brothers under similar economic conditions getting different outcomes after they parted and followed two different lines. In Yongwu Township, Gui County, for another example, because of scattered management of agriculture, although irrigation works were built, the problem regarding a ditch could not be solved. After the establishment of cooperatives it was solved quickly. As a result of such education of the peasants, the masses' thinking underwent a profound change. The mobilization of the masses to join cooperatives was done not only through public meetings, but also though private contacts.

The report by the Sichuan Provincial Committee said: In the fall 27,270 agricultural cooperatives were set up throughout the province. Right now there are altogether 57,581 cooperatives in the province. Including the peasant households that joined the enlarged cooperatives before the fall, there were altogether 2,286,297 households in the cooperatives comprising 17.4 percent of all peasant households. While the number of cooperatives increased by slightly less than 100 percent compared to those before the fall, the number of households [in APCs] increased slightly more than 100 percent over those in the cooperatives prior to the fall. Another 70,000 cooperatives are all actively being prepared for construction in the next period.

The Guangdong Provincial Committee reported: "After the movement reached the township level, the number of cooperatives established in most regions surpassed the planned figures. The number of cooperatives, including old cooperatives, has increased to 93,939 throughout the province before spring 1956 (the original planned figure was 85,000) and the cooperative membership accounts for 35.98 percent of peasant households (the original planned figure was 33 percent). In some counties the quotas were surpassed by far more. In Lianjiang County, for example, the original plan was to have 35 percent of peasant households join cooperatives prior to spring 1956, but the results of township planning increased the percentage to 44.7 percent. In Qujiang County, taking into account both new and old cooperatives, the percentage of the peasant households with cooperative membership increased from the originally planned 44.9 to 52 percent." "After a series of meetings, wide publicity, and comprehensive planning and implementation, especially after Chairman Mao's relayed instruction concerning the question of agricultural cooperativization was heard in broad countryside, the cadres and masses are in very high mood, the socialist atmosphere in the countryside is unprecedentedly strong, and peasants' socialist consciousness is greatly enhanced. As a consequence whole villages and whole townships of peasants ask to join cooperatives. . . . However, because of inadequate preparation, there are still many problems." "The provincial committee has made the following decision. In order to ensure the quality of cooperatives in view of the continuous surpassing of the planned figures, suitable control of the number of cooperatives to be established is entirely necessary. The number of cooperatives to be set up before the spring of 1956 is finally fixed at no more than 90,000. The cooperative membership should on average cover 35 percent of peasant households. This percentage could be lower in some areas but should not be less than 30 percent. It should be higher in some areas but should be no more than 37 percent. For any percentage over 37 percent application should be made for approval by the provincial party committee. . . . Prior to the fall the number of newly established cooperatives should not exceed 35,000. Those cooperatives that had not been completed can be done after the fall." It seems that at that time the Guangdong Provincial Committee was relatively sober.

However, the actual development of the movement was much faster than the plans drafted by each province. In competition with each other, by the end of 1955 over 1.904 million agricultural cooperatives had already been established throughout the country (among that 17,000 were higher stage cooperatives). More than 75 million peasant households, covering 63.3 percent of peasant households in the whole country, had already joined the cooperatives. This figure already came close to the targeted 70 percent set in the resolution of October for the advanced areas prior to spring 1957. The situation developed so rapidly that Mao Zedong had to rewrite his preface of September 25 for *How to Run APCs* and change the title to *Socialist Upsurge in the Chinese Countryside*. In explaining why he had to rewrite the preface, he wrote:

> The problem is not simply about materials. The problem is that in the second half of 1955 the situation in China has fundamentally changed. Up to the now—late December 1955—among the 110 million Chinese peasant households, more than 60 percent of them, that is, 70 million households have joined semisocialist APCs in response to the call of CCP center. In my report regarding the question of agricultural cooperativization of July 31, 1955, I mentioned that there were 1.69 million peasant households in cooperatives. During the past few months 50-odd million peasant households recently joined cooperatives. This is a tremendous event. This event tells us that it will take only the one year of 1956 to accomplish basically semisocialist agricultural cooperativization. In another three to four years, that is, by 1959 or 1960, we can basically complete the change over from semisocialism to socialism. This event tells us that China's socialist transformation of handicrafts and capitalist industry and commerce needs to be completed a bit ahead of schedule in order to suit the needs of agricultural development. This event also tells us that the scale and speed of industrialization and of the development of science, cultural affairs, education, public health, and other fields of work in China should not follow what was originally thought out. These should be appropriately expanded as well as speeded up.

The development of the situation again exceeded Mao Zedong's estimation. By the end of May 1956, 110.13 million peasant households, accounting for 91.2 percent of total peasant households in the country, had already joined APCs. Among them 74.72 million households, constituting 61.9 percent of total peasant households, joined higher stage APCs, while 35.42 million households, accounting for another 29.3 percent of total households, joined elementary APCs. By the end of November 1956, the number of APCs throughout the country reached 764,000, and that of peasant households in the cooperatives totaled 116.74 million, accounting for 96.1 percent of the total peasant households of the whole country. Among the established APCs there were 488,500 higher stage APCs whose members covered more than 100 million peasant households, accounting for 83 percent of peasant households in the country, with an average of 206 households per APC.[37] In this way the socialist transformation of agriculture, the changeover from private ownership to collective ownership that was originally planned to be finished within fifteen years (Mao Zedong in his report "On the Question of Agricultural Cooperativization" still said after 1960), was hastily completed within a brief period of four years.

Mao Zedong spoke highly of this 1955 upsurge of the agricultural cooperativization movement that was facilitated by antiright-deviationism within the party.[38] He said:

> In short, in the second half of 1955 a fundamental change took place in the balance of class forces in our country. Socialism soared and capitalism plunged. Given another year of hard work in 1956, the foundation basically will have been laid for the socialist transformation in the transition period. In China, 1955 has been the decisive year for the struggle between socialism and capitalism. The decisive battle unfolded first of all at the three conferences called in May, July, and October by the CCP center. In the first half of 1955 the atmosphere was foul and dark clouds threatened. But in the second half of the year there has been a complete change and the climate is entirely different. In response to the call of the party center tens of millions of peasant households have swung into action and carried out cooperativization. At the time the editor is writing these lines more than 60 million peasant households have joined cooperatives all over the country. This is a raging tidal wave sweeping away all demons and monsters. People of all sorts in our society have been clearly revealed for what they are. It is the same in the party. By the end of this year the victory of socialism will be largely assured. Of course, many more battles lie ahead and further efforts must be made to carry on the fight.

That the victory of socialism was already within our grasp was the conclusion Mao Zedong drew from the development of the socialist transformation of agriculture in 1955. This conclusion incisively revealed his psyche at the time. History proves that the rapid development of left-deviationist thinking within the party in the mid and late 1950s began right here.

[In the remainder of this chapter the authors examine the speeding up of socialist transformation in other areas with particular emphasis on the late

1955-early 1956 period following the dramatic acceleration of agricultural cooperativization.]

Notes

[The notes that are numbered page by page in the Chinese text have been renumbered consecutively throughout this translation.]

1. *Nongye jitihua zhongyao wenjian huibian* (A collection of important documents on agricultural collectivization), vol. 1, pp. 248–49.

2. Ibid., p. 260.

3. Ibid., p. 321.

4. It was also suggested that by the end of winter 1954, 7 billion jin of grain was overpurchased throughout the country. It is recorded on p. 66 of *Zhonghua Renmin Gongheguo guomin jingji he shehui fazhan jihua dashi jiyao* (Summary of major events of the national economy and the planning of social development of the People's Republic of China) that by the end of 1954, "103.6 billion jin of grain was purchased and 110 percent of the plan was achieved." On the basis of the above data, 10 billion jin was overpurchased.

5. *Nongye jitihua*, vol. 1, pp. 291–93.

6. Rural Work Department of the CCP Central Committee, *Nongcun gongzuo tongxun* (Rural work newsletter), no. 32.

7. *Nongye jitihua*, vol. 1, p. 290.

8. *Zhongguo nongye hezuoshi ziliao* (Materials on the history of Chinese agricultural cooperation), no. 2 (1982), p. 13; *Nongye jitihua*, vol. 1, pp. 290–91.

9. *Sanzhong quanhui yilai zhongyao wenxian huibian* (Collection of important documents since the Third Plenum), vol. 2, p. 955.

10. *Zhonggong dangshi jiaoxue cankao ziliao* (CCP history teaching reference materials), vol. 20, p. 478.

11. *Nongye jitihua*, vol. 1, pp. 227–84, 295–98.

12. *Zhongguo nongye hezuoshi*, no. 5 (1988), p. 4.

13. *Nongye jitihua*, vol. 1, pp. 308–10.

14. See the April 12, 1955, letter to Tan Zhenlin by Yuan Chenglong, the deputy section chief of the Second Office of the Central Secretariat, in *Dangshi yanjiu ziliao* (Research materials on party history), no. 5 (1981), p. 4.

15. *Zhongguo nongye hezuoshi*, no. 5 (1988), pp. 4–5.

16. *Nongye jitihua*, vol. 1, pp. 327–28.

17. The editorial departments of the *People's daily*, *Red flag* magazine, and the *People's Liberation Army daily*, "The struggle between the two lines in the Chinese countryside," *Renmin ribao* (People's daily), November 23, 1967.

18. *Dangshi yanjiu ziliao*, no. 5 (1981), pp. 5–6.

19. *Zhongguo nongye hezuoshi*, no. 5 (1988), p. 9.

20. *Nongye jitihua*, vol. 1, p. 260.

21. *Dangshi yanjiu ziliao*, no. 5 (1981), pp. 3–4.

22. *Dangshi yanjiu* (Research on party history), no. 1 (1981), pp. 2–9; *Nongye jitihua*, vol. 1, pp. 333–41; *Zhongguo nongye hezuoshi*, no. 5 (1988), p. 6.

23. First Secretary of the CCP Central Committee's Shanghai Bureau. [The Shanghai organ was the single exception to the elimination of all regional party bureaus in 1954–55—Eds.]

24. *Dangshi yanjiu ziliao*, no. 5 (1981), p. 6.

25. *Nongye jitihua*, vol. 1, pp. 331–32.

26. *Zhongguo nongye hezuoshi*, no. 5 (1988), p. 6.

27. Ibid.

28. Ibid., p. 13.

29. *Dangshi yanjiu ziliao*, no. 5 (1981), p. 8.

30. *Mao Zedong xuanji* (Selected works of Mao Zedong), vol. 5, pp. 168–91.

31. Ibid., pp. 195–217.

32. *Xinhua yuebao* (New China monthly), no. 11 (1955), pp. 9–13.

33. *Mao Zedong xuanji*, vol. 5, pp. 171–72, 188–89.

34. *Nongye jitihua*, vol. 1, pp. 377–425.

35. Ibid., pp. 460–61.

36. Rural Work Department of the CCP Central Committee, *Nongcun gongzuo tongxun*, no. 45.

37. 1957 *Renmin shouce* (People's handbook), pp. 197, 474.

38. *Mao xuanji*, vol. 5, p. 233.

5

Bo Yibo

Selection from *Reflections on Certain Major Decisions and Events**

**Chapter 15: A turning point in the acceleration
of the socialist transformation of agriculture**

Since the 1951 dispute over the development of agricultural producers'
cooperatives (APCs) in Shanxi, the transformation of agriculture in our
country had been proceeding at a relatively high tempo. By December 1951
when the "Resolution on Mutual Aid and Cooperation in Agriculture
(Draft)" was announced, the number of APCs was more than 300. By June
1952 it grew to more than 3,000, to more than 14,000 by December 1953
when the "Resolution on the Development of APCs" was formally promulgated, to 100,000 by spring 1954, and to 670,000 by spring 1955. However,
after summer 1955 the pace of development was suddenly speeded up. By
the end of that year more than 60 percent of peasant households had joined
the cooperatives. Nationwide cooperation in an elementary form had been
basically accomplished by the end of April 1956, and cooperation in an
advanced form was achieved in most provinces and municipalities by the end
of October 1956.

The rapid development of socialist transformation of agriculture brought
forth rapid progress in socialist transformation of capitalist industry and
commerce and of handicrafts. Prior to summer 1955 socialist transformation
of capitalist industry and commerce in our country basically proceeded from
low, through middle, to high levels, from major to minor sectors, and from
big to medium and small cities. The First Five-Year Plan required that by
the end of 1957 most of the privately owned industrial enterprises should be
transformed into state capitalism in various forms and that more than half
of the privately owned commercial enterprises should be transformed into
state capitalist ones or cooperative ones. However, after summer 1955,

---

*Bo Yibo, *Ruogan zhongda juece yu shijian de huigu* (Reflections on certain major decisions
and events), vol. 1. (Beijing: Zhonggong zhongyang dangxiao chubanshe, 1991), pp. 326–55,
366–75.

pushed forward by the high tide in agricultural cooperativization, upsurges in the transformation of capitalist industry and commerce were set off in the cities throughout the country in winter 1955. By the end of January 1956 joint state-private ownership of enterprises in all sectors had been basically completed in big and medium cities across the country. By the end of 1955 the number of organized handicraftsmen in the whole country was approximately 2 million, accounting for 25.47 percent of all handicraftsmen. Under the influence of the high tides in the transformation of agriculture and capitalist industry and commerce, the percentage increased to 90 percent by April 1956.

The turning point in the acceleration of socialist transformation in our country was the criticism of so-called "walking like a woman with bound feet" within the party in summer 1955.

The criticism of "walking like a woman with bound feet" was proposed by Chairman Mao in his report, "On the Question of Agricultural Cooperativization," delivered on July 31 at a conference of secretaries of provincial, municipal, and autonomous region party committees. In this report he expounded upon the possibilities and necessities of agricultural cooperativization in our country, reiterated the principle of voluntary participation and mutual benefit, proposed the principle of implementing cooperation first and mechanization second under the conditions in our country, and demanded that leadership and overall planning of cooperation should be stepped up. All the above points are doubtlessly correct. However, since the keynote of the report was its criticism of the right-deviationist view of "walking like a woman with bound feet" that kept escalating after the conference and reached a climax at the Sixth Plenary Session of the Seventh Central Committee and later with publication of *Socialist Upsurge in China's Countryside*, an atmosphere in reality formed throughout the country in which whoever did not march double time was "walking like a woman with bound feet." Such an atmosphere brought forth not only rapid development of agricultural cooperativization, but also rapid development of socialist transformation as a whole and rash advance in economic development during 1956.

The above criticism within the party reflected a significant difference between Chairman Mao's view and that of Comrade Deng Zihui, director of the Central Rural Work Department, vice premier, and concurrently director of the Seventh Office of the State Council, concerning overhauling and consolidating APCs in Zhejiang Province and the pace of the development of agricultural cooperativization in the whole country. Reflecting upon and analyzing the beginning and end of the debate over the above two issues and the essence of the difference in their views over the two issues may be of some value in going a step further in summing up the experience and lessons of our country's agricultural cooperativization.

I. On overhauling and consolidating cooperatives in Zhejiang

This issue was made a sensation by Lin Biao and the Gang of Four during the tumult of the Cultural Revolution. As a matter of fact, the so-called reactionary policy of "stop, shrink, overhaul" and the cutting down of "200,000 cooperatives" in the November 23, 1967, article, "The Struggle between Two Lines in China's Countryside," jointly by the editorial departments of two newspapers and one journal, referred to this issue.

Here I will first look back on the origins of the issue.

In December 1954 the center approved the proposal put forth in the report to the Fourth National Mutual Aid and Cooperation Conference that prior to the 1955 fall harvest the number of APCs should increase to about 600,000, that in the old [liberated] areas about 30 percent of peasant households should join cooperatives, that most townships in the new [liberated] areas should have cooperatives, and that the total number of cooperatives would increase by 500 percent over the 100,000 cooperatives of spring 1954 and by about 200 percent over the cooperatives set up before the fall 1954 harvest. The report said that if these 600,000 cooperatives were well run, we could be assured that by 1957 more than 50 percent (the First Five-Year Plan required about one-third) of peasant households could be organized to join elementary APCs so that APCs in the existing form would become the main form of organization of production in major agricultural regions throughout the country.

On January 4, 1955, Comrade Deng Zihui reported to Premier Zhou and the party Central Committee in a bulletin of the Seventh Office of the State Council about the implementation of the plan for developing cooperatives. The gist of the bulletin is as follows. Since the lower levels' enthusiasm was very high, the original 600,000 target had already been raised to 700,000. However, it now seemed that it was not at all that easy to run 600,000 cooperatives well because county and district cadres spent almost twelve months, that is, the whole [previous] year, on economic work such as state monopoly purchase and marketing of grain and could only spend a short period of time on developing cooperatives. For the 380,000 new cooperatives established at the time throughout the country (there still were 100,000 old APCs), most of them had not found a foothold and no one helped them to overcome various kinds of difficulties during the early stage following their establishment. In addition to the above problem, state monopoly purchase and marketing of grain was under way and some peasants were severely resentful over it. Combined with their fear of nationalization, their resentment resulted in fairly widespread activities detrimental to production, such as sluggishness in collecting manure and making compost, the massive sale of livestock, and spending their money not on purchasing means of production but on items not needed urgently, or even on renovating graves, purchasing coffins, and so on. These activities warn us against the wavering attitudes of small owners toward socialist transformation.

Two proposals were made in the bulletin to ensure a healthy development of the movement and two documents drafted on behalf of the center were included in the appendixes. First, the bulletin suggested the formulation of a national charter and included a draft "Model Regulations for APCs." The aim in making the regulations was to stipulate clearly the semisocialist nature of cooperatives and to prevent cadres from making laws blindly and the masses from having confused misgivings. Second, it proposed to bring the cooperative movement into a stage of controlled development where consolidation was emphasized. It also included in its appendixes a draft "Circular on Overhauling and Consolidating APCs." The general spirit of the circular was that it would naturally be good to reach the target of 600,000 cooperatives according to the original plan; however, if it could not be accomplished, it should also be regarded as the greatest victory to set up 500,000 cooperatives as long as no waste [poorly run] cooperatives were formed.

The center accepted the proposals by Comrade Deng Zihui. Through discussion the Politburo decided that people concerned would be organized to revise the draft model regulations and that a slightly-revised "Circular on Overhauling and Consolidating APCs" would be signed and sent out by Comrade Liu Shaoqi on January 10. The circular made the following statements. At present the number of APCs in the whole country had increased to 480,000 plus. Among them some of the 300,000 plus new cooperatives were set up without preparation or with very poor preparation. As a result newly established cooperatives collapsed and members withdrew from them one after another in many places. Therefore, "the cooperativization movement at present should basically shift to a stage in which development is controlled and consolidation is emphasized." Wherever the original plan for the development of APCs had been basically accomplished or overfulfilled, development should be halted and all efforts should be devoted to consolidation.

In the areas where there was still a long way to go before the plan was fulfilled, already established cooperatives should be carefully consolidated and during consolidation preparations for continuing development should be made. If some provinces thought that the original plan was too high, they could report to the Central Rural Work Department and apply for its approval of an appropriate reduction. In the areas where the movement spread hastily without adequate preparation (such as the situation in certain counties of Hebei and Zhejiang), on the basis of the principle of not dampening the activists' enthusiasm and at the same time ensuring the quality of the newly established cooperatives, the number of the existing cooperatives and APC-member households should be reduced reasonably.

The circular also required that in consolidating cooperatives emphasis should be placed on publicizing the principle of voluntary participation, that the broad masses should be allowed to speak about the doubts and worries in their minds, and that education work should be conducted in the light of their thinking that had been exposed. It pointed out that the voluntary union of all the members was the most fundamental guarantee for running cooperatives well.

After the circular was sent out, the number of APCs kept increasing. It grew to 580,000 in early February and to 670,000 in April.

In accordance with tasks proposed in the circular of January 10, the Central Rural Work Department concentrated on helping Hebei, Zhejiang, Shandong, and other provinces, in particular Zhejiang, to make a good job of overhauling and consolidating APCs.

The problems in Zhejiang were very prominent. According to the report by the Rural Work Department of the Zhejiang Provincial Committee, in Zhejiang after opposing Rao Shushi's erroneous thought, blind enthusiasm for cooperativization emerged; some prefecture [party] committees raised the misleading slogan of "grasping two ends to bring along the middle" (relying on the poor peasants, struggling against the rich peasants, and bringing along the middle peasants) and so on, which the Provincial Rural Work Department did not rectify in time. Before the fall 1954 harvest, there were 3,800 APCs in the whole province. By spring 1955 the number increased to 50,950, and adding 4,800 spontaneous cooperatives, the total number reached 55,000. Due to rapid expansion and too many cooperatives, commandism and many other problems occurred. For example, meetings were held in some counties at which the rich peasants in the whole district were publicly denounced and the following was announced: "Whoever takes the socialist path should set up cooperatives whereas whoever does not join the cooperatives should be struggled against like the rich peasants."

When carrying out the state monopoly purchase of grain in Zhejiang in 1953, local production output was to be uniformly assessed according to the output of the cooperatives (which was greater than that of peasants who farmed on their own). [Moreover,] in some places the output of peasants who farmed on their own was set higher than those of the cooperatives, so, out of fear of suffering losses when the state purchased grain, peasants asked to join the cooperatives. After land reform there were many backward villages in Zhejiang. During the transformation of backward villages, out of the fear of being assigned another class origin, peasants implored urgently to join the cooperatives. Due to rough implementation of the policy of mutual benefit, some poor peasants mistakenly thought that joining the cooperatives meant partnership on the basis of an even distribution of property. As a result, once the APCs were set up the practice of living on first the middle peasants' investments and then on state loans spread gradually. After spring plowing started, since little preparation was done for farming, the new cooperatives set up by coercion could not be run any longer. They accounted for about 10 percent of all cooperatives. Cooperatives that were set up under inadequate conditions and could not be well run even after the leadership was strengthened accounted for 30 percent of all APCs. The peasants were slack in production, which was particularly reflected in the fact that they were at loggerheads over investment and neither purchased nor repaired any farm tools. In his letter of April 12 to Comrade Tan Zhenlin, Comrade Yuan Chenglong, the deputy section chief of the Second Office of the Central Secretariat, mentioned that the big expansion of cooperatives in Zhejiang was largely caused by some cadres' commandism. He said that in encouraging the peasants to join cooperatives, some cadres in charge of setting up APCs openly announced that whoever joined the cooperatives would be assigned a smaller quota for grain sold to the state whereas whoever did not join would be assigned a bigger quota. In many areas it was required that for the establishment of cooperatives the land should be joined together into a single piece, and many peasant households that did not join cooperatives were forced to exchange their land with others. Some cadres even blackmailed the peasants who did not join APCs. As a result, many peasants joined them out of fear and with anxiety.

To help Zhejiang make a good job of overhauling and consolidating agricultural cooperatives, in late March Comrade Deng Zihui, along with Comrade Tan Zhenlin, deputy secretary-general and director of the Second Office of the Central Secretariat, invited Comrade Jiang Hua, secretary of the Zhejiang Provincial Committee, to attend a meeting to carry out a study [of the situation]. On the basis of opinions from the discussion, they wrote "Opinions about Current Cooperativization Work in Zhejiang Province" and sent it to the Zhejiang Provincial Committee by telegram in the name of the Central Rural Work Department on March 25.

[Bo here quotes in full the text of "Opinions." This text is reproduced in the original documents section of this volume, pp. 165–67. The gist of the document is that in light of the tensions in the province's rural areas a reduction in the number of APCs was called for, but a reduction that should vary according to actual conditions in different areas. Attention was to be given to the feelings of the peasants and voluntary participation adhered to. An estimate that 30,000 APCs could be consolidated was given and retaining 10 percent of peasant households in the cooperatives would be regarded as a great achievement.]

According to concerned comrades, after writing out the draft of this telegram, Comrade Deng Zihui asked Chen Boda (at that time head of the Policy Research Office of the Central Committee and deputy director of the Rural Work Department) to take it to Chairman Mao for approval.

After sending out the telegram, Comrade Deng Zihui went abroad.

Comrade Tan Zhenlin convened a meeting of the responsible persons in the Second Office of the Central Secretariat and the Rural Work Department, at which it was decided that Comrade Du Rensheng, the secretary-general of the Rural Work Department, and Comrade Yuan Chenglong, the deputy section chief of the Second Office of the Central Secretariat, would be sent to Zhejiang to explain the gist of the telegram. As Comrade Du Rensheng admitted later during the Sixth Plenary Session of the Seventh Central Committee, he told the comrades at the Zhejiang Provincial Committee the following: "It was correct for you to be strategically brave in developing cooperatives between last winter and this spring. However, tactically speaking preparation was inadequate." "In a batch of APCs, instead of investing in them, the middle peasants demanded to withdraw from the cooperatives while the poor peasants were short of grain ration and asked the APCs for payment in advance. They were not in a stable mood. For this batch of cooperatives, once they got on the horse, it was difficult for them to get off. However, if they do not get off, they will miss spring plowing and the worker-peasant alliance will be negatively affected." "To retreat from the positions where we cannot find a foothold is for the purpose of consolidating those we already have and for developing new ones." On April 11 Du Runsheng and Yuan Chenglong together wrote a report to the two institutions that dispatched them and proposed that in order to overhaul and consolidate the cooperatives in Zhejiang, "in addition to straightening out the implementation of the policy of voluntary participation and mutual benefit, a policy of devoting all efforts to consolidation and resolute contraction is needed." They also pointed out that currently many cooperatives asked the government for money and grain and remarked: "Since middle peasants are not investing and poor peasants are asking for payment in advance, they are sitting idle and eating up the whole fortune." [They concluded that] "Since the whole year's work depends on a good start in the spring, we should get off the horse right away."

After receiving the telegram from the Central Rural Work Department and listening to the explanation by Comrade Du Runsheng, the Zhejiang Provincial Committee unanimously agreed. It convened a four-level cadre conference at which work was assigned. Before that conference, Comrade Du Rensheng had hurried back to Beijing to ask Comrade Tan Zhenlin whether the contraction measures in Zhejiang were feasible. Additionally, Comrade Jiang Hua called the provincial party committee from Beijing, telling them that "rash advance in cooperativization in Zhejiang was the most serious in the whole country" and urging them to accept the proposal of the Rural Work Department. After one month's work, the number of APCs in Zhejiang decreased from 53,144 to 37,507, a reduction of 15,637. The claim during the Cultural Revolution that Zhejiang "cut down 200,000 cooperatives" was sheer exaggeration and dishonest.

By the end of June there were 650,000 agricultural cooperatives in the whole country, a drop of only 20,000 from the 670,000 in April. In addition to the reduction of 15,607 APCs in Zhejiang, the number of cooperatives in Shandong decreased by 4,000 and in Hebei by 7,000. In fact, they were increasing in Shanxi, Henan, Jilin, Yunnan, and other provinces.

Most of the 15,000 APCs cut down in Zhejiang were changed into mutual aid teams. In his report to the Central Rural Work Department by telephone, Comrade Huo Shilian of the Zhejiang Provincial Committee said that by so doing it enables comprehensive propaganda on the party's policy, makes the cadres realize the disadvantages of encroaching upon the middle peasants' interests, clears up some poor peasants' misunderstanding that cooperation meant partnership on the basis of equal distribution of property and some middle peasants' misunderstanding that cooperation was a "second land reform," and thus was extraordinarily beneficial for both social production and cooperativization. He also said that make-up policy propaganda work should be done not only for those cooperatives that should be cut, but also for those that should be consolidated. In his inspection report in Hangzhou on June 21, Comrade Tan Zhenlin reported on the situation after overhauling APCs in Zhejiang: "At present APC production is going very well. For most of them an increase in output can be assured, and [cooperative] operation and management is also good in most of them. However, the policy of mutual benefit has not been thoroughly implemented. The investigation found the reason to be mainly that since the class line was implemented last year the idea of taking advantage of middle peasants had already emerged and nobody was willing to treat middle peasants equally and share benefits with them. According to my understanding, unless the problem is solved the existing cooperatives cannot be fully consolidated and a batch of them will collapse after the fall." On July 6 he also reported that peasant households in APCs in Zhejiang declined from 28 to 18.6 percent. While the policy of voluntary participation and mutual benefit and the slogan of voluntary withdrawal and changing the cooperatives into mutual aid teams were widely publicized, a large number of cooperative members withdrew from the cooperatives and the policy of mutual benefit still had not been carried out. In his report of July 28 to the Shanghai Bureau of the party center by telephone, Comrade Lin Hujia, member of the Standing Committee of the Zhejiang Provincial Committee, made the following remarks regarding cooperatives: "We think that resolute contraction is correct, but in the process of contraction there are shortcomings. Some cooperatives that should not have been cut down were cut down and it became a campaign in many places during which most of the efforts were devoted to contraction; some of the APCs were cut down in a hasty manner and the work dealing with the aftermath was not well done; and some peasants suffered losses that dampened their enthusiasm. These defects have been corrected after the May conference held by the center."

Having sensed the problem of the reduction of cooperatives in Zhejiang, Chairman Mao gave Comrade Deng Zihui the following warning: "Do not repeat the 1953 mistake of dissolving a large number of cooperatives. Otherwise, you will have to make a self-criticism again." Regarding the time when he gave that warning, Chairman Mao said in his report of July 31 that it was in April 1955, whereas Comrade Deng Zihui said at the Sixth Plenary Session of the Seventh Central Committee that it was in early May. According to *A Chronicle of Major Events of the Center in 1955*, at 21:30 p.m. on May 5, "the chairman talked with Comrade Deng Zihui at Yinian Hall." Thus Deng Zihui's recollection is probably correct.

At the end of July when he came to Beijing for a conference, Comrade Ke Qingshi, secretary of Shanghai Bureau of the party center, passed on to Chairman Mao the record of Lin Hujia's telephone report to the Shanghai Bureau. Chairman Mao immediately made a comment: "It should be printed and distributed to the secretaries of each provincial and municipal committee and other people attending the conference." He also made the following comment next to the sentence in the original record that "We think resolute contraction is correct": "This estimation is not correct—Mao's note."

On July 31 in his report Chairman Mao made [the following] criticism: With the adoption of a policy that was called "resolute contraction" in Zhejiang (not by the decision of Zhejiang Provincial Committee), out of 53,000 APCs, 15,000, comprising 400,000 peasant households, were dissolved at a single stroke. This caused great dissatisfaction among the masses and cadres, and it was altogether the wrong thing to do. This policy of "resolute contraction," [he said,] was decided on in a state of panic. To take such a major step without the approval of the center was wrong too. To become dizzy with success, which leads to swelled heads and left-deviationist mistakes is, of course, bad. To be scared of success, which leads to resolute contraction and right-deviationist mistakes is just as bad. [He claimed that] the trouble now was of the latter kind, for some comrades had become scared of the several hundred thousand small cooperatives.

Chairman Mao summed up the difference in views over this issue as a dispute between getting off and getting on the horse. In his report he stated: Some comrades take a wrong approach to the vital question of the worker-peasant alliance, proceeding from the stand of the bourgeoisie, rich peasants, or well-to-do middle peasants with their spontaneous tendencies toward capitalism. They warn us: "If you don't get off the horse quickly, we run the danger of breaking up the worker-peasant alliance. We think, exactly the opposite. If we don't get on the horse quickly, there will be the danger of breaking the worker-peasant alliance. There is a difference of only a single word here—one says 'off' while the other says 'on'—yet it demonstrates the difference between the two lines."

On September 26, in examining a draft speech by Comrade Deng Zihui for the Sixth Plenary Session of the Seventh Central Committee on the question of overhauling APCs in Zhejiang, Chairman Mao wrote the following comments: "Why do you always like to frustrate the socialist element but not the capitalist one? You have not answered this question. The answer should be that the capitalist thinking in your mind is so serious that you do not think that the socialist element is lovely at all and thus are hardhearted enough to frustrate it." "You have been infected by the spontaneous tendencies of the well-to-do middle peasants who account for 20 to 30 percent of the total number of peasants, and therefore, you 'go off in the opposite direction instead of protecting,' turn a blind eye to and 'dare to frustrate' and write off the enthusiasm of the poor and the lower middle peasants, who account for 60 to 70 percent of the total number of the peasants. Does this happen accidentally?"

On October 11 in his concluding speech at the Sixth Plenary Session of the Seventh Central Committee, in referring to the formulation that "if we do not get off the horse quickly, the worker-peasant alliance will be broken up," Chairman Mao said: "I think that this statement is in the main 'correct' only after a single word is changed, that is, change the word 'off' to 'on.' "

The differences of opinion over this issue were essentially about the following two problems. First, how to handle the cooperatives that were not well run. Second, how to evaluate the development of agricultural cooperativization in Zhejiang after fall 1954.

It seems nowadays that we cannot say that concerning the first problem there was nothing wrong with the telegram to the Zhejiang Provincial Committee by the Rural Work Department and with the statements by Comrade Deng Zihui and some other comrades. For example, it was proposed in the telegram of March 25 that "if 30,000 APCs can be consolidated and if more than 10 percent of peasant households can be preserved in cooperatives on the basis of voluntary participation" in Zhejiang, it would be "a great achievement." It thus explicitly asked that more than 20,000 APCs should be cut down in Zhejiang. Although it was suggested that the quota for cutting down should be "known only within the party," this did not seem necessary. For another example, regarding the definition of contraction, Comrade Zihui made only a rather ambiguous explanation. He said: "Contraction applies to the cooperatives that actually are not well run and that cannot be well run after tremendous efforts have been made. They should be thrown out." He also said: "Why should we keep those cooperatives in which there are many problems, about which the masses have complaints, and in which only a small number of members are willing to stay whereas most of them are not? A simple solution is for members to be allowed to withdraw (and the cooperatives will be dissolved). They can feel free to come and go, we need not wait until August 15 before we dissolve the cooperatives." This statement left everyone with the following two impressions. The first one was that contraction meant the dissolution of cooperatives. The second one was that whether a cooperative ought to be cut down, that is dissolved, should be decided by most of its members. I think that Comrade Zihui's statement is not as good as Chairman Mao's.

Chairman Mao said: "Only those APCs where all or almost all members are determined not to carry on will be dissolved. If some members are determined to give up, let them withdraw while the majority stays and carries on. If the majority is determined to give up but the minority is willing to carry on, let the majority withdraw while the minority stays and carries on. Even if things are going that badly, it will be better [than to dissolve these cooperatives altogether]." Using a small cooperative in Nanwang Village, Anping County, Hebei Province, as an illustration, Chairman Mao said: "The three old middle peasants were firmly against carrying on and were allowed to withdraw, but the three poor peasant households said they would continue whatever happened. They stayed and the cooperative was preserved." At least over the issue of dissolving APCs, Chairman Mao's above statement could better reflect the principle of voluntary participation and free withdrawal than Comrade Zihui's statement that the minority should obey the decision by the majority. As for the phrases "getting off the horse of cooperativization," "cutting down cooperatives," and so on by Comrade Du Runsheng, their inappropriateness is more manifest, for they could easily be misunderstood.

The telephone report by Comrade Lin Hujia that in Zhejiang contraction "became a campaign" and was done "in a hasty manner" and that thus "the enthusiasm of some peasants was dampened" was also supported by facts. Some investigations done afterward show that some peasants were seriously dissatisfied with the dissolution of the cooperatives. They said: "It was you who asked us to set up cooperatives. It was also you who asked us to dissolve them." Some peasants even said: "We can neither speak out fully for three years nor will we forget all our lives our anger toward resolute contraction." The above examples show that commandism had occurred in dissolving 15,000 APCs. We cannot deny that such commandism in practical work had nothing to do with inappropriate statements by Comrade Deng Zihui and other comrades. At this point I think that we should not deny the truth in Chairman Mao's criticism of Comrade Zihui and other comrades simply because we have to draw a lesson from that criticism.

Practice indicates that Comrade Zihui's opinion was correct regarding the evaluation of the development of agricultural cooperativization in Zhejiang Province after fall 1954. Abundant materials show that it was indeed rash advance for cooperative membership as the percentage of peasant households to increase suddenly from several tenths of 1 percent to more than 30 percent in Zhejiang Province after fall 1954. On the basis of the this estimation, it was necessary for the Rural Work Department to put forward proposals to the Zhejiang Provincial Committee that in the main were also correct. Among the 15,000 cooperatives dissolved in Zhejiang, although some of them should not have been dissolved in a simplistic manner, most of them could not have been sustained. Before the Rural Work Department sent the telegram to the Zhejiang Provincial Committee, the center circulated the experience of Sichuan Province that allowed the county governments to issue a proclamation announcing that participation in cooperatives should be voluntary. This proclamation was issued in fifty-five counties in Zhejiang Province. By the end of February, 19 cooperatives were dissolved on a voluntary basis, and by the end of March the number increased to 264. It showed that the cooperatives that were set up against the principle of voluntary participation due to commandism, or under various kinds of political and economic pressure, could not survive with vitality. Neither to dissolve cooperatives in a forcible manner nor to set up cooperatives in a forcible manner was correct.

Although the path of mutual aid and cooperation is the inevitable way from a small-scale peasant economy to socialism, ultimately the peasants' own will must be respected over the issues of whether or not and when they join the cooperatives. The party should inspire them only through demonstration by examples or ideological education to take this path, not through commandism. In December 1953 the center formally promulgated the "Resolution on the Development of APCs" that explicitly pointed out: "The development of agricultural cooperativization should be based on the principle of voluntary participation by the peasants regardless of time and place." "If commandism is used to transfer the peasants' means of production into public ownership, it can be only regarded as a crime to sabotage the worker-peasant and the poor and middle peasant alliances, thus sabotaging agricultural cooperativization. It cannot have any advantage for agricultural cooperativization." Some of the phrases in the above statements may have been too sharp, but the reasoning behind them was correct. The crux of the problem of the rash advance in agricultural cooperativization in Zhejiang after fall 1954 can be found here. The same thing can be said about a variety of setbacks in agricultural cooperativization and later communization in our country.

On March 9, 1981, the General Office of the Central Committee transmitted a "Report for Approval concerning the Question of the Rehabilitation of Comrade Deng Zihui" submitted by the party group of the State Agricultural Commission and the comments on the report by the center in approving it. The report described the situation, which was confirmed by investigations, after overhauling and consolidating APCs in 1955 in Zhejiang Province as follows: "Relatively good results were achieved, the mistakes of encroaching on the interests of the middle peasants were rectified, the once tense relationship of the middle and poor peasants was very well resolved, the peasants' enthusiasm for production recovered, and the cadres' level of policy awareness was raised. Practice proves that handling the problem in that way met the masses' demands. Due to poor preparation, rough implementation, and a crude work style, however, some cooperatives that should not have been cut down were eventually dissolved. These were mistakes in the concrete implementation of policy." This conclusion conforms to reality.

It seems nowadays that Chairman Mao's inappropriate criticism of Comrade Deng Zihui mainly lies in the fact that he failed to get a comprehensive understanding of the progress of agricultural cooperativization in Zhejiang and other places. As a result, he failed to notice the fact that in some areas rash advance had already happened and failed to sense the abnormalities in the dramatic increase in the percentage of peasant households in APCs in Zhejiang and other provinces. On the contrary, he regarded it as a sign of the arrival of "a high tide of socialist cooperative transformation in the countryside" and considered the arrival of the high tide in these areas as a sign of the coming of a high tide of cooperativization in the whole country. On the basis of the above estimation, he took the criticism of rash advance by Deng Zihui and other comrades concerning the cooperativization movement in a small number of counties and provinces such as Zhejiang as concerning the cooperativization movement in the whole country. Similarly, he took as demanding "getting off the horse" in the whole country, the idea that applied exclusively to a small number of cooperatives in Zhejiang where the middle peasants were "at the loggerheads over investment" and "whose members were sitting and doing nothing, eating up the whole fortune." He thus misinterpreted Comrade Deng Zihui's actual thinking, for Comrade Zihui repeatedly stated that the development of the cooperativization movement after fall 1954 was healthy, that achievements were the main aspect, that most of the more than 600,000 APCs could be consolidated, and that rash advance only happened in a small number of counties and provinces such as Zhejiang, Hebei, and Shandong.

The above differences in their understanding of the issue also involve more profound issues, such as that of class policy in the countryside, of how to understand the poor peasants' enthusiasm for socialism, and so on. I will reflect upon them below.

II. The debate over the pace of development of agricultural cooperativization

Following the differences in their opinions over the issue of overhauling cooperatives in Zhejiang, starting in late June 1955 Comrade Deng Zihui engaged in another debate with Chairman Mao over the pace of development of APCs. Chairman Mao summed it up as a debate over big or small development.

On June 14, chaired by Comrade Shaoqi, the Central Politburo held a meeting to hear a report by Comrade Deng Zihui concerning the Third National Rural Work Conference and to examine the control figures and guiding policy for the expansion of APCs in the second half of the year. The following was agreed at the meeting: "Although some trouble occurred in the work of agricultural ccoperativization during the past years, great achievements have been made and most of the cooperatives have increased their yields. A big expansion should be made in the coming year. The policy is that existing cooperatives should be consolidated while attention should be paid to establishing new cooperatives and the number of APCs should reach 1 million prior to the fall 1956 harvest." "The principle of mutual benefit and voluntary participation should be adhered to in our cooperativization work. The statement in the past that 'the middle peasants should suffer some losses in the cooperatives' was wrong and should be rectified." The target of 1 million cooperatives was suggested by the Central Rural Work Department. During the discussion Comrade Shaoqi said that after development reaches 1 million cooperatives, we can close the door for a while until the middle peasants knock at it of their own accord.

Upon returning from his inspection tour outside Beijing in late June, Chairman Mao invited Comrade Deng Zihui for a talk. In the talk he said that the increase from the existing 650,000 to 1 million APCs in the second half of the year, that is, an increase by 350,000 cooperatives, or slightly more than 50 percent, seemed too small. He proposed that the number of cooperatives should increase by 100 percent, that is, an increase to about 1.3 million cooperatives and that there should be a big expansion of cooperatives in the new [liberated] areas and further expansion in the old [liberated] areas. Comrade Deng Zihui insisted that it was better to maintain the plan of 1 million cooperatives, that there should be a small or appropriate expansion in the new [liberated] areas where the movement should proceed slowly at the beginning and fast later, and that expansion should be halted in the old [liberated] areas before a new decision was made. They got into a dispute over the issue.

On that occasion Comrade Deng Zihui provided three reasons for his argument. First, the cooperativization movement as a whole should keep in step with the pace of industrialization. During the First Five-Year Plan, only a preliminary basis could be laid for industrialization, technological transformation of agriculture would just start, and cooperativization could only rely on manual labor. Under the above conditions, the expansion of cooperatives should not be too hasty or too fast. According to investigation materials from various places, during the first or second year after their establishment, the existing APCs could increase their output by 20 to 30 percent. However, after that, if technological transformation did not keep abreast, an increase in output could hardly be sustained. Second, there were many problems with and a very heavy task of consolidating the existing 600,000 plus cooperatives. If the expansion of cooperatives was too fast, development and consolidation would have to be undertaken at the same time. This would go beyond the level of the masses' consciousness and the cadres' experience. As a result, not only expansion and consolidation, but also agricultural production, would be negatively affected. Third, the main task between 1955 and 1956 was to lay a foundation for having one-third of peasant households join cooperatives and prepare well for full cooperativization in the future. Although the percentage of peasant households joining cooperatives in the old [liberated] areas had reached 20 to 30 percent, because in recent years the leadership concentrated on setting up cooperatives, little consolidation work had been done and the basis for the cooperatives was extremely fragile. Therefore, there should be about one year for consolidation.

In the light of the experience of the old [liberated] areas, the main task in the new [liberated] areas, where there were no habits or tradition of mutual aid and cooperation, was to assign some places for model experiments, set up a batch of new cooperatives in an appropriate manner, and devote all efforts to running them well so as to train cadres, set a good example, and lay the basis for accelerating the spread of development from the experimental points to a wide area. As for remote areas and national minority regions, in some of them land reform had not yet been carried out, production technology was still at the level of slash-and-burn cultivation, and even an accountant was difficult to find. It was thus very difficult to set up cooperatives there. Therefore, a longer time should be allowed for these areas to make preparations. At that time Comrade Deng Zihui had just returned from his visits to the Soviet Union and Hungary. In his talk with Chairman Mao, he also referred to the lessons of hasty cooperative transformation of agriculture in those two countries.

In his opening speech of April 21 and his concluding speech of May 6 at the Third National Rural Work Conference that the center entrusted the Rural Work Department to convene, Comrade Deng Zihui had already elaborated upon his above opinions. His thinking can be described as follows. Since socialist revolution was a long-term struggle, in a country like China without an industrial basis, it would be good enough if agricultural cooperativization could be accomplished, as originally planned, within fifteen years. Running cooperatives was different from land reform. The latter would be finished after the masses were mobilized and the land was distributed. During cooperativization, however, the establishment of a cooperative was only the beginning. It was more difficult than land reform to run a cooperative well, maintain solidarity within it, put the work onto the right track, actually increase output, and conduct good education of the cooperative members. After a peasant joined the cooperative, although he could get a payment for the means of production that were still owned by him, it was no longer at his disposal. Since he had already handed over the property of his whole family to you, if you could not run the cooperative well, at least those peasants who were the heads of their households would not sleep well. This was materialism. The peasants' socialist consciousness was based on what they saw, not what they heard. It would be somewhat idealistic not to judge their socialist consciousness on a materialist basis (the good or bad operation of the cooperative, the extent of increase or decline in the members' income, etc.). The good operation of a cooperative did not depend solely on the peasants. Average peasants had very rich experience in making a good job of the production of a single family or household. However, they did not have any experience in taking charge of the production of 30 to 40 households. The cooperative members would naturally feel uneasy in seeing that the director of their cooperative was incompetent. Therefore, without a group of full-time cadres with a certain cultural and theoretical level, a large number of cooperatives could not be run well. Even where an old cooperative had been set up for a few years, many new problems could not be solved by the APC itself if no cadres were there to take care of it for half a year. Where no cooperatives had been set up, there should be a period for trial establishment when a model was made to show the cadres and masses before [the cooperative movement] was spread. After the cooperatives were set up for a period of time, they should be consolidated for another period of time. The movement should not advance through tumbling and crawling. Otherwise, we would have to wipe clean our bottoms [after shitting in this manner] and the longer we did so the more wiping clean we would have to do. In the present period only the lower-stage APCs should be set up in which private ownership of land and dividends on land shares would be maintained.

On July 11 Chairman Mao invited Comrades Deng Zihui, Liao Luyan, Liu Jianxun, Du Runsheng, Tan Zhenlin, and Chen Boda for a talk at Yinian Hall in which he reiterated his opinions and quite severely criticized Comrade Deng Zihui and other comrades. However, Comrade Zihui still insisted on his own opinions. The talk lasted more than five hours. According to some comrades' recollections, Chairman Mao told Comrade Zihui: "Your mind needs to be shelled by artillery."

On July 18 Chairman Mao wrote to Comrade Du Runsheng saying: "Please send me for review all materials from the last rural work conference, such as reports and each participant's speeches and conclusions. I am looking forward to them." "The last rural work conference" in his letter referred to the Third National Rural Work Conference that proposed the following guiding policy: development should be halted before the fall, all efforts should be devoted to consolidation, the movement should be contracted appropriately in the provinces and counties where development was fast and many problems had appeared, and it could be expanded appropriately in the new [liberated] areas after the fall. In view of the opinions Comrade Deng Zihui expressed to his face and the conference materials, Chairman Mao started to write his report "On the Question of Agricultural Cooperativization."

On July 31, in his report "On the Question of Agricultural Cooperativization," Chairman Mao pointed out: "A high tide in the new socialist mass movement is imminent throughout the countryside. But some of our comrades, tottering along like a woman with bound feet, are complaining all the time, 'You're going too fast, much too fast.' Too much carping, unwarranted complaints, boundless worries, and countless taboos—all this they take as the right policy to guide the socialist mass movement in the rural areas." "No, this is not the right policy. This is wrong." (*Selected Readings from Mao Zedong's Works*, Version A, vol. 2, p. 406).

After Chairman Mao's criticism, Comrade Deng Zihui gave a speech in which he expressed his support for Chairman Mao's criticism and admitted that his previous analysis of the situation was not comprehensive and that the policy of allowing a small, not big, expansion of the movement in the new [liberated] areas was relatively passive.

On August 1 at the conclusion of the conference of provincial, municipal, and autonomous region party committee secretaries, Chairman Mao made the following remarks: The debate with Comrade Zihui has already been resolved. In April the center had one opinion whereas Comrade Zihui had another and the Rural Work Department did not implement the former's opinion. Prior to May 17 (when the conference of secretaries from fifteen provincial, municipal, and autonomous region party committees was held), it was said that the expansion of cooperatives in the new [liberated] areas was very bad. At the present conference, everyone spoke very well. Now it has been proved that the movement can be expanded in the new [liberated] areas and developed rapidly in the coming winter, spring, and summer. Rash advance would not happen if preparations and consolidation are done. The first preparation is to criticize mistaken thinking. Collectivism is better than dispersionism and personal decision, and we should observe this discipline. No department should issue orders arbitrarily.

On August 26 Chairman Mao instructed Comrades Deng Xiaoping and Yang Shangkun as follows: "Please inform the Central Rural Work Department by telephone that during the coming several months the center will write telegrams in direct response to the telegrams on agricultural cooperativization from provincial, municipal, and autonomous region party committees; also tell the concerned comrades not to write 'To be handled by the Rural Work Department' when sending this kind of telegram."

Between August 13 and October 2 prior to the opening of the Sixth Plenary Session of the Seventh Central Committee, Comrade Mao Zedong himself wrote comments for the center and made comments in authorizing the dispatch of reports by ten provincial party committees, such as Hubei, Liaoning, Anhui, Shanxi, Henan, and Zhejiang, concerning the study of "On the Question of Agricultural Cooperativization," criticizing right-deviationist conservative thinking, and readjusting and accelerating the pace of the development of cooperativization.

On August 31, in authorizing the dispatch of a report by the Anhui Provincial Committee, Chairman Mao pointed out: "The Anhui Provincial Committee sharply criticizes right-deviationist opportunist thinking concerning agricultural cooperativization. Such criticism is completely necessary." This was the first time a central document proposed criticism of right-deviationist opportunist thought. In its report, the Anhui Provincial Committee thought that in Anhui there were "women with bound feet," a "reorganization faction" [that maintained that in some areas APCs should be changed back to mutual aid teams—Eds.], and big feet. In order to make the bound feet bigger and turn the reorganization faction into natural feet, it was necessary to combine a profound self-examination with the study of Chairman Mao's instructions to expose further and criticize "women with bound feet."

On August 26 Comrade Mao Zedong wrote a "Circular" on behalf of the center that asked that the revised report "On the Question of Agricultural Cooperativization" be formally distributed to provincial, municipal, and autonomous region party committees and asked them to print it and distribute it to the party committees at all levels down to the rural branches. Compared to the report of July 31, the revised report added parts four, six, and seven. Parts six and seven were mainly criticism of "some comrades" who used Soviet experience to conceal their "crawling thought."

On September 7, in his comments written for the center on the report by the Fujian Provincial Committee, Chairman Mao comprehensively expounded his views on the class policy for agricultural cooperativization, especially the policy toward the middle peasants. His views persuaded many comrades to support the acceleration of cooperativization.

On September 26, in going over the manuscript of a speech of self-criticism by Comrade Deng Zihui prepared for the Sixth Plenary Session of the Seventh Central Committee, Chairman Mao wrote a long comment regarding Comrade Zihui's admission that in discussing the plan for expanding APCs he neither paid enough respect to the center and Chairman Mao nor paid enough attention to the different opinions of the comrades in the department. Its main idea was: "You [plural: Mao appears to be addressing other leaders in the Rural Work Department as well as Deng—

Eds.] have a line and a policy that contradict those of the center. Therefore, for a long time, the center could not persuade you, even through severe criticism." This reflected "not that you did not have adequate respect for the opinions of the center, but that you basically had no respect at all for them." Your refusal to listen to "slightly different opinions at your department" was directly related to the fact that you were only willing to subject yourselves to the influence of the well-to-do peasants who had a spontaneous tendency toward capitalism but not to that of the numerous and widespread positive elements in the countryside." "Since you even do not want to accept the severe criticism by the comrades at the center and the rejection of your proposal by the Secretariat and Politburo, what could some comrades in your department do with you?"

The enlarged Sixth Plenary Session of the Seventh Central Committee, one of whose main topics was agricultural cooperativization, opened October 4. In 248 speeches or written speeches, participants expressed unanimous support for Chairman Mao's report "On the Question of Agricultural Cooperativization" and criticized without naming names right-deviationist conservative thought, "a woman with bound feet," right-deviationist opportunism, "a man who shares his breath with the bourgeoisie," "a capitulationist to bourgeois thought," and so on. My speech was one of the 248. The gist of my speech was about the relationship between agricultural cooperativization and agricultural technological transformation. From today's perspective, the exploration of that relationship in my speech was necessary and the contents of the speech were all right. However, I made some inappropriate remarks in stating my position at the beginning. Among the 248 was also Comrade Deng Zihui's self-criticism. He said that he examined his other "mistake in principle" "in deep grief" and that he should assume full responsibility for the forcible dissolution of APCs in some areas of Zhejiang.

On [October] 11 Chairman Mao concluded the conference by delivering a report entitled "The Debate on Agricultural Cooperativization and the Current Class Struggle." [The text states September 11 but this is clearly a misprint as Mao spoke a month later; see *Selected Works of Mao Tsetung*, vol. V (Peking: Foreign Languages Press, 1977), p. 211—Eds.] He said: "Our present session has been a great debate. This debate concerns the question of whether our party's general line for the transition period from capitalism to socialism is entirely correct or not." Summarizing Comrade Deng Zihui's and others' views into thirteen points, he refuted them one by one. Finally he pointed out that "the mistakes Comrade Deng Zihui committed this time are right-deviationist and empiricist in nature."

In the "Resolution on Agricultural Cooperativization," passed at the Sixth Session of the Seventh Central Committee, the guiding policy for agricultural cooperativization of Comrade Deng Zihui and others was termed "a policy of right-deviationist opportunism." The resolution claimed that the increasing consolidation of cooperatives, the increase in production, and [the fact that] many peasants were actively joining the cooperatives "declared the bankruptcy of right-deviationist opportunism."

The publication of *Socialist Upsurge in China's Countryside* in early 1956, especially its prefaces, notes, and materials on typical cases, pushed further and deeper the criticism of "a woman with bound feet" and spread it throughout the country. The tone of criticism became sharper.

In his speech of January 20, 1956, at the conference on the question of intellectuals convened by the center, Chairman Mao said: "Our Rural Work Department should have been a department promoting advance. Within a certain period of time, however, it became a department promoting retreat."

When Chen Boda was delivering his speech at the Chengdu Conference on March 18, 1958, Chairman Mao added an occasional remark: "Regarding the difference of opinions over cooperativization, the key person opposing cooperativization was Deng Zihui."

On the surface the debate over the pace of expanding cooperatives seemed to be over whether to double the number of cooperatives or increase it by 50 percent and whether to increase it to 1.3 million or 1 million. However, it was essentially a debate between two types of guiding thought for cooperativization.

Comrade Deng Zihui was one of our party's outstanding leaders of the peasant movement. As I mentioned above, he shared the same view with Chairman Mao that the accomplishment of agricultural cooperativization in China was the fundamental path and direction for agricultural development. There was no difference between them over this point. There was also no divergence over the point that the development of cooperatives must have a control figure. However, there was an obvious difference between their guiding thoughts concerning the pace of the expansion of APCs. From the First National Rural Work Conference of 1953 onwards, Comrade Deng Zihui had been proposing adoption of a policy of steady progress and avoiding acting with undue haste in the mutual aid and cooperativization movement in China. Although the Chairman also talked about steady progress, the emphasis of his basic guiding thought was reflected by the following remarks: "As long as the cooperatives are well run, the more the better, as Han Xin said about the number of troops he could command." "If the number of the cooperatives is to be doubled, quotas can be allotted. If it is to be tripled, then there is room for consultation." "Overfulfillment will greatly increase people's enthusiasm." If the divergence of their views in 1953 over opposing "rash advance" and opposing "getting off the horse" was the first round in the debate between these two guiding thoughts, then the debate over "a great expansion" and "appropriate development" in summer 1955 was the second and more important round of their dispute.

The difference in the two types of guiding thought reflected their understanding of a number of issues related to the pace of the development of agricultural cooperativization.

They placed a different emphasis on the goal of agricultural cooperativization.

Comrade Deng Zihui emphasized that the transformation of the relations of production should keep in step with the development of productive forces in order to increase production. In 1953 he proposed: "The movement of mutual aid and cooperation should advance step by step in the light of the needs of production, not solely according to subjective demands. Otherwise, the goal of increasing production will not be achieved." In his concluding speech at the Third National Rural Work Conference of 1955 he pointed out three goals for agricultural cooperativization: to develop agricultural production; eventually to wipe out capitalism; and to consolidate thoroughly the worker-peasant alliance by eliminating the contradictions between the workers and peasants. Among them, however, he emphasized that developing agricultural production so as to satisfy the needs of the state and the people was the main goal. When he criticized rash advance in Zhejiang and other areas and when he proposed small, instead of great, expansion, his focus was to ensure an actual increase in cooperative production.

Chairman Mao, on the other hand, emphasized that productive forces could be developed quickly through accelerating the transformation of the relations of production. In his report "On the Question of Agricultural Cooperativization," he pointed out that although it took the Soviet Union seventeen years, that is, between 1921 and 1937, to accomplish cooperativization, the main work of cooperativization was done within six years, that is, between 1929 and 1934. The Soviet experience thus proved that it was correct to adopt the policy of big expansion in cooperative transformation in our country. In talking about the impetus for accelerating agricultural cooperativization in his concluding speech at the Sixth Plenary Session of the Seventh Central Committee, he said: "On this matter we are quite heartless! On this matter Marxism is indeed cruel and has little mercy, for it is determined to exterminate imperialism, feudalism, capitalism, and small production to boot. In this respect, it is better not to have much mercy. Some of our comrades are too kind, they are not tough enough, in other words, they are not so Marxist." Chairman Mao had made a number of penetrating theoretical expositions on the dialectical relationship between the relations of production and productive forces. He knew deeply that the relations of production should suit the level of development of the productive forces and that to reform relations of production was to better protect and develop productive forces. However, his criticism of Comrade Deng Zihui actually left people with the impression that the relations of production could be changed regardless of the state of the productive forces and that the faster it was changed, the more the productive forces could be developed.

They also had different understandings about the possibilities of accelerating the pace of the development of APCs.

Comrade Deng Zihui placed more emphasis on the possibilities provided by objective conditions. In 1953 he proposed three requirements for expanding cooperatives: production needs, the masses' consciousness, that is, their realization of the advantages of the cooperatives through personal experience, and the cadres' leadership capabilities. His suggestion of steady expansion in 1955 was still based on the above three requirements. After the dispute with Chairman Mao, he prepared a "Draft Speech" (judged from its content, it was probably for the conference of secretaries of provincial, municipal, and autonomous region party committees convened on July 31). He made the following points in the draft. Up to the present, the plan submitted by the provinces was to increase the number of cooperatives to 1.05 million, that is, in addition to the existing 650,000, to set up another 400,000 APCs. This plan conformed to practical needs and thus was feasible. He hoped that provinces, municipalities, and autonomous regions would pay attention to the following four conditions in approving concrete local plans: first, the degree of consolidation of the existing cooperatives; second, the scale of development of mutual aid teams; third, the strength of the cadres; fourth, whether the original groundwork was good or bad, for example, in the backward villages where land reform was not thoroughly carried out, the expansion of cooperatives should proceed slowly. Thus we can see that even after being criticized, Comrade Deng Zihui still emphasized that attention should be paid to the possibilities permitted by objective conditions in developing APCs.

Chairman Mao, on the other hand, emphasized that the masses' enthusiasm for the socialist road constituted the greatest possibility for accelerating the expansion of APCs. In reading the material entitled "A Summary of the Recent Situation in Agricultural Cooperativization" on July 29, he wrote a very long comment. In its first paragraph he expounded on the above point. He said: "There are two problems, that is, 'no advance' and 'rash advance' concerning the development [of cooperatives]. The problem now is not that of having to criticize rash advance and 'going beyond objective possibilities,' but that of having to criticize failing to realize and make use of 'objective possibilities,' that is, failing to see and make use of the broad peasant masses' enthusiasm for the socialist road due to insufficient land, poverty, or their not well-off lives. However, some of us fail to realize and utilize such existing objective possibilities." In his report of July 31, Chairman Mao further elaborated on this point. He pointed out that the objective conditions highlighted by Deng Zihui were merely "countless taboos."

During the period of his debate with Chairman Mao, some comrades at the Central Rural Work Department complained that Deng Zihui should not have gotten into the debate with Chairman Mao over the issue of a mere several hundred thousand cooperatives. Comrade Deng Zihui replied: "This is not a question of several hundred thousand more cooperatives. What is critical is that he thinks even those conditions for running cooperatives are not necessary. How could I not make myself clear?"

Chairman Mao also raised a new viewpoint concerning class policy for agricultural cooperativization.

In commenting on and distributing the report of the Fourth National Mutual Aid and Cooperation Conference of December 1954, the center proposed the following class policy in the countryside: "Relying on the poor peasants (including all new middle peasants who were formerly poor peasants, these poor peasants account for 50 or 70 percent of the rural population) and firmly uniting with the middle peasants so as to limit step by step and eventually eliminate exploitation." Comrade Deng Zihui endorsed and adhered to this class policy. He also put forward an important view that the poor and middle peasants "both will benefit if they cooperate and will suffer if they separate from each other." He suggested that Zhejiang adopt the contraction policy mainly because the relationship between the middle and poor peasants was severely strained. He did not endorse a big expansion of cooperatives also largely because at that time the middle peasants had doubts and a wavering attitude toward joining APCs. At the Third National Rural Work Conference he said: "I do not quite believe your remark that they (the upper middle peasants) are willing to join cooperatives, for their levels of production are higher than that of the cooperatives and will not be surpassed by the latter even if the APCs have been set up for three to four years. They will not comply if we ask them to join APCs and distribute their output equally. Of course, watching the general trend is a special feature of the middle peasants, but another special feature is that they calculate their gains and losses. If, after they finish their calculation of gains and losses with their abacus, they find that what they will gain falls short of what they are expecting, they will not join the cooperatives. Even if they eventually join, they are forced to do so." "It will lead to error if we think their consciousness has been enhanced by merely looking at their surface behavior and seeing that they asked to join the cooperatives with both hands raised in happiness or even in endless weeping and wailing." "Similar things happened last year in Guangdong. When the state purchased grain from the peasants, a middle peasant, weeping and wailing endlessly, obstinately asked our cadres to persuade the work team to allow him to join the cooperative. At first glimpse he seemed to have a high level of socialist consciousness. After some time, when he was asked about his own opinion, he said: 'Comrade, to tell you the truth, I did so at that time in order to get over the hurdle of grain purchase.' You say whether this was coerced or voluntary." "Besides, in some areas, settling accounts with the rich peasants is as a matter of fact 'killing the chicken to frighten the monkey.' A cadre thrust a knife at a rich peasant in the presence of the middle peasants. Can you say that this was not commandism?" Comrade Deng Zihui thought that "poor peasant cooperatives" in which no member was a middle peasant would lack means of production and thus could hardly be run well. On the other hand, he believed that if middle peasants were forced to join coopera- tives against their will, a good job could not be made of production either. Therefore, he concluded, the good operation of a cooperative depended on the unity of the poor and middle peasants. Regarding the issue of whether "new middle peasants who were originally poor peasants" were those on whom we should rely or those with whom we should unite, like many other comrades, his answer was that they were both.

In view of Comrade Deng Zihui's opinion, in his report of July 31 and his comments on the report of September 7 by the Fujian Provincial Committee, Chairman Mao differentiated the middle peasants according to their attitudes toward cooperativization and their degree of wealth into a number of strata, including new middle peasants, old middle peasants, new lower-middle peasants, old lower-middle peasants, middle-middle peasants, new upper-middle peasants, and old upper-middle peasants. He thought that since their lives were still difficult or not well-off, the poor peasants, the lower-middle peasants (including the middle-middle peasants) among the new middle peasants, and the lower-middle peasants among the old middle peasants were "enthusiastic about establishing cooperatives" and that therefore we should rely on them for cooperativization and absorb them in batches into cooperatives according to their level of consciousness. For the well-to-do middle peasants, with the exception of those who were really enlightened, none of them should be absorbed into the cooperative for the time being. According to this analysis, it was not all the middle peasants, but a small part of them, that is, well-to-do middle peasants with a spontaneous tendency toward capitalism (the so-called well-to-do middle peasants, according to the interpretation in the "Resolution on Agricultural Coopera- tivization," were the upper-middle peasants among the new middle peasants and the upper-middle peasants among the old middle peasants), who held doubts and a wavering attitude toward cooperatives. Chairman Mao said: "Some people say that the slogan 'rely on the poor peasants and firmly unite with the middle peasants' seems to have been abandoned in our present formulation. This is not true. We have not given up the slogan but rather made it more precise in light of the new conditions, that is, we count the lower middle peasants among the old middle peasants as a section of the people on whom we should rely, but not the well-to-do peasants among the new middle peasants." This new class analysis and argument by Chairman

Mao persuaded Comrade Deng Zihui and many other comrades to support his view on cooperativization at the July 31 conference of secretaries of provincial, municipal, and autonomous region committees and the enlarged Sixth Session of the Seventh Central Committee in October. In making his self-criticism at the Sixth Session of the Seventh Central Committee, Comrade Zihui focused on this issue and tried to dig out the root of his mistakes. He said: "Due to my lack of correct class analysis, I failed to distinguish the well-to-do strata of the middle peasants from the people on whom we should rely and vaguely included all new middle peasants as those on whom we should rely. As a consequence, the well-to-do peasants were absorbed into cooperatives too early everywhere and the difficulties in running them were thus increased. On the other hand, I indiscriminately treated the well-to-do peasants' wavering positions as those of all middle peasants, . . . and the former's spontaneous capitalist thinking as that of all middle peasants and thus underrated the new and old lower middle peasants' enthusiasm for socialism."

At that time the problem of the poor peasants taking advantage of middle peasants was very severe in some areas. Comrade Deng Zihui emphasized that middle peasant interests must be protected and that poor peasants must be educated not to take advantage of others. Chairman Mao, however, emphasized that both poor peasants and middle peasants should be educated to take into account the situation as a whole and a full compromise with the middle peasants should be opposed. In his comments on "A Summary of the Recent Situation in Agricultural Cooperativization," he said: "Since the problem of 'taking petty advantage' has occurred, we should educate the peasants not to 'take advantage,' correct all our policies, and support the poor peasants in the form of loans. Meanwhile, on the other hand, we should educate the middle peasants to take the situation as a whole into consideration and not to care too much about minor injustices to them when they joined cooperatives as long as production and their income from production output increased over the past. In short, instead of having a so-called full compromise with the middle peasants, both [poor peasants and middle peasants] should be educated to take into consideration the situation as a whole. Full compromise would not lead to socialism. Our policy is to unite with the middle peasants while also struggling against them."

Regarding the debate over the pace of the expansion of agricultural cooperativization, the party center approved the report by the party group of the State Agricultural Commission in March 1981 and affirmed that Comrade Deng Zihui's insistence on following the plan approved by the Politburo meeting of June 14 was correct. I think this is a realistic assessment.

["Section III. Where the fault lies," has not been translated. Here, although asserting that Mao's path from individual farming to agricultural cooperativization was completely correct, Bo addresses the reasons for the improper criticism of Deng Zihui and notes two main causes: (1) inadequate understanding of the arduous, complicated, and long-term nature of the socialist transformation of agriculture that led to impatience for success; and (2) the treatment of different opinions within the party as a line struggle.]

IV. An analysis of the "change in May"

Concerning the two big issues of overhauling and consolidating the existing APCs and developing new cooperatives, Chairman Mao did not criticize Comrade Deng Zihui from the outset. As a matter of fact, he had supported him, and we can even say very actively, for a certain period of time.

On March 3, 1955, Chairman Mao signed an "Urgent Directive by the CCP Central Committee and State Council on Prompt Assignment of Grain Purchase Work and Stabilizing the Peasants' Production Spirit" that had been proposed at the National Financial and Economic Conference and discussed and revised by Comrades Liu Shaoqi, Zhou Enlai, Chen Yun, Deng Xiaoping, Peng Zhen, Deng Zihui, Li Xiannian, Tan Zhenlin, and Yang Shangkun. It was stipulated in the directive that the quota for grain purchase in the second half of the year was reduced to 90 billion jin (it was further reduced another two times) and that while making a good job of purchasing grain, "the pace of agricultural cooperativization should be slowed down since it had great significance for alleviating tension in the countryside and stabilizing the peasants' production spirit." [Before this] it was suggested in the proposal made at the Fourth National Mutual Aid and Cooperation Conference approved by the center in December 1954 that we should strive for an increase of the percentage of the peasant households with cooperative membership to 50 percent by 1957. About the time of his signing the urgent directive of March 3, Chairman Mao sought out Comrade Deng Zihui for a talk in which he told him that it would be all right to have one-third of the peasant households join cooperatives by 1957 and that the percentage need not be 50 percent. At that time Comrade Zihui still insisted on the plan of 50 percent. Comrade Mao Zedong disagreed. He thought that since grain purchase had already reached [the maximum] limit and the task for grain purchase was 90 billion jin, that even one more jin should not be allowed, and that cooperativization should also be slowed down. In his concluding speech at the Third National Rural Work Conference of May 6, in referring to this talk with Chairman Mao, Comrade Zihui said: "Chairman Mao's proposal is very important" for "at that time we only thought that this year's plans of some provinces were a bit too big and still did not expect that it would be impossible to have 50 percent of the peasant households join APCs by 1957." "Thus we can see Chairman Mao's foresight!"

Afterward Comrade Shaoqi sought out Comrade Zihui for a talk in which he proposed to increase [the percentage of peasant households with cooperative membership] to one-third in the First Five-Year Plan, then add a further one-third in the Second Five-Year Plan, and another one-third in the Third Five-Year Plan. Today some works take for granted that Chairman Mao made that remark. Even at that time there was similar hearsay. After I checked the records for meetings of the Central Rural Work Department held in August 1955, I found that to counter this hearsay Comrade Zihui stated several times that it was Comrade Shaoqi, not Chairman Mao, who made the remarks about the three one-thirds.

Still, in early March Chairman Mao listened to the work report by Deng Zihui, Chen Boda, Liao Luyan, and Du Rensheng. In talking about the policy for developing APCs, Chairman Mao said: "The policy is a 'three-word scripture,' that is, stop, shrink, develop." It was decided at that time that the movement should contract a little in Zhejiang and Hebei Provinces, in general it should stop in the Northeast and North China, and it should develop appropriately in other areas (mainly new [liberated] areas). The three words "stop, shrink, develop" are a simplified formulation of the three guiding policies of halting development, appropriate contraction, and appropriate development of the movement to be adopted in different areas that had been proposed by the center in the January 10 "Circular on Overhauling and Consolidating APCs." The charge during the Cultural Revolution that the policies of "stop, shrink, and overhaul" were so-called reactionary policies was a purely groundless and distorted accusation.

Some peasants created disturbances in some areas during spring 1955. Some comrades used the term rebellion to describe the relatively large-scale peasant disturbances in certain areas. In the above-mentioned talk, Chairman Mao thus borrowed the word rebellion to make the following penetrating exposition of the slaughter of pigs and oxen by the peasants: "Relations of production should suit the development of productive forces. Otherwise, productive forces will rise up and rebel. Currently, the slaughter of pigs and oxen by the peasants is the uprising and rebellion of the productive forces."

When referring to Chairman Mao's opinion concerning the policy for the development of cooperatives in spring 1955 in his concluding speech of May 6 at the Third National Rural Work Conference, Comrade Deng Zihui said: "Originally we said that [expansion] should stop in the coming fall. Later Chairman Mao said that we could simply stop it (right now) and wait until the fall of next year, [in other words,] we would stop [expansion] for one and one-half years."

On April 20 the Central Secretariat held a conference to listen to the report by the responsible person of the Rural Work Department concerning preparations for the Third National Rural Work Conference to be convened the next day. In accordance with the gist of the Chairman's several talks, it was proposed at the Secretariat conference that the present "general policy" for agricultural cooperativization was to "stop the development of cooperatives and devote all efforts to consolidation." The conference proposed: "Up to the present 670,000 cooperatives have been set up. In those provinces with too many cooperatives, where the numbers of cooperatives exceed the plans by 20,000 to 30,000, our subjective strength cannot keep development under control, [so] we must contract a bit." The Third National Rural Work conference was convened according to the spirit of the above statement.

The change in Chairman Mao's understanding took place in May 1955.

After his warning of May 6 to Comrade Deng Zihui not to dissolve a large number of cooperatives [see above, p. 129, where Bo gives May 5 as the likely date of this warning—Eds.], on the evening of May 9 Chairman Mao invited Comrades Deng Zihui, Liao Luyan, Li Xiannian, and Chen Guodong (vice minister of the Grain Ministry) for a meeting. Premier Zhou Enlai was also present. Chairman Mao suggested that the amount of grain to be purchased, which was originally set at 90 billion jin, could be reduced to 87 billion and that such a reduction could be exchanged for socialism and an increase in agricultural production so as to lay a foundation for agricultural cooperativization. He said that since the coming two or three years would be a crucial period for agricultural cooperativization, the foundation for cooperativization should be laid down during these three years. He asked whether we could have 40 percent [of all peasant households] join the cooperatives by 1957. Comrade Deng Zihui replied: Last time we said one-third, it is better to stick to one-third. Chairman Mao said reluctantly: All right, one-third.

At the May 17 conference of secretaries of fifteen provincial and municipal party committees convened at Hangzhou, Chairman Mao said that there were not a few disturbances involving cooperatives, but [the APCs] were on the whole good. If we did not emphasize that point, [he said,] we would make mistakes. [He stated that] there was a passive sentiment about the issue of cooperativization, and in [his] opinion it must be changed; otherwise, we would make a big mistake. In his speech, although he reiterated the three-word policy of "stop, shrink, develop," he placed stress on "development." He said: "Regarding cooperatives, [our policy] is first stop, second shrink, third develop. As far as contraction is concerned, there can be complete contraction, half contraction, big contraction, and small contraction. If the APC members are determined to withdraw from the cooperatives, what can anyone do about them[?] Contraction should be done in the light of practical conditions. One-sided contraction will inevitably dampen the enthusiasm of the cadres and the masses. In the areas that were liberated later, [cooperatives] simply must be developed, not stopped or contracted, but basically they should be developed. In some places [the movement] may need to be halted, but in general it should be developed. Even in some old liberated areas in North China and the Northeast there is the need to expand. Take Shandong as an example. Thirty percent of its villages do not have cooperatives. [The cooperativization movement] should by no means either stop or contract [in such areas]. There are no cooperatives there. What should we stop? There [the catchword] is simply to develop. [To summarize,] wherever the movement ought to be stopped, we should stop it; wherever it ought to be contracted, we should contract it; wherever it ought to be developed, we should develop it." After discussion, he proposed in his conclusion control figures for the expansion of APCs in provinces of the new [liberated] areas for the next year (from the end of fall 1955 to the beginning of fall 1956) as follows: "70,000 cooperatives in Henan, 45,000 each in Hubei, Hunan, and Guangdong Provinces, 35,000 each in Guangxi and Jiangxi, and 65,000 in Jiangsu." He said that if you were willing, we could strike a deal and fix the above figures. He also said that as far as the Northeast, Northwest, Southwest, and North China were concerned, we would have Lin Feng, Ma Mingfang, Song Renqiong, and Liu Lantao convene meetings [upon their return] at which they would relay the gist of this conference and discuss the solution. He added we must guarantee that 90 percent of the APCs that are developed are reliable.

The above two talks, especially that at the May 17 conference, signify that Chairman Mao's views concerning agricultural cooperativization had already changed significantly and that he shifted from initial support to criticism of the work plan of Comrade Deng Zihui.

Deng Zihui and other comrades also sensed the change in Chairman Mao's thinking. Some historical research works in recent years call it the "change in May." However, they have not explored or explained clearly the causes of the change. To find out the causes of the change is an issue that we should not avoid in studying the history of that period. Now I will try to offer some analysis and conjecture concerning the causes of this change on the basis of the materials I have read and my own recollections.

Throughout the history of our party the proposal of each task and the assignment of work in order of importance and urgency have always been related to the analysis and estimation of reality and the situation. Whenever the situation is relaxed, the proposed task will be a bit high and the pace a bit fast. Whenever the situation is tense, the guiding thinking will be very cautious so as to allow for a steady pace. On the basis of my experience, I infer that Chairman Mao's shift from support to criticism of Comrade Deng Zihui's work is probably related to the change in his estimation of the situation in the countryside.

In spring 1955 Chairman Mao supported the slowdown of the pace of agricultural cooperativization. The pace he backed was so slow that sometimes even Comrade Deng Zihui did not expect it. His support probably lay in his consideration of the severe situation in the countryside.

In 1954 the middle reaches of the Yangtze River, the Huai River valley, and the north China plain suffered from the biggest flood of the century. In other areas crop yields were the same as or increased over that of the previous year. Since the state had to make up for the losses in yields in areas with bad harvests by purchasing more grain from areas with good harvests, it purchased 7 billion jin of grain above the plan from the areas that did not suffer floods. In some areas, even the peasants' grain rations were purchased. In Guangdong and Guangxi Provinces and some areas in southern Hunan in particular, a drought lasted from September 1954 until early May 1955. As a result, the rice seedlings could not be transplanted during that spring. Additionally, severe cold weather destroyed the sweet potatoes that were supposed to be harvested in the spring. Therefore, there were serious tensions in the countryside in spring 1955, especially in Guangdong and Guangxi and the areas in Hunan affected by the cold weather and drought where the tensions were the most severe. In addition to natural calamities, the tensions could indeed be traced first to excessive targets for grain purchase that resulted in the second nationwide grain agitation since 1953, and also to too rapid development of agricultural cooperativization since fall 1954. Due to intense grain purchasing work, almost all county and district cadres were engaged in grain purchase. No one could pay attention to the expansion of cooperatives. Therefore, many newly established cooperatives were run in a very rough manner and many problems regarding economic policies were handled inappropriately. The peasants' misunderstanding that cooperativization meant "to eat rice from a big pot," was not cleared up and consequently their enthusiasm for production was negatively affected. For example, in some areas the slogan "accomplish cooperativization within three years" was put forward and it was stipulated that the ratio for drawing dividends on land and labor shares followed the principle of "three to seven in the first year, two to eight in the second year, and turning over to the state in the third year" (that is, the ratio between the dividends on land and labor shares would be 3:7 in the first year and 2:8 in the second year, and land dividends would be completely abolished in the third year). As a result, the peasants not only did not spray fertilizer on the land, but they were also in the grip of great anxiety, and rumors spread everywhere. For "the livestock were turned over to the cooperatives at too low a depreciated price too early and too hastily, and payment was not made as scheduled; or the remuneration by cooperatives for using privately owned farm animals was too low, and the peasants owning farm animals more often than not sold them before they joined cooperatives" (quoted from CCP center, "Urgent Directive on Making Great Efforts to Protect Farm

Animals," January 15, 1955). This aggravated the dramatic drop in the price of and reckless slaughtering of farm animals.

In spring 1955 Chairman Mao did not hesitate to believe the situation Comrade Deng Zihui and the Rural Work Department reported to him. In the "Urgent Directive by the CCP Central Committee and State Council on Prompt Assignment of Grain Purchase Work and Stabilizing the Peasants' Production Spirit" of March 3, which he personally signed authorizing distribution, it was pointed out at the very beginning: "At present the situation in the countryside is rather strained in that in many places the peasants have slaughtered a large number of pigs and oxen, are neither enthusiastic about collecting fertilizer and preparing for spring plowing nor are in high spirits for production. We should realize that this situation is serious and that although it may result from resistance and sabotage by a small number of rich peasants and other bad elements, it is on the whole a warning from the peasant masses, especially from the middle peasant masses, due to their dissatisfaction with certain measures taken by the party and government in the countryside. It arises from many causes, such as too hasty and too fast development of the mutual aid and cooperative movement in some regions, some unreasonable measures, defects with supplies to the countryside, and so on." This estimation of the situation in the countryside was basically identical to that in the brief report of January 4 by Comrade Deng Zihui.

During April and May Chairman Mao traveled outside Beijing to inspect work. Starting in May his estimation of the situation in the countryside changed significantly. He held that: "It is said that the peasants are slack in production. I think they are the minority. I have seen on my way that wheat has grown to a person's waist. How can we say the peasants are slack in production?" "The so-called grain shortage is most cases fictitious; the clamor about it is raised by landlords, rich peasants, and well-to-do peasants." He also thought that the grain shortage was an offensive "launched by the bourgeoisie under the disguise of grain problems" and that the report by the Rural Work Department that some cooperatives could not be run any longer was "blowing a wind of rumors."

The speech on October 4 by Comrade Shaoqi at the Sixth Plenary Session of the Seventh Central Committee roughly explains the change in the understanding of the center and Chairman Mao concerning the situation in the countryside. He said: when spring was changing into summer in 1955, "when the clamor 'very bad' came into our ears from everywhere in the country, we first of all judged that the clamor about the grain problem was not true, or in most cases not true. At the beginning, we also had some doubts concerning the clamor about cooperatives. However, not long after, Chairman Mao also found out that such clamor was not true and refuted it so strongly that he charged the Central Rural Work Department with "blowing a wind of rumors."

Let us first look at the change in their understanding of the grain issue. In March and April, when the sale of grain in the countryside increased dramatically and the clamor about the grain shortage was becoming louder and louder, the center received some materials about typical cases that showed that not all cases of grain shortage were true. Among them was material about Songdian Township, Wenxi County, Shanxi Province. That township originally asked for 10,170 jin of grain. After monopoly sale work was overhauled, it not only did not ask for grain supplies, it also came up with 6,200 jin of grain reserved for emergency use. What happened was as follows. Some households were able to be self-sufficient, but seeing the others buying grain from the state they went along and clamored about a grain shortage. Some other households had surplus grain but they intentionally yelled about a grain shortage with the others out of the fear that the others would criticize them for selling too much grain to the state or would come to them to borrow their grain. Although knowing that the clamor about a grain shortage was false, some cadres still turned a blind eye to it since they had overpurchased grain for themselves or gave leeway to their relatives for their overpurchase of grain. Besides, due to lack of experience and irregular methods for the sale of grain, unfairness in supplying grain and the practice of budgeting liberally and spending sparingly were also encouraged. The people who falsely yelled about a grain shortage came from all strata. However, the well-to-do peasants outnumbered those from other strata.

A number of materials about typical cases such as Songdian Township led Chairman Mao and the party center not only to make the judgment that "the clamor about a grain shortage was in most cases made by landlords, rich peasants, and well-to-do peasants," but also to decide to make great efforts to overhaul the work of monopoly grain sale. On April 24 an editorial, "Immediately Rely on the Masses to Overhaul Monopoly Grain Sale Work," was published in the *People's Daily*. On April 25 Comrade Li Xiannian made a report at Zhiguang Hall to explain to personalities from various circles the truth about the grain problem and the significance of overhauling the sale of grain. On April 28 the CCP Central Committee and State Council jointly issued a "Directive on Grasping Firmly Monopoly Grain Sale Work." The result of overhauling was as had been expected. Starting from May the sale of grain eventually decreased dramatically. It made Chairman Mao further believe that the original estimation of the tensions in the countryside was an overstatement. It was at that time that among high level nonparty personages more people came out to speak for the peasants. Some of them made some remarks similar to Mr. Liang Shuming's in 1953 that "The peasants are living a bitter life." Although these comrades did so out of good will, as everyone knows Chairman Mao did not like to hear such remarks. At that time he formed an impression that those who talked about the bitterness of the peasants' lives regarded themselves as representatives of the peasants, but actually they did not represent the peasants, and that they made those remarks because they did not want to have industrialization and socialism. Additionally and more importantly, Ke Qingshi, secretary of the Shanghai Bureau of the party center, once spoke about the situation with Chairman Mao saying that through investigation he found that 30 percent of the cadres at county, district, and township levels reflected the peasants' demand for freedom and unwillingness to practice socialism. Ke figured out very well Chairman Mao's thinking and what he liked. His above remark left a deep impression on Chairman Mao. Chairman Mao immediately thought that there were people who were "unwilling to practice socialism" not only at the lower level and provincial level, but also among cadres in central organs.

After Chairman Mao reflected upon what he heard about the above state of affairs, he not only changed his view concerning the spring situation in the countryside, he also started to apply the viewpoint of class struggle to the estimations by different people about the situation in the countryside.

On his inspection tours in different areas and at the May 17 conference, Chairman Mao found that comrades in many places were enthusiastic about establishing and running APCs. In his own words, everyone thought that agricultural cooperatives were very good. At the May 17 conference some provinces even made a few complaints about the Central Rural Work Department. This made Chairman Mao think that the report on the situation of agricultural cooperativization by the Central Rural Work Department was not true either.

Since the pace of cooperativization was originally slowed down mainly in the light of the tensions in the countryside, and since at that time the understanding of the situation in the countryside had changed, it seemed natural to have an acceleration of the pace of cooperativization. However, Comrade Deng Zihui could not catch up with this change. I think that this is probably the major reason why Chairman Mao shifted from support to criticism of Comrade Deng Zihui's work.

Chairman Mao's tour outside Beijing at this time to inspect work was a turning point in his understanding of the situation in the countryside. From what he saw and heard, he came to understand and discover many fresh aspects about the situation. Some of them he had not understood or discovered before; in some others he discovered facts with discrepancies from what he had understood previously. What he said concerning everyone being enthusiastic about running cooperatives was one of them. Here I think of one problem. Most of the materials reported to Chairman Mao on his tour were doubtless true. However, it seems that we cannot rule out the possibility that some of the materials were not so authentic, or contained certain subjective elements on the part of those making the reports, or treated a particular case as the entire situation, or contained empty boasting. Real life and innerparty life are very complicated. Although the ideological line of the party is to seek truth from facts, it actually is not easy to carry it out.

[Bo concludes the paragraph and chapter with some general observations on the need for both high and low levels to pay attention to actual facts and avoid situations where leaders are given only what they want to hear or what lower-level officials believe will impress them.]

Part II: Original 1955 Documents

6

DENG ZIHUI

State Council Seventh Office
Work Bulletin No. 1
(January 4, 1955)

Premier:

Recently we have paid attention to two things. One is directing the cooperativization movement, the other is learning about the situation of state monopoly purchase and marketing of grain. A separate report will be made on the latter issue. Here we will only report on the cooperativization movement as follows.

In October last year, the center approved the establishment of 600,000 APCs in all provinces throughout the country. The enthusiasm of the lower levels is so high that they increased the target to 700,000. Now it seems that it is not at all easy to run 600,000 cooperatives well. The reason is that county and district cadres spent almost twelve months, that is, the whole [previous] year, on economic work such as state monopoly purchase and marketing of grain and, therefore, they could spend only a short period of time on developing cooperatives and could not direct the production activities of the cooperatives in a regular and systematic manner. Up to the present, 380,000 new APCs have been established throughout the country (there still are 100,000 old cooperatives). Most of these new cooperatives have not found a foothold and no one has helped them overcome various kinds of difficulties during the early stage following their establishment. In this period, state monopoly purchase and marketing of grain was under way and some peasants were severely resentful over it. Combined with their fear of "nationalization," their resentment results in fairly widespread activities detrimental to production, such as sluggishness in collecting manure and making compost, the massive sale of livestock, slaughtering pigs and sheep, and spending the money they make not on purchasing means of production but on items not needed urgently, or even on renovating graves, purchasing coffins, and so on. These activities warn us against the wavering attitudes of small owners toward socialist transformation. For this reason, we adopt the two following measures:

First, a national charter should be made to specify the semisocialist nature of cooperatives so that cadres will not make laws blindly and the masses will not have confused misgivings. Now a draft is written. We ask the party center to distribute it to all regions in the country for trial implementation. After that, opinions will be collected, the draft will be revised, and a new version will be sent to the People's Congress or its standing committee for formal approval and promulgation.

Second, in view of the fact that the expansion of cooperatives up to the present is not far from the planned target of 600,000, that the Northeast, North China, and South China have already reached the assigned target, and that the Central-South, Southwest, and Northwest only need a little further development, the overall movement should shift to controlled development and enter a stage of consolidation. In some places, such as Shandong, Henan, and Hebei, since the original targets are a little bit high and cannot be accomplished, they have willingly reduced them after consultation with us. The general spirit is that it would be good to establish 600,000 APCs, [but] it should also be acknowledged as the greatest victory to set up 500,000 cooperatives as long as no waste [poorly run] cooperatives are formed. A directive has already been drafted and sent to the center for approval. In so doing the two tensions caused by state monopoly grain purchase and cooperativization will not combine and more activities detrimental to production can be avoided. Considering that state monopoly grain purchase, conscripting recruits, establishing and operating cooperatives, and collecting the grain quota for the state are all heavy tasks, that the exchange of commodities between the urban and rural areas is not smooth, and that lower-level cadres' coercion and commandism will inevitably happen, [we can hardly expect] that only a few problems will occur. Therefore, we should pay close attention to [the cooperativization movement].

A couple of other things we have done are: convening the forum on fishery and forestry work, helping the Agriculture, Forestry, and Water Conservancy Ministries prepare for the conference at which work will be assigned at the beginning of the coming year, preparing for the organization of an investigation group on the question of basic level construction, and so on.

Deng Zihui
January 4, 1955

7

Circular of the CCP Center on Overhauling and Consolidating Agricultural Producers' Cooperatives (January 10, 1955)*

Shanghai Bureau, all subbureaus, and provincial (and municipal) committees:

I. At present the number of APCs in the whole country has increased to 480,000-plus. Among these cooperatives, about 100,000 were set up in spring and summer 1954 and another 300,000-plus were newly established around the time of the fall harvest. Since a considerable portion of these new cooperatives were set up without preparation or with very poor preparation and, in addition, in November and December 1954 the whole party was concentrating on the state monopoly purchase of grain and was unable to overhaul them, as a result, the collapse of newly established cooperatives and the withdrawal of members from them happened one after another in many places. It has already become an urgent task to overhaul and consolidate the above 400,000 and several 10,000 cooperatives.

II. Since a large number of peasants eagerly join the APCs because they realize that cooperativization not only provides economic superiority but is also a general trend, there has been a rapid development of cooperatives within a brief few months. This is naturally a good thing but a comprehensive estimate of the favorable situation is needed. Neither should we applaud blindly nor should we look at the work of cooperativization in an oversimplified manner and neglect the likely serious doubts and worries of the peasants, especially middle peasants, during the change in the relations of production and the likely consequent shocks in the countryside. Recently

---

*Reprinted from the original archival document.

the massive sale of farm animals, slaughtering of sheep, cutting down of trees, and other events of this sort have happened in many places. Indeed, there are many causes for them. But it should be understood that one of the important causes is the peasants' fear that their property would be nationalized during the great development of the cooperativization movement, and the peasants try to make some quick money before that happens. If we fail to aim at the state of the peasants' actual thinking, conduct ideological education repeatedly, carry out organizational work painstakingly, solve critical economic problems in cooperatives carefully, and organize present production activities well, then inevitably immature outcomes will occur, the cooperativization movement would be prevented from advancing continuously, and severe consequences unfavorable for production might follow. It should not be taken for granted that no deviations will occur because the party enjoys high respect from the peasants and the present semisocialist policy of cooperativization receives the support of the peasants. In the period when the cooperativization movement develops rapidly, if we do not do our work well and let deviations occur, we will encounter various phenomena unfavorable to production. However limited and short-lived these phenomena might be, they will cause great losses. For this reason, we should make every cautious and conscientious effort to avoid them.

III. In light of the above two points, the center believes that it is necessary to reiterate the policy that we are obliged to run [the cooperatives] well; anything short of this is unacceptable. [Also,] the cooperativization movement at present should basically shift to a stage in which development is controlled and consolidation is emphasized. [The following measures should be adopted] in accord with [conditions in] different areas.

1. Wherever the original plan for the development of APCs has been basically accomplished or overfulfilled such as the provinces in the Northeast, North China, and East China (with the exception of Inner Mongolia), development should be halted and all efforts should be devoted to consolidation. We will again consider whether or not to continue development only after all the existing cooperatives have on the whole been overhauled.

2. In areas where there is still a long way to go before the plan is fulfilled, such as the provinces in the Central-South, Southwest, and Northwest, already established cooperatives should be carefully consolidated and during consolidation preparations for continuing development should be made. The original plan for the development of cooperatives should be strictly observed and not overfulfilled. If some provinces or municipalities think the original plan is too high, they can report to the Central Rural Work Department and apply for its approval of an appropriate reduction. For example, Shandong Province has already decided to reduce its APCs to 80,000 from the 100,000 originally planned and Henan Province [will

similarly cut down] to 40,000 from 50,000. Such reductions are appropriate.

3. In areas where the movement unfolded hurriedly without adequate preparation (such as the situation in certain counties in Hebei and Zhejiang), the provincial committee concerned should earnestly help county committees overhaul the cooperatives. Under the principle of no damage to the enthusiasm of activists and guaranteeing the quality of the newly established cooperatives, the number of cooperatives and that of peasant households in cooperatives should be reasonably reduced.

IV. During the work of consolidating cooperatives emphasis should be placed on publicizing the principle of voluntary participation, the broad masses of cooperative members should be allowed to speak about the doubts and worries in their minds, and education work should be conducted in the light of their thinking that has been exposed. It should be made clear to the broad ranks of cadres that they should not fear even if a small number of people wish to withdraw from the cooperatives because the voluntary union of all the cooperative members is the most fundamental guarantee of well-run cooperatives.

Recently the masses had to set up some nominal cooperatives that existed in name but not reality in some places under the pressure of the cadres. For this kind of cooperative it will be good if they can continue to operate after being reorganized with [our] help. If they still cannot be run after receiving help, they should be allowed to change back into mutual aid teams and [hopefully] become cooperatives again in the future.

In many places some rich peasants, landlords, or counterrevolutionaries sneaked into cooperatives because the masses were not fully mobilized. [In these cases] the masses should be educated to identify and expel them from the cooperatives. In those fake cooperatives controlled by hostile elements, the masses should be won over in order to reform or dissolve them.

V. Another important aspect of consolidating cooperatives is to handle correctly the major economic issues within the cooperatives.

Since the evaluation of land yield and remuneration concerns each member's basic interests, it should be dealt with carefully.

At present particular attention should be paid to the issue of turning over private livestock to cooperative ownership. In places where the prices of farm animals drop dramatically such as Henan and Hebei, a normal price above the present abnormal price should be negotiated publicly for the renting or collectivizing of livestock. The above measure can on the one hand prevent middle peasants from having regrets afterward and on the other hand contribute to the stabilization of the public mood. It should be carried out after the poor peasants are consulted and persuaded to accept it. In the past, when livestock was collectivized, some old cooperatives negotiated a price and payment by installments. However, the payment was not actually made and the promise to the former owners of the livestock was broken. This is quite wrong. Unless severe disasters happen whereupon payment can be delayed upon negotiation, under normal circumstances payment should be made according to the originally negotiated schedule in order to honor the promise.

At present, we do not encourage turning over to cooperative ownership some means of production that can be easily damaged such as flocks of sheep and trees. This can done after the situation has stabilized.

We must pay attention to correcting two deviations: either the cooperative members keep excessively large private plots or they are not allowed to keep any.

VI. Consolidation and continued development of cooperatives should be conducted in the light of winter production. Concerning all kinds of phenomena unfavorable for production, we should conduct studies to locate the causes and to propose feasible and efficient solutions for improving the situation in accord with the thrust of the instructions of the party center approving and promulgating the circular by the Ministry of Commerce on the present market situation for cows and sheep and the production of pigs.

VII. Currently about half of the provinces have on the whole completed monopoly grain purchase work, and the remaining half of the provinces will not finish it until the end of this month. After the spring festival we still must devote [great] efforts to the conscription of recruits in due course. Hence the tasks for rural work in the lead up to spring plowing are extraordinarily heavy. We expect provincial and prefectural committees to make overall plans and appropriate arrangements for rural work [to make sure that] a suitable effort is put into the establishment of cooperatives in good time. Prior to spring plowing a period of time should be devoted to helping a large number of cooperatives organize their labor force and implement labor contract measures in order to avoid the terribly chaotic situation in the management of labor within newly established APCs that has happened in past years.

The CCP Center
January 10, 1955

8

CENTRAL RURAL WORK DEPARTMENT

Circular of the Central Rural Work Department on Consolidating Existing Cooperatives (March 22, 1955)*

Shanghai Bureau, all subbureaus, and rural work departments of all provincial (and municipal) committees:

I. Now the time for spring plowing has arrived. Up to now 600,000 APCs have been set up and the original plan has been fulfilled. Regardless of locality, no more cooperatives should be established and all efforts should be devoted to the work of spring plowing and consolidating existing cooperatives.

II. There are a great many difficulties concerning this year's spring plowing. The tensions in the countryside still have not been completely alleviated, there is a shortage of fertilizers and insufficient farm animals, and some areas even suffer from a spring crop failure. The present need is to stabilize the peasants' morale concerning production, overcome difficulties, and fulfill the tasks for spring plowing and sowing. The cooperatives have already become a major factor providing impetus for agricultural production as a whole and a socialist banner on the agricultural production front. Therefore, if the cooperatives' productivity is obstructed, not only will the organization of the cooperatives become slack but production as a whole will be affected. For this reason, to organize well spring plowing and sowing should become the crucial link in the effort to consolidate cooperatives. Thus close attention must be given to [these tasks] so that a foundation can be laid for the cooperative economy that could in turn facilitate the development of production by mutual aid teams and individual [private] peasants

III. Effective measures should be adopted to deal with the common problem that some people joined the newly established cooperatives on an

---

*Reprinted from the original archival document.

involuntary or not quite voluntary basis. The principles for dealing with this problem are as follows:

1. With the prerequisite of strengthening the education [of cooperative members], we should pay attention to solidifying members who joined the cooperatives out of their own free will and to strengthening members who joined less willingly so that the mass base for the cooperatives can be consolidated. On such a base the problem of involuntary participants [in the cooperatives] will be handled. After explaining to them the advantages of joining and the disadvantages of withdrawing from the cooperatives, they should be allowed to decide of their own free will whether to stay in or withdraw from the APCs. No excuse should be used to control, restrict, or harass them, let alone punish them. It must be understood that if we respect their will today, even if they cannot be persuaded to stay in the cooperatives, they can be drawn politically closer to the party so that it will be easier to persuade them to rejoin in the future.

2. Solutions should be prescribed on the basis of diagnosis and analysis of what is behind the unwillingness [to join APCs]. Some people are truly not willing to join the cooperatives and were forced to join them. Some others were not unwilling to join but are not willing to stay because they do not like the internal policies of [certain] cooperatives. There are also some who regret their participation in the cooperatives and want to withdraw from them after seeing deficiencies in the arrangement of APC production. Some, resenting the bad attitude of certain working personnel, leave the cooperatives out of spite. The matter will not be settled well if we only say to them that they can leave of their own free will and that is the end of the matter. Instead, we should, in view of their different states of mind, patiently exchange views and discuss solutions with them, and, in the light of different cases, determine solutions to change their wavering thinking and strengthen solidarity within the cooperatives.

3. Concerning those nominal cooperatives that assume the title in order to appease their superiors and are not yet actually set up, or those nominal organizations in which production has not been done collectively, the empty titles should be removed and the members should be allowed to engage in production on their own.

After the great development of cooperatives it is necessary to overhaul and consolidate them and to have a reasonable reduction in the number of cooperatives and APC member households. It is not right for some places not to implement the principle of voluntary participation for fear of a decline in the number of cooperatives and the percentage [of peasant households with cooperative membership]. Such practices should be rectified.

IV. Rural work departments at the provincial and county levels should send some cadres to lower levels to help certain cooperatives make their own regulations and to organize studies and discussions concerning already made regulations in the adjacent cooperatives in order to solve in a timely manner some pressing problems. For example, seeds and fodder can be collected by assigning quotas to each mu [1 mu = 0.067 hectares—Eds.] of cultivated land and in addition by encouraging cooperative members to invest. As far as farm animals are concerned, in order to alleviate anxiety outside the cooperatives and to overcome the difficulties of poor feeding and heavy debt within APCs, in the initial stage of the cooperatives we should promote adoption of private ownership and feeding and public use rather than the premature measure of public ownership and feeding. Regardless of whether fertilizers, fodder, farm animals, or farm tools are concerned, a fair price or remuneration should be given to ensure mutual benefit between the poor and middle peasants by repeating the democratic procedures of manifold discussions and consulting [APC members] household by household. The criterion for mutual benefit is that both the poor and middle peasants as APC members earn more in estimated income than they do when they work on their own and that neither side will suffer [economically in joining the cooperatives]. Only mutual benefit will enable cooperatives to continue to operate. To have cooperatives operate is indeed in the basic interests of the poor and middle peasants, and [the principle of mutual benefit] also sets the basic limit to our policies.

V. We should make several months available for the leading bodies to send people [to the grass roots] to conduct comprehensive surveys and select backbone cadres to run the existing cooperatives, mainly the chairmen, vice chairmen, and accountants. For those cooperative backbone cadres who are good all round or who are basically qualified, we should continue to promote [their capabilities for leadership] by helping them to do a good job in their work and to strengthen their ties with the masses of APC members. Concerning those backbone cadres who are not competent or cannot act in a fair manner, new activists can be selected and fostered and a new core of leadership can be gradually formed through painstaking work with the masses, the method of individual contact during concrete work, and preparations to change the leadership at an appropriate time by democratic election. Without good backbone cadres it is certain that cooperatives cannot be run well. In some places, especially those where the number of cooperatives increase too rashly and too rapidly without careful preparations, not enough effort is made to select the backbone cadres while setting up the cooperatives. It already constitutes a problem left behind for which make-up work should be done and that should be solved in good time.

VI. Under the unified leadership and planning of the party committees, all the forces that can be mobilized should be put into the work of production, consolidating cooperatives, and overhauling mutual aid teams. We should ensure that all aspects of work are taken care of and that work is advanced according to the regular pattern of spreading over a whole area from a single point.

It is hoped that this circular will soon be distributed to the counties and districts.

Central Rural Work Department
March 22, 1955

9

Opinions of the Central Rural Work Department about Current Cooperativization Work in Zhejiang Province (March 25, 1955)*

Rural Work Department of the Zhejiang Provincial Committee:

According to the materials we have, tensions in the countryside in your province are still continuing and spreading and the peasants' morale regarding production is still very unstable. Apart from grain work, one important cause of tension is the too-rapid development of APCs that have advanced with a stride that is too big and too impatient (the proportion [of households in cooperatives] increased from 0.06 to 30-plus percent). In light of this, we suggest you reduce the number of cooperatives by differentiating according to area. Those [cooperatives] with the right conditions must be consolidated, whereas we ought to take the initiative to change back into mutual aid teams or individual farming those without such conditions for consolidation. You should consolidate the number you can and should not try to sustain a facade of false achievements.

The worries expressed by comrades from the provincial rural work department that reducing the number of cooperatives will lead to the mistake of divorcing ourselves from [cooperative] activists are indeed well grounded. However, if the masses remain unwilling to join cooperatives and if the cooperatives cannot be consolidated further, [persisting with such unsuitable cooperatives would result in] the activists themselves becoming divorced from the masses for a long time, and eventually we ourselves would be cut off from both the activists and masses causing tremendous losses in social productivity. Therefore, the correct policy can only be: Make every

---

*Reprinted from *Nongye jitihua zhongyao wenjian huibian* (A collection of important documents on agricultural collectivization), vol. 1, edited by Office of the State Agricultural Commission, October 1981.

effort to run well those cooperatives with appropriate conditions, make no rash retreat. Concerning those lacking adequate conditions for being run well, we should straighten out the thinking of the basic level backbone and cooperative activist elements, unite with them, and with them jointly lead the masses to reorganize [the cooperatives]. We also need their leadership [in helping] the peasants who withdraw from the cooperatives to engage in production.

Regardless of whether these peasants decide to go back to the mutual aid teams or to individual production, we should help them to do well in production. We should all along stay in good contact with them and not in any case hurt their feelings, so that we can continue striving to run the cooperatives well in the future. We can come forward and mediate in order to help out grass roots cadres and activists as they step down in these places. We must explain to the masses: Since cooperativization is for the sake of the peasants' interests it should be carried out completely in accord with the free will of the masses. While the work style of basic level cadres and activists is inappropriate and has shortcomings, this is related to the excessively high demands of their superiors and they cannot bear the whole blame. [We should take some of the blame] so that they can continue to work with the masses from now on. For cadres at the provincial and lower levels, their superiors at each level should bear the responsibility for unduly rapid development of the movement so that they can work without any chips on their shoulders.

In handling the economic problems concerning withdrawal from and dissolution of cooperatives, we should formulate fair and reasonable regulations after taking into account the interests of the masses from all quarters, profoundly investigating typical cases, and coming up with new experiences from them. [These regulations should] not hurt anyone's feelings so that they can cooperate with each other and avoid any possible conflict in the future. We have learned that under the policies for the cooperative economy implemented in your province, in some places remuneration for land is obviously low and cooperative members have no grain left after delivering their quota to the state. Even trees and silkworm breeding sideline occupations have been prematurely turned over to cooperative ownership. These policies are inappropriate and should be reviewed and rectified without delay for the benefit of our solidarity with the middle peasants and the consolidation of the alliance between the poor and middle peasants. There are some cooperatives that, although enjoying sufficient conditions for continued operation, suffer from a great shortage of grain. [In these APCs] the poor peasants lack grain rations and seeds, while the middle peasants are reluctant to provide loans [to the cooperative] with their own produce. [In these cases] the state should provide support both for purchasing and selling grain and for low-interest loans. (The bank should make feasible plans for providing loans.)

It is estimated that, after strengthening the leadership, 30,000 APCs can be consolidated and more than 10 percent of peasant households can be preserved in cooperatives on the basis of voluntary participation. This, despite the fact that we have been zigzagging a bit, could still be regarded as a great achievement, not a failure in any sense, though it would be of course better to have more cooperatives consolidated. The above number for reduction need not be passed down [to lower levels] and should be known only within the provincial committee. People at the lower levels should be told to consolidate as many cooperatives as they [reasonably] can and not to force themselves to maintain those APCs that cannot possibly be run well. [In short,] they should make every effort to consolidate those cooperatives that can be consolidated, and [stick to the principle of] seeking truth from facts. We hope you will tell us your opinions quickly by telegraph.

(This telegram is approved by Comrades Tan Zhenlin and Jiang Hua.)

Central Rural Work Department
March 25, 1955

10

Du Runsheng and Yuan Chenglong

A Report on the Situation in the Countryside of Zhejiang Province (April 11, 1955)*

Central Rural Work Department and
Second Office of the Central [Secretariat]:

I. After our arrival in [Zhejiang] Province, we have already passed on to the provincial committee the opinion agreed to at the conference in Beijing.

II. The tensions in the countryside in Zhejiang Province have indeed not yet calmed down and in certain areas they are escalating to a very high level. Due to the good foundation that was laid in our work in the past as well as work achievements, no severe incident has occurred so far. However, our estimate is that production will inevitably be affected.

III. As far as grain is concerned, the estimated output was higher than the actual one. In many places the purchase of grain is excessive, the scope of state monopoly grain sales [to the peasants] is too broad, ([enough to feed] over 80 percent [of the entire population]), and our relationship with both the poor peasants and middle peasants is seriously strained. [There is also the problem of] excessive development of the cooperatives. The number of APCs has increased from 2,000-plus, covering .6 percent of total peasant households last spring, to 50,000-plus, incorporating 20 to 30 percent of total peasant households (there are twenty-nine counties where more than 30 percent of total households have joined the cooperatives). Some cooperatives are good. However, because of inadequate preparation of policy, there are many problems and severe chaos in economic policies. Some of the cooperatives cannot be run any longer, or even if they can, they cannot be run well. Facing tensions over both grain and cooperatives, [responsible cadres cannot but] attend to one thing and lose sight of the other,

---

*Reprinted from *Nongye jitihua zhongyao wenjian huibian* (A collection of important documents on agricultural collectivization), vol. 1, edited by Office of the State Agricultural Commission, October 1981.

consequently becoming passive in carrying out overall work. In addition to this, the class policy was not carried out comprehensively in the past year. The main deviation was neglecting unity with the middle peasants. As a result, the tensions between the party and the middle peasants and between the poor and middle peasants have been aggravated. [This is reflected in the fact that] now many cooperatives ask the government for money and grain "since middle peasants are not investing while poor peasants are asking for payment in advance," [and consequently these cooperatives] are sitting idle and eating up the whole future. While the old relations of production have been changed, a new productive order is yet to be firmly established. If the present situation persists, it will lead to the danger that we will be cut off not only from the middle peasants but also from the poor peasants, and that our party will be placed in an isolated position. In contrast, becoming passive in our work is merely a minor matter.

IV. Since the whole year's work depends on a good start in the spring, we should get off the horse right away. The provincial committee has foreseen [the problems] and adopted some measures in the past, and is adopting further measures. [Now we have to] get off the horse concerning grain. The province is determined to do well, rationally, and reasonably the work of selling grain, but this will probably require the support of the center. The present situation is that the stock of pigs and sheep has decreased by one-third to one-half, and various [depressing] phenomena have appeared one after another, such as selling one's furniture, eating seed grain, begging for food, selling one's children, making petitions, the aged and the weak lying in bed and dying from hunger, and so on. All these phenomena are signs of instability, hence it is difficult to ensure fulfillment of the grain sale plan. [We also have to] get off the horse concerning cooperativization. This can be sorted out by the province itself. In addition to straightening out the implementation of the policy of voluntary participation and mutual benefit, a policy of devoting all efforts to consolidation and resolute contraction is needed. This means abandoning false achievements while concentrating all efforts on consolidating real achievements, and avoiding the all-embracing effort to sustain, however inadequately, [every cooperative]. If we disperse our forces, nothing can be done well and the tense situation will be prolonged.

V. Contraction implies giving some room to the individual economy in order to consolidate the already established position of cooperation. The provincial committee agrees with this policy. What deserves careful consideration are the measures to implement [the policy]:

1. Prolong the process [of implementation] by taking an easy approach in order to avoid a chaotic retreat and deviations.

2. Settle quickly those things that ought to be settled quickly, while dealing slowly with those that do not require quick solutions. What should

be done quickly is to publicize through propaganda the point that our policy meets [the demands of] the broad masses. Those cooperative members who want to change back [to mutual aid teams] or to withdraw [from the cooperatives] are allowed to do so and to do so quickly. What can be done slowly is dealing with those remaining cooperatives and cooperative members that want to change or withdraw yet encounter difficulties in doing so. This can be dealt with slowly since our top priority is to shift our work to full-scale consolidation. In areas where chaos is most severe, measures should be taken quickly. In areas where rash advance is not serious, things can go slower. [In other words] no one will be forced stay [in the APCs], neither will anyone be forced to withdraw. In this way a swift and safe solution can be achieved. In view of the overall situation, the second method has greater advantages. The provincial committee is inclined to adopt it. It is about to formulate different programs by taking into account differences in areas and types of problems. It is also considering sending high ranking officials to the countryside to set a good example and implement the measures.

VI. The provincial committee has both the determination and the solutions for handling the present problems. While dealing with the problems, its attention centers on current concerns and interests, namely, to boost production. It follows closely a number of principles and methods, such as resolutely rectifying mistakes while promoting achievements, drawing a line between right and wrong while assuming responsibility according to rank in the hierarchy, and protecting the cadres' enthusiasm while helping them to get rid of blindness in their work. Judged by the performance of the cadres at and above the county level, they are all sober and united.

If anything is inappropriate in the above [report], please give us your instructions.

Du Runsheng and Yuan Chenglong
April 11, 1955, Hangzhou

11

Deng Zihui

Opening Speech at the Third National Rural Work Conference [Excerpt] (April 21, 1955)

[Deng began by listing five agenda items for the conference and noting some organizational details. The agenda items were: (1) the current situation of cooperativization and the policy of consolidation; (2) fundamental questions and plans of cooperativization; (3) revising the draft APC regulations; (4) the state monopoly purchase and marketing of grain, cotton, and other agricultural products and the transformation of rural private commerce; and (5) cooperation in forestry, animal husbandry, and fishery.]

Now I am going to raise several issues for your discussion here.

I. The current situation of the development of cooperativization and the policy of overhauling and consolidating cooperatives from now on

This is the main content of this conference.

We should affirm that during the past half year cooperativization has been rapid and great achievements have been made. We have established 670,000 cooperatives across the country exceeding the original plan for setting up 600,000 APCs. Among them 90,000 are in the Northeast, 144,000 in North China, 250,000-plus in East China, 118,000 in the Central-South, 43,000 in the Southwest, and 25,000 in the Northwest. The movement in most areas proceeds in a normal way and most of the cooperatives are good and can be consolidated. As a result, a stronghold has been built for agricultural cooperativization, laying down a preliminary foundation for the forthcoming socialist transformation of agriculture. Growth in agricultural output is further ensured, and a lot of experience favorable for the future development of cooperativization has been gained. In recent months [our] tasks have been very demanding and the work of state monopoly purchase and marketing of grain has been very pressing. Despite this it should be acknowledged that the above achievements have been great. However, it should also be admitted tension exists in the countryside at the moment.

During February and March of this year the center already pointed out in an urgent instruction that tension existed to varying degrees in the countryside at present. This is reflected in the strained relationship between the party and the peasants, in the strained and unharmonious relationship between the poor and middle peasants, and in the strained relations among the cadres themselves and between higher and lower levels (although the nature of the tension in the latter case is different from those of the former two kinds). [These cadres,] although they refrained from speaking their minds, hold some grievances [against the party]. All the above tensions essentially center on the issue of the worker-peasant alliance.

After the center promulgated the three-fix policy ([of quotas for] production, purchase and marketing) and stipulated that prior to 1956 the amount of grain to be purchased by the state would be around 90 billion jin, tension in general has been alleviated to some extent, yet it has not been removed. It is still developing in a small number of provinces and a small number of counties in some provinces. If the situation is not changed, agricultural production will be affected. The center has already pointed out that the peasants have given us warnings not merely by cynical remarks and complaints, but also by their actions. Vigorous actions are collective riots by hundreds or thousands of peasants that occurred in Guangdong, Hubei, and all the provinces. Recently 5,000 peasants participated in an upheaval in Xiao County, Jiangsu, and rumors spread. Passive actions are absence from work, slaughtering livestock, killing pigs and chickens, sluggish preparation of fertilizers, and cutting down trees such as fruit trees and mulberry trees. In addition to the negative impact on production, another consequence is the damage to the worker-peasant alliance. If grain output declines, the grain price will become unstable, prices of other goods will not be stable, and banking, finance, and national construction will thus be affected. Moreover, if the production of industrial raw materials is insufficient, light industry will also be affected.

Last night I reported to the chairman and made an analysis of the following three causes of tension:

1. Most obvious is the state monopoly purchase and marketing of grain.

2. The transformation of private business in the cities and countryside is proceeding so fast that the circulation of goods between the two areas is "obstructed in small respects although open on the whole," affecting fiscal and tax revenue in recent months and causing the unemployment of some people in urban areas. In the villages there is also a section of the peasants, especially poor peasants, who suffer a decline in their income from sideline production.

3. Even more fundamentally there is something wrong with the socialist transformation of agriculture (mainly in terms of production cooperation).

Under the category of socialist transformation all three above factors were basic causes creating tension. However, cooperativization was the most basic cause, while at present the grain [question] is the most obvious cause. The peasants could engage in production and solve living problems for their families when they were farming individually as long as they owned their land, draft animals, and farm tools. A fundamental change happened when they joined cooperatives. Although they still owned the means of production and could get payment for them, they could not freely control them. The right of control went to the APC. This was a fundamental change. The peasants naturally would be very concerned with the means of production they owned after they handed them over to the cooperatives. The above change was the most profound revolution that would have a huge impact on the peasants as a whole despite the fact that at the time not many peasants had joined the APCs. For example, it was reported that in the Northeast livestock generally lost weight after they were incorporated into cooperatives and some of them laid down with sickness while a few even died. Upon seeing this, how could the peasants not get scared and worried? This was materialism. At least the peasants who were the heads of their households would not sleep well. How could they not worry when they saw that there was little hope of an increase in production?

The major and fundamental cause for the tension between workers and peasants, between poor and middle peasants, between cadres and the masses is shortcomings in cooperative production. Of course achievements [in cooperativization] are predominant. However, mistakes do exist and more mistakes are made this year than last year. There are three defects in the work of cooperativization:

1. Last year's plan for establishing 600,000 APCs was a little too big and plans in some provinces were both too ambitious and too "rash." The plans of most provinces were appropriate. However, plans in some counties and districts were adventurous while those in some [other] counties and districts were too low. All in all the situation was not uniform. The big plans were the 105,000 cooperatives in Hebei, 96,000 in Shandong, 57,000 in Zhejiang, 42,000 in Henan, etc. Cooperative membership as a percentage of peasant households increased from a few tenths of a percent to more than 30 percent in some provinces and from a few percent to more than 30 percent in others. Last year in some provinces cooperatives were developed quickly even though the groundwork was poorly laid.

For this situation the responsibility should first be borne by the Rural Work Department and I should be the first one to bear responsibility since I was the one who reported the plan to the center for approval. At that time I was a bit optimistic. Although at the Fourth Mutual Aid and Cooperation Conference of last year I already pointed out that "It is easy to set up cooperatives yet difficult to consolidate [them]," the plan that was agreed on was still [too big]. Now it seems that the shortcomings would not have been so serious if we [planned in a less ambitious way to] set up 400,000 or 500,000 APCs or a bit more. Although I also said that the tasks during the winter were more pressing and like other campaigns, such as the reduction of rent and interest, had seasonal ups and downs, yet cooperativization is nevertheless quite different. [It was my fault] to have judged that tension in cooperativization was due to seasonal factors that was also the cause of our sluggishness [in rectifying the situation]. [Clearly,] when the task exceeds certain limits it naturally drags our policy away from the right track and leads to commandism at the lower levels. The causes [of the excessively big plans] are:

a. The estimation of our subjective strength is too high. The establishment of cooperatives cannot solely depend on the peasants. It should be under the leadership of cadres capable of theoretical understanding of the policy. Overly ambitious plans will pose great difficulties in terms of our subjective capabilities. [That is to say] cooperatives have been developed in such a way that goes far beyond the capabilities and leadership of our cadres. [Normally] in a district, only three to five cadres are capable of leading cooperatives. However, there are some districts where hundreds of cooperatives have been set up. The cadres simply cannot handle all of them and have to deal with them in a slapdash manner. As a result, by the end of the year they do not know in how many cooperatives production has increased and in how many it has decreased. Some cadres have to visit fifteen APCs per day by bicycle. They call it "looking at flowers while riding on horseback." I am afraid that they would not be able to look at anything. Since the work load exceeds the capacity of the leadership, mistakes can hardly be avoided.

In his concluding speech at the National Party Conference the chairman answered the question of what is leftism and what is rightism as follows: "Leftism goes beyond the actual situation and possibilities while rightism lags behind the actual situation and possibilities."

b. The estimate of the masses' consciousness is too high. Last year I said that we should not look at the masses' good behavior only on the surface level. After publicizing the general line, the masses' socialist consciousness has indeed been enhanced. As a result of their enhanced consciousness some poor peasants, new middle peasants, and lower middle peasants among the old middle peasants asked for cooperatives. However, as we pointed out at the time, peasants are not born socialists; it is hardly easy for individual farmers to accept socialism. The peasants, including even the poor peasants, will not believe in socialism right away. As peasants judge things by their eyes and not by their ears, their socialist consciousness is based on what they see and not on what they hear. Since "it is better to see once than hear a hundred times," we ought to let the peasants see in order to have them believe. While it is easy for poor peasants and relatively easy for lower-middle peasants among the middle peasants to accept cooperatives, it is difficult for the majority of old middle peasants and well-to-do middle peasants, and for upper-middle peasants including new middle peasants, to do so, for the newly established cooperatives might not produce higher yields than they did. Some comrades tend to be a bit idealist in making high estimates and in failing to judge the rise in peasants' socialist consciousness on a materialist basis (in terms of the poor or good performance of cooperatives).

c. Taking lightly [the task of] running cooperatives well. At present cadres have little or even no experience in running cooperatives. Average peasants have very rich experience in making a good job of the production of a single family or household. However, they do not have any experience in taking charge of the production of 30 to 40 households. The cooperative members would naturally feel uneasy in seeing that the director of their cooperative was incompetent. There is a difference between cooperativization and land reform. During land reform, when land certificates were issued, work groups could be recalled. At most only several persons needed to stay and settle the remaining problems. During cooperativization the establishment of cooperatives merely means the beginning of our work. Although we have said that "it is easy to set up cooperatives yet difficult to consolidate them," even I initially did not fully anticipate the difficulties.

Because of the above three considerations the plan was set too high. In some areas, unrealistically no restrictions were imposed on expanding APCs and too much emphasis was placed on the speed of the movement and the number of cooperatives. For all these mistakes the Rural Work Department should first of all be held responsible, [and] I myself am responsible. For example, we reported to the center that last year 90 percent of the 108,000 APCs [sic] increased their output. Later we found out that only 70 percent of them had done so. Naturally those [overambitious] plans were made by the provincial authorities so we should have shown them respect [as we did]. Nevertheless, we offered our advice on these plans.

[In short,] various kinds of problems emerge because we have set ourselves a massive task. One striking point about [our] party's work style is that we tend to accomplish surely and overfulfill whatever the task once it has been assigned. Such a spirit is great. However, if tasks are so heavy to the extent that they exceed the possibility of being realized, deviations from policy and mistakes in work will become inevitable. For example, since the center stipulated that the top end of our policy on grain purchase is to collect 90 billion jin of grain, if we had set the limit at 400,000-odd or 500,000 for the number of cooperatives to be established, much less trouble would have occurred. However, after we set it at 600,000, we end up with 670,000 APCs.

2. The principle of voluntary participation and mutual benefit is violated in policy [implementation]. First of all, the policy of mutual benefit (that is, the principle of mutual benefit between middle and poor peasants) is violated, and in some cooperatives there are only unilateral rather than mutual benefits. In some of them the middle peasants gain benefits while poor peasants get nothing (that happened more frequently the year before last than this year). In some of them only the poor peasants benefit or they gain most of the benefits whereas the middle peasants gain no or [only] a little benefit (that happened quite often this year).

These phenomena are reflected in the following aspects of the relations of production:

The assessment of land productivity: [If land productivity is assessed] according to current output the poor peasants will suffer losses, [if it is evaluated on the basis of] land quality the middle peasants will suffer. This is a contradiction. In my opinion the stipulation in the draft regulations for cooperatives that productivity is judged on the basis of land quality with reference to regular yields can be better reformulated so that land productivity is assessed on the basis of regular yields with reference to land quality. Otherwise the middle peasants will not accept it and commandism will result.

Dividends from land and labor: In the past, in some areas the land drew 80 or 70 percent [of the profit of cooperatives] while labor got only 20 or 30 percent. There the exploitation by the land owner was too much. At present in the north the practice in general has been changed so that land draws 40 or 45 percent [of the profit] while labor gets up to 60 or 55 percent. In the south land and labor each get 50 percent. In other places, however, land draws [only] 30 or even 20 percent of the profit while labor gets 70 or even 80 percent. In still other areas the ratio changes from year to year. It resembles a saying in the Northeast last year: "In the first year land draws 30 percent and labor 70 percent; in the second year land 20 percent and labor 80 percent; in the third year all cooperative profits will go to the state." [Such practices] inevitably result in commandism, contradictions between middle and poor peasants within the APCs, and fear on the part of middle peasants still outside the cooperatives. Some common people even [cry out]: "Cooperativization in three years, then our doomsday in 1957."

The premature turnover of farm animals to the ownership of the cooperatives for monetary compensation: As a result, some livestock get thinner, some come down with illness, and some even die. [Such losses] have increased the burden on cooperatives. The prices for farm animals turned over to the cooperatives are lower than market prices. Some of the prices are 30 percent or even more than 30 percent lower than market prices. In some places it is common for [peasants] to sell out their big livestock, buy small livestock, and put the surplus money into their own wallets. In some places in Henan and Hebei Provinces the market prices of livestock are about half the normal prices. Although this may be caused by the shortage of fodder due to the state monopoly purchase and marketing of grain, the main cause is that monetary compensation [for livestock turned over to the cooperatives] is too low and rashness occurs [in cooperativization]. So far 2 million or more livestock have been lost across the country. At present we rely heavily on livestock [for production] and their death has cost us dearly. [When livestock are turned over to collective ownership], the period for payment [was set variably,] ranging from three years through five years to even one hundred years. [These transactions] have been termed "loans" to the cooperatives that, however, do not seem to have any intention of returning them [to their owners]. Furthermore, no interest is paid for payment by installments, or payment is made in the form of shares. Since they can be withdrawn only upon withdrawing from cooperatives, they are virtually scrap shares.

There is no interest on investment. When fruit, date, and mulberry trees are turned over to the ownership of the cooperatives no remuneration is made and land quality for the trees is discounted. As a result, many fruit trees are cut down and silkworm breeding is abandoned.

For the aforementioned we should also be held responsible. [As far as I myself am concerned,] last year I misinterpreted the chairman's instruction about semicompromise with the middle peasants. So-called total compromise is to abandon socialism and cooperativization and to allow the middle peasants to follow their own inclination toward capitalism. Semicompromise means that as long as the middle peasants take part in cooperativization we should guarantee that they will not suffer losses over any other issues. But last year I interpreted semicompromise as letting the middle peasants suffer losses somewhat. Comrades here should now explain this to the lower levels.

For this reason there is a defect in the draft regulations. Assessment of land productivity should be based on regular yields [of average harvests] with reference to land quality. This can be taken to mean our semicompromise with the middle peasants. Whether the land draws 40 percent and labor 60 percent of [cooperative] profit or land 45 percent and labor 55 percent with all the surplus going to labor in cases of overfulfilling the production target, the percentage obtained by labor can be further lowered. However, peasants' actual income should not be lower than what they experienced before. Besides, the ratio for the land dividend should not be lowered year by year. In the past some people proposed to change the remuneration for land in three to five years. In my opinion we should not specify the exact time and should instead talk about changing it in a given period. In short, we must be cautious because the middle peasants are particularly concerned about this issue. If we handle this issue badly there will be no way for us to achieve a compromise with the middle peasants. Within the first year of setting up a cooperative it is not always necessary to turn the livestock over to cooperative ownership for monetary compensation. Compensation during the winter should be higher than market prices. On this issue we must ensure that the middle peasants won't suffer losses.

Since there are shortcomings in my interpretation [of the chairman's instruction], I would like to make a self-criticism here. A mistake is a mistake. Yet this mistake was naturally aggravated due to the poor policy understanding of comrades at the lower levels. Once I gave a bit of a wrong interpretation they made the deviation from policy much greater.

The middle peasants not only watch the general trend, they also calculate their gains and losses. If we overestimate their looking out for the general trend and underestimate their economic interests, the policy of mutual benefit cannot be implemented well. When the middle peasants are reluctant to join cooperatives and the time for establishing cooperatives is short and tasks are massive, if we still urge them to join the APCs we cannot but violate the principle of voluntary participation. Various kinds of commandism would naturally occur, for example, putting them in a meeting for three days and nights, exerting pressure on them by means of the state monopoly purchase of grain, and so on.

3. The mass line is not followed in [our] work. In some areas the tradition of the mass line gives way to the increasing use of administrative orders. Since last October there has been the state monopoly purchase and marketing of grain, followed by the conscription of recruits on top of the heavy task of setting up cooperatives. Some cadres thus leave aside the question of how to approach their work, how to conduct mass work, and how to follow the mass line. Instead, they resort to general calls to the masses. The case of putting up a poster to raise an army is merely one of the less bizarre approaches.

Moreover, since in these places cadres with experience in mass work are transferred elsewhere, only a few experienced cadres are left. In one instance only the county [party] secretary was left and was too busy to take care of all the work. Their work at the grass roots level is hardly that of visiting the poor or knowing the distressed, or private contacts. [Let me] tell you a joke. Some of our work is so shallow that we cannot even emulate Catholics, Christians and the [folk religion] Yiguan Sect (though the nature of their work can in no way be compared to ours). Actually their work style was quite arduous and penetrating. They established private contacts and carefully selected their key members. In this respect we should learn from them. If we fail to stick to our tradition of mass work, rely simply on administrative orders, fail to mobilize the masses' thinking or to make individual contact, and even fail to choose good leaders for the cooperatives, the APCs will collapse easily once problems emerge. Consequently middle peasants in cooperatives will become disgruntled, those [who have not yet joined] will get scared, APC members will refuse to invest, and peasants outside the cooperatives will cut down their fruit trees, and [everyone's] production spirit will be low. These factors, plus rumormongering by bad elements in society will naturally cause problems [for us].

II. The future policy of consolidating cooperatives

The day before yesterday I made a report to Comrade Shaoqi. Yesterday Comrade Shaoqi convened a Secretariat meeting. Through discussion the following instructions were made:

The overall policy hereafter is: stop further development and concentrate all efforts on consolidation.

1. The expansion [of cooperatives] should stop for the time being; a new decision will be made after the fall in light of the current situation. In certain counties, districts, and townships where conditions are ripe yet no cooperatives have been set up, cooperatives can be experimentally run on an individual basis. Three to five cooperatives may be set up within each of these districts to gather experience and prepare the ground for future development. To stop development is for the purpose of consolidating existing cooperatives and strengthening achievements. We should proceed with further development only after consolidation as we used to do in the past, [namely] consolidate a batch of cooperatives and then develop a batch. In provinces in the Southwest and the Central-South where the grain task is not heavy, the movement can be developed a little bit further, but not too rapidly.

2. In order to consolidate hundreds of thousands of cooperatives we should first handle production well and help solve the problem of shortages of livestock and fodder. We should also reassign cadres and ensure an increase, or at least no decline, in output in [every] cooperative. These are things of crucial importance for the consolidation of APCs.

3. Appropriate contraction is applied only to areas where excessive development has occurred such as Hebei, Shandong, Anhui, Zhejiang, Henan, etc. In some counties where development has been excessive it should also be contracted appropriately.

Some cooperatives must change their present course. If they don't they will still be forced to do so due to their own worsening situation. At present, although some areas such as Cao County that attempt to keep their APCs afloat may be able to do so for another year, [I am afraid that] their cooperatives won't last long.

Only when further development is stopped can we consolidate cooperatives right away. Otherwise we won't be able to consolidate even those cooperatives that are worthy of consolidation. Contraction is thus for the sake of further development. As Lenin said, we should "take a step backward before we take two steps forward." If we do not make up our minds [to do so] now, the problems with cooperatives will become more serious next year and some of them will keep collapsing. Therefore, it would be better to contract some [APCs] this year.

The center has [already] made it clear that wherever the number of cooperatives is excessive or they are riddled with problems, where running them is beyond our subjective capability, there should be appropriate contraction. [The center] also suggested that we can even afford to lose the majority of cooperatives in Cao County. [In short,] it will be the greatest success if we can get 500,000 APCs consolidated.

It should not be taken for granted that contraction [targets] will be distributed proportionally among the areas. In some provinces where few cooperatives have been developed the cooperativization movement should, of course, not be contracted. Nevertheless, in some prefectures and counties where development is excessive it should be contracted accordingly and appropriately. Contraction is done for the sake of consolidation. Therefore, it should be done step by step under appropriate arrangements.

Comrade Shaoqi instructed that all those cooperatives that enjoy conditions for consolidation should be consolidated with all our efforts, that in the course of consolidation our policy must communicate with the masses and we must declare to them the principle of voluntary participation, and that consolidation without communication is merely false communication. Announcing the principle of voluntary participation does not mean paying lip service, [persuasion and education] work are still needed following the announcement. If members are indeed reluctant to remain in a cooperative, the whole cooperative should be dissolved or part of the members allowed to withdraw from it. For those members who choose to withdraw from APCs, their problems should be settled reasonably. For instance, concerning wheat that is planted jointly, labor contributions should be calculated and the accounts settled. These matters should not be dealt with perfunctorily. For some members, settling labor accounts should be done before their withdrawal. Others can be allowed to withdraw before the account is settled. When there are many middle peasants withdrawing from a cooperative, a great deal of support should be provided for the poor peasants who are left with great difficulties, such as renting livestock for them from the middle peasants who are withdrawing from the cooperative, or providing them loans for purchasing livestock, grain, seeds, and so on.

To conclude, the gist [of our policy] is to get [the cooperatives] consolidated with great enthusiasm instead of contracting passively. [Our policy] is designed to consolidate better the cooperatives whenever possible and to carry through better cooperativization. It is not rash retreat. We should not bypass the principle of voluntary participation under the disguise of consolidation. However, promotion of the principle of voluntary participation does not mean that no more work needs to be done. On the contrary, we should care for the cadres' enthusiasm while asking those cadres who committed severe commandism to make self-criticisms to the masses. Contraction is by no means easier than setting up cooperatives. However, for those APCs that simply cannot go on with any certainty, it would be better if they were contracted. That we draw back from the front line is solely in order to secure our position. It is not giving up our position.

[The third and final section of the Chinese text, "Consolidate with All Efforts those Cooperatives that Can Be Consolidated," deals in particular with issues concerning cadres, the question of state support in finances, grain and materials, and methods of carrying out the mass line.]

12

DENG ZIHUI

Concluding Report at the Third National Rural Work Conference (Excerpt) (May 6, 1955)

Part I. First an analysis of the current situation

At this conference the opinions of comrades from all regions are in general identical rather than divergent. However, I would like to make several points clear. I am going to do so point by point.

1. First of all, it should be affirmed that our achievements are the main thing. We have made great achievements from last year to this year (from 1954 to 1955). The simple fact is that despite time being short and tasks heavy, and also that the plan had to be fulfilled and the resolution realized, in general the development of the movement has been going well with most [APCs] set up on the basis of mutual aid teams and particularly the [already] successfully established 100,000 cooperatives, even though excessive development and minor problems occurred in some places. Therefore, it should be affirmed that most of this year's more than 600,000 cooperatives can be consolidated. I made this point in my first speech here, and in my report to the center. We cannot deny our achievements because we are now a bit tense and some places made mistakes. Nor can we say that defects are the main aspect. I think that we should affirm this view. We have very strong backing for future cooperativization simply because we formed several hundred thousand cooperatives, i.e., last year we set up several hundred thousand socialist strongholds in the countryside and took the preliminary step in forming a battlefront for agricultural cooperativization.

As long as we run the cooperatives well we can extend the party's edu-
cation among the peasants and expand its influence. This is the general case although a bad impression of the party has also been created in some areas. However, generally speaking the peasants are educated, the party's influence has been extended, and favorable conditions have been created for the socialist transformation of agriculture in the future. Then where do our achievements come from? I think that they come from the following facts:

We have a foundation of 100,000 cooperatives and the mutual aid teams formed in the past several years whose good operation is the essential aspect; the party's policy of relying on the poor peasants and firmly uniting with the middle peasants is clear; through the work of these years the masses' consciousness has been raised, in some areas to a high level; and work in other aspects, such as that of the state monopoly purchase and marketing of grain, has helped us and pushed forward cooperativization. Also, we have been supported by work in some other aspects, such as party rectification and party building, propaganda and education, Youth League work, and the suppression of counterrevolutionaries. Without the support of these departments we could not have done our work well. Besides this, we, the rural work departments, have really worked arduously and made a good job of mass work in many areas by following the mass line. Again, I think that we should affirm this point.

2. Concerning the question of the present tense situation. Is there any tension? Obviously there is. Of course the tension varies in degree [and from one area to another]. For example, it is relatively mild in the Southwest, although not entirely absent. The other day the comrades from Yunnan Province said that tension also existed in some places in their province. The situation in Sichuan Province is probably the same. All other provinces have strained situations to a considerable extent; their differences are only a matter of degree. I think we should admit this fact. Not admitting this will neither do our work any good, nor give rise to our vigilance.

What is the essence of the tension in the countryside? It is the strained relationship between the workers and the peasants as well as between the middle and poor peasants. The causes of tension, as many comrades correctly pointed out in their speeches, should be seen in two aspects. On the one hand, they reflect a sentiment of resistance by the rural small producers against socialist transformation and are part of an inevitable process due to the dual character of small producers. The socialist transformation includes not only cooperativization, but also the state monopoly purchase and marketing of grain, and the transformation of private commerce, naturally with cooperative production as the central [issue]. A number of socialist revolutionary measures, namely the various forms of cooperation in production, supply and marketing, credit and the handicraft industry, the transformation of private commerce, and the state monopoly purchase and marketing of grain, have changed peasants' habits that they have had for many years. Their resistance due to these habits is inevitable. This is indeed the essence of [our] peasants. When you carry out socialist transformation they just do not feel accustomed to it and thus express nervousness about it. This is an objective fact. Besides, there was something wrong with our propaganda, especially [our slogan] "accomplish cooperativization in three years." Of course the lower levels should not be blamed for it. It is we who proposed that 50 percent of peasant households join the cooperatives by 1957! We proposed to accomplish 70 percent in old [liberated] areas in three years. There were also some other inappropriate propaganda, such as [choosing between] "two roads," the road of Taiwan, or even following Truman or Eisenhower [if one didn't choose the socialist road]. Thus it highlighted all the more the masses' fear and wavering and aggravated tensions. This constitutes the first type of cause for [rural] tension.

On the other hand, we made mistakes in our policy and work. What were the mistakes? They were that plans [for cooperativization] in some areas were so big that deviations could hardly be avoided, that the policy of mutual benefit and voluntary participation was not fully implemented or even violated, and that administrative commandism in our work and the failure to do careful mass work were widespread. To conclude, since the rural petty producers harbored feelings of resentment against socialist transformation and since we made mistakes in our work and policy, tension naturally emerged.

Why did these mistakes occur in policy and its implementation? We leaders [at the upper levels] should bear the general responsibility. As far as the lower ranks are concerned, mistakes can be attributed to one of three causes: heavy tasks, inadequate experience, and the failure of our present organizational forms to match the current revolutionary tasks. Comrades from Heilongjiang have pointed out rightly that our present organizational mechanism can no longer keep up with the current revolutionary task. The organizational mechanism is still the one formed during the stage of the democratic revolution, yet today we have already entered into the stage of the socialist revolution. Some areas have advanced very far with the socialist revolution yet their organizational mechanism remains outdated. An organizational mechanism should be at the service of political tasks. It should be suited to political tasks. If political tasks change while the organizational mechanism remains unchanged, problems will naturally arise. At this moment the center is carrying out studies concerning changes in the various establishments at the provincial, county, district, and township levels. This task [of reorganization] is complicated and heavy. It is not only a tough business, it is also new stuff. We have no previous experience. This is a new situation not only for our common people and for our cadres, but for ourselves as well. For everybody, this is a situation in which the struggle is bound to be very complicated due to lack of experience.

Basically there are three tasks: one is cooperativization, another is the state monopoly purchase and marketing of grain, and the [third] is the [socialist] transformation of private commerce. In addition there was the conscription and demobilization of soldiers, but these three were the major ones. The three were all tasks of the socialist revolution. Whether it was monopoly purchase and marketing of grain, or the transformation of private commerce, or cooperativization, they all fall under the category of socialist transformation. Since all of them were new tasks and were to be fulfilled at the same time, the burden was very heavy. I agree with the opinion expressed by you, comrades, that these three were fundamental causes of tension.

Naturally we should admit that cooperativization was the most fundamental cause. As socialist transformation in the countryside, [i.e.,] cooperative production, cooperative supply and marketing, cooperative credit, and state monopoly purchase and marketing of grain, pivoted on cooperative production, the latter was the key link in the transformation of the relations of production and therefore the most fundamental cause of tension. It is not right if everyone refuses to admit it. At the beginning [of cooperativization] I said that the transformation of private commerce and monopoly purchase of grain were [mere] temporary factors. I [now] take back my statement because the comrades' opinions are correct. However, we should not see them as three equal factors.

Cooperativization is very important for rural work departments. Although the most obvious problem at present is the grain issue, the most fundamental issue is cooperativization. That is to say, we should do a good job of handling this issue by acting cautiously and advancing steadily. If anything goes wrong over this issue it would be nothing short of a disaster, for example, the slaughter of livestock and cutting down of trees. Indeed, these questions are linked to the grain issue, but primarily with cooperation. This is not merely evident in the sphere of cooperative production, it is even evident in the case of cooperative forestry in the south (more on this later). I am afraid that we need to reconsider whether to proceed with cooperative forestry under present circumstances. If we want to afforest a bare mountain [in a cooperative manner], this won't cause any big hassle. Yet if we collectivize existing [private] trees, [then we will find great difficulty]. For it would be very easy to strike a deal based on a compromise price that could readily lead to the situation of the have-nots taking great advantage of the tree owners. The [current] incidents of setting fire to mountains must have something to do with this. Therefore, this thing [i.e., cooperativization] is the main aspect in the transformation of the relations of production. I think it would be unrealistic if we refuse to concede this point, or if we fail to understand this point. Before last December I too felt the pressure of the grain issue. But since then, especially since this January, the more I see the more I feel that cooperativization is the essential cause.

Some of us who happen to be here visited our hometowns and found that the situation was good and no trouble existed wherever cooperativization had not taken place. Although in those areas the state monopoly purchase and marketing of grain was carried out, the owners of livestock were hardly scared or worried simply because there was no cooperativization. There was not even a single cooperative. Of course, the massive slaughter of livestock did have something to do with the state monopoly purchase and marketing of grain. We cannot say there is no relationship. However, cooperativization is the most fundamental cause. Thus we of the rural work departments should be more cautious. We cannot say that our work on cooperativization does not matter as long as you do a good job of state monopoly purchase and marketing of grain. This way of looking at things is wrong. We must correctly understand that cooperativization is a fact and the most fundamental force for changing the relations of production. It is also true that grain is currently the most obvious issue, especially in some provinces such as Zhejiang, Heilongjiang, Hebei, Shandong, Hubei, Guangdong, and Guangxi. These provinces are troubled by the monopoly grain sale this year and the monopoly purchase last year. Of course, this is the most obvious factor at this moment. However, the most fundamental one is still cooperativization. In short, falling under the category of socialist transformation all of the above three factors are fundamental causes of tension, among which cooperativization is the most fundamental and the grain issue is the most obvious. Everyone should look into this matter to see whether such a statement conforms to the facts or not. If it does not we can change it again, that's quite OK. [The more important thing] is to distinguish between right and wrong and to have our views conform to the facts.

3. Is there really any rash advance? Everyone is terrified of the two words "rash advance." Indeed everyone will have a hard time carrying that label. However, we should first be clear what is meant by rash advance. The chairman said in his concluding speech to the National Party Conference that it was leftism and rash advance to go beyond practical possibilities. It is rash advance to go beyond the level of the cadres' experience and the masses' consciousness, to do more than what can actually be done, and to go beyond practical possibilities. If this definition is correct, then it should be said the phenomenon of rash advance is not evident nationwide, [only in a small number of provinces is rash advance a little bit serious]. In these provinces the number of APCs is relatively large, but most provinces are not like this. For example, the 28,000 cooperatives in Sichuan Province are not a large number since the province has 60 million people, 16 prefecture party committees, and more than 100 counties, and since the cadres there are able to control them. For another example, there are a large number of peasant households [in cooperatives] and more than 700 cooperatives in Beijing, so naturally although there are slightly too many peasant households [in APCs] the cadres there are able to handle the situation. Hence no serious trouble happens there.

According to the above definition it should be noted that at present rash advance is not a nationwide phenomenon. It is only evident in a small number of provinces. Even in these provinces [cooperativization] does not proceed evenly. There is rash advance in some areas and normal development in others. For example, in Zhejiang, Shandong, Hebei, and Anhui Provinces where more rash advance can be found, the movement develops unevenly. In Shandong, in two to three prefectures more than half the peasant households have joined the cooperatives while in others the percentages of the peasant households in the cooperatives are not so high so that the cadres there can bring the situation under control and the movement turns out to be normal. In other provinces, although the total numbers of cooperatives are not large, yet they are too big in some of their counties. For example, the cadres in [a certain] county in Hubei Province feel that they have too many cooperatives. Similarly, uneven development is also evident in Yunnan Province. In short, rash advance, that is, going beyond practical possibilities, happens in some provinces or some counties. In addition, I think I should also say that some counties and localities possibly still [suffer from] the laissez-faire phenomenon. Of course this is not widespread, but it does exist. What are your opinions about this analysis? Does it conform to the practical situation? To repeat, rash advance is not nationwide but limited to a small number of provinces and counties. In some areas there is also the laissez-faire tendency. However, I feel that the mood of rash advance is widespread among the cadres. If we do not spell out the fact of rash advance and overcome it, it will emerge again in the future. Even if it does not emerge today, it will tomorrow; even if does not this year, it will next year. Rash advance will only do harm to our work, cause difficulties for our future, and for a long period prevent the newly established cooperatives from being consolidated.

Why, then, is the rash advance phenomenon comparatively widespread among our cadres? I think that there are two reasons: The first reason is that we overestimate the peasants' socialist consciousness and fail to understand adequately the small producer nature of the peasants. In fact, peasants are not that ready to accept socialism. It is true that after our propaganda on the general line exerted a positive effect on the peasants, especially the poor and new middle peasants, their consciousness was raised. It cannot be denied that in some areas the peasants' consciousness reaches a high level, for example wherever the cooperatives are well run and the old cooperatives and mutual aid teams have a good foundation. The peasants' consciousness has risen wherever mutual aid teams have been set up in large numbers and run well, thus providing good examples for the socialist banner.

However, it would be wrong to claim that the rise in peasants' consciousness is widespread and high tides sweep everywhere and to fail to see the uneven development across the country. Such a view is superficial, failing to grasp [the peasants'] essence. Since this view overestimates the upsurge of the movement and the peasants' socialist consciousness it is idealist. It is not in line with Marxism-Leninism, nor is it a realistic approach. Instead, it is misled by appearances at the surface level. People with this view fail to see the essential aspects from a materialist viewpoint, such as how many cooperatives are really well run, how the mutual aid teams and cooperatives are actually run, and how many cooperatives had already been set up previously. It will lead to error and encourage the cadres' rash advance sentiment if we think their socialist consciousness has been enhanced by merely looking at their surface behavior and seeing that they asked to join the cooperatives with both hands raised in happiness or even in endless weeping and wailing. It looks as if their consciousness is high. But is it really a good thing? It may look good but is it really wonderful? Not necessarily. Is the situation really wonderful everywhere? Again, not necessarily. We have to examine how well your mutual aid teams and cooperatives are respectively run and how good your work foundation is. Otherwise it is always unreliable to make a judgment only in light of appearances. We should admit that the masses' consciousness has risen, especially that of the new middle peasants, the lower middle peasants, and the middle middle peasants. We are not denying this fact. To deny it is unrealistic and neither objective nor materialist. However, it will not do us any good and will only contribute to the cadres' rash advance sentiment to declare in an empty sense the rise in the peasants' consciousness and to consider blindly such a rise common and widespread everywhere, [finding it] here and there. This is the main reason why rash advance sentiment occurs among our cadres.

The second reason is that due to our lack of understanding that cooperativization is meant to change the relations of production and is a socialist revolution and the most profound class struggle, we, including myself, fail to appreciate adequately the great difficulties of running the cooperatives well and increasing production. For we do not have experience and thus take lightly the task of running the cooperatives. We think the APCs are well run and that the peasants are tough enough to run them well. In fact, running cooperatives is not an easy matter. This is because unlike the Soviet Union and Hungary that are industrialized countries (in Hungary industry accounts for 70 percent of the national output), we run APCs on the basis of a small peasant economy. We do not have similar conditions and lack a [solid] material foundation. We are trying to industrialize on the basis of a small peasant economy. In light of this situation it must be an arduous task to improve genuinely the crop yields of the cooperative, though indeed it is not impossible. We should not be pessimistic and disappointed either. However, unless the Good Lord warrants it, it would be too optimistic to think that as long as cooperatives are set up their crop yields will automatically increase. It can hardly be regarded as materialist to think that crop yields will be raised as long as the socialist banner is planted. In short, it is not an easy matter to run the cooperatives well, to have a real increase in yields, to have a sense of solidarity among APC members, and to get things done in a regulated as well as systematic manner.

Of course, it is completely impossible to overcome these difficulties that are like the road to Sichuan Province [merely by setting up APCs]. [As the old saying puts it,] "To pass through the road [to Sichuan] is more difficult than reaching the blue sky." [But] it can be affirmed that as long as you are willing to try and able to accumulate experience, you can run cooperatives well, make a good job of uniting with the middle peasants, increase yields, and consolidate the APCs. On the other hand these tasks of running the cooperatives well, uniting with the middle peasants, and increasing cooperative production cannot be accomplished easily if we take this matter lightly. We should admit that this is more difficult than land reform, that it is a long-term project that cannot be achieved within one or two years, and that cooperatives should be run for the full course instead of only for several years. [Our objective] is a "long life" [to the cooperatives]. I think that the failure to see this constitutes the second cause of the rash advance sentiment among the cadres.

It is a good thing that comrades from each province have come to understand the above two causes of the rash advance sentiment. This point should be made clear to the cadres in charge of running cooperatives, especially to those work team cadres who are sent to set up cooperatives as well as county and district cadres. This conference is very important in that it has enabled us to understand clearly the above two causes so that our minds will be a little bit more sober and we won't be misled by superficial phenomena.

Part II. Four future policies

1. In general we must halt development. Originally we said that [expansion] should stop in the coming fall. Later the chairman said that we could simply stop it and wait until the fall of next year, [in other words] we would stop for one and one-half years. Why should it be stopped in general [but not everywhere]? This is because in a small number of provinces, such as those of the Central-South and Southwest, the number of cooperatives is not large, with the exception of Henan in the Central-South. [In Henan] there are already more than 40,000 APCs and that is quite enough. [What Henan should do] is to overhaul these 40,000-plus. In the other five provinces [of the Central-South], where only 10,000-plus cooperatives have been set up, expansion can therefore be considered. Regarding how many more APCs should be developed, comrades from each province should look into the matter carefully but should not rush into decisions for the time being. It will be fine if you make the decision by July or August, or by June or July. Your decision should be made on the basis of the losses caused by this year's [natural] disasters so as to lay a solid foundation for the movement. Of course, in certain provinces where further expansion is needed preparation should be made prior to the fall, otherwise you will be caught in a passive position.

Now it is May. [You comrades] should look into the matter upon your return and put forward opinions by July or August, preferably prior to July. After that is done we can get together again to discuss it. In principle expansion should not be too big and should proceed from small to large scale and from a small number to a large number of cooperatives. Besides, each province should be in control of its districts and townships, especially the backward ones, and should not allow development in the latter until the situation there has been changed. No expansion should be pursued without a change of circumstances in the first place. While development should be pursued in those districts and townships where cooperatives are non-existent, the following two principles should be observed.

The first principle is that where no cooperatives have been set up, there should be a period for trial establishment in which it would be good enough to run experimentally one or two, instead of too many, cooperatives. This is because it won't do to be without perceptual knowledge. It is better to set up a couple of models to demonstrate [advantages] to the cadres and the masses before pursuing the large-scale expansion of cooperatives. This principle must be confirmed.

The second principle is that after the cooperatives are set up for a period of time, they should be consolidated for another period of time. The movement should not advance through tumbling and crawling. To advance this way is like shitting without wiping clean our bottoms. The more shitting like this the more bottoms that need to be wiped clean. Now we are not increasing the numbers [of APCs] by leaping forward by 200 or 300 percent. We are increasing the percentage of peasant households in cooperatives by 10 percent or a little bit more each year. As far as the number of households in APCs is concerned, its rate of increase is from one-fourth to one-third each year. We are going to draw in seven or eight more households into cooperatives with thirty households and five or six households into cooperatives with twenty households. Expanding in this way is much easier for us to absorb. If the increase is blindly pursued, indigestion will be the only outcome. Halting development in general is thus a policy. The aim of halting development is for consolidation, not for marking time or letting things drift. It is for the sake of consolidating the existing cooperatives, especially in those provinces with an unduly large number of cooperatives, that APC development must be stopped this year.

2. We shall work on production right away and consolidate it with all our strength. The 100,000 old cooperatives and more than 500,000 new cooperatives should be consolidated. The existing new cooperatives in particular must be consolidated. If these APCs are not overhauled and overhauled urgently after being set up, the socialist foundation will not be in good shape in the future. In fact, they will not become a foundation at all but will become a burden instead. Therefore, to consolidate the existing coopera-

tives, especially the existing new cooperatives, is to lay down a good socialist foundation, set a good example, become the starting point for consolidation and advance, and do good groundwork for our smooth progress in the future. [In short,] it is necessary for the foundation to be well set. If old cooperatives are well run many cadres can be released from their work [in these cooperatives], a source for new cadres will thus be provided, and we will be able to develop key cooperatives that can become leading examples for ordinary cooperatives. This was the way our party [successfully] built our army. Instead of expanding the army constantly we consolidated some military forces after they were formed. We did the same thing in building our base areas. Wherever a base area was expanded we next consolidated it so that we could advance on our way from a solid basis. When expanding to some extent we then would stop, and after again mobilizing the masses, making a good job of our work, and consolidating the base area, [our] forces were consolidated and grew stronger, and we once more moved ahead to expand further [the base area].

All of you know that consolidation of the cooperatives today will do us good and thus constitutes a very important issue, for we cannot advance if the hundreds of thousands of cooperatives are not well consolidated. However, you also have to realize that it is not easy to consolidate well this number of cooperatives and that we have to have cadres, especially a group of transferred cadres who will concentrate on this issue, and have [enough] time, in order to make a good job of it. It deserves special noting that in some places old cooperatives have not been well run from the beginning and are fraught with trouble. It will be more difficult to consolidate them and will cause more problems if we keep moving forward [in these places].

3. In a small number of provinces and counties the movement should be contracted appropriately. What is contraction for? We do not contract because we are pessimistic or because we want throw in the towel. If so, then we are clearly in the wrong. We contract in order to release [and reserve] some of our forces so as to make a good job of consolidating cooperatives. To throw out some baggage is not a retreat out of pessimism, but [to achieve] smoother advance and better consolidation. As each region has been instructed, we should be resolute, not hesitant. We should tell [our local cadres] not to consolidate reluctantly nor attempt to save face. Otherwise cooperatives cannot be eventually consolidated, and our cadres will bear the burden for a long time to come. And they would need to wipe clean their bottoms every year, [i.e., they would have too many catch-up tasks to do]. In the end there would be no way to get the cooperatives consolidated. It would be awful if they finally contract after the collapse of APCs that could and should be consolidated now. The current problem is not that we feel we have too many cooperatives, but that we have to throw out a group of cooperatives [in order to set up more cooperatives in the

future]. This is because we would eventually be dragged down if we attempt to consolidate those APCs that are not worthy of consolidation. This point should be heeded not only by provinces with a big expansion but also by some particular counties and districts in other provinces, especially those with excessive development. Neither rigid stipulations nor equal quotas shall be distributed concerning how much contraction there should be. It depends solely on the local situation. In short, wherever consolidation cannot be carried out the method of contraction should be applied.

Contraction should be applied only to cooperatives that cannot be run well even after the greatest efforts have been made. These APCs should be simply thrown out. [To repeat,] this applies only to those cooperatives that cannot be consolidated at all. Every cooperative that can be consolidated in any way should be consolidated. We should tell those peasants who displayed unhappiness after joining the APCs that they may withdraw and join again next year. In those problem-ridden cooperatives the masses are very critical [of the situation]. Only a minority are willing to stay in the cooperatives. The majority of the masses are reluctant to remain. What is the point of making them stay in this case[?] It would be better simply to let them withdraw. It is good for them to come, and also good for them to leave. What is the point of postponing the dissolution [of APCs] until after August 15, [i.e., the Moon Festival on the lunar calendar]? Why not the Dragon Festival, [i.e., May 5 on the lunar calendar]? Friendly dealing, friendly intercourse, in this way no one's feelings are hurt. Make sure both joining and leaving take place on good terms. Do not end up fighting. We shall have no reluctance to part with such [hopeless] cooperatives. We do not feel sorry [about their dissolution]. For such reluctance we would have to pay the price of wasting three or four months time [on hopeless APCs] while missing the chance to consolidate cooperatives that could have been consolidated.

Previously, in my opening speech, I mentioned the following point. In 1945 the center decided that our army needed to abandon the territory south of the Yangtze. Thus the New Fourth Army retreated to north of the Yangtze from south of the Yangtze. Elsewhere our army in the Northeast abandoned the city of Siping. All these moves were precisely for the sake of reinforcing our armies in order to advance better. They were not meant as passive retreat. Of course, we now encounter various difficulties. My proposed policy is indeed a little bit overdue. It would have been good if I made the proposal two or three months earlier, namely in February this year.

Before anything else we should make clear to the masses the principle of voluntary participation and mutual benefit. Like Zhejiang, every province and county should make a public statement in a comprehensive way on this principle. Whoever is unwilling to stay can feel free to withdraw. Lord Jiang fishes with a hook and line, [i.e., without bait]. Whoever is hooked must be hooked out of his own free will. [There is no coercion] for those who do not want to be hooked. Our mutual benefit policy must be spelled out as clearly as this. For this policy to make contact with the masses we have to take quick and resolute measures to deal with hopeless APCs in the manner of using a sharp knife to deal with thorny hemp. No public announcement is needed if the bad situation is not countywide. Yet it should be clear that we can announce their dissolution wherever there are pseudo-cooperatives, cooperatives so riddled with problems they are going to collapse, impossible cooperatives despite every effort to consolidate them, or cooperatives controlled by bad elements. Concerning these [kinds of APCs] we need to fight with time to deal with them. Never leave them unattended to for long. Consolidate the APCs whenever possible. During the process of consolidation there may be some cooperatives that cannot be consolidated. We shall bypass them and deal with them later. Members of this type of a small number of APCs can feel free to withdraw. We won't coerce them in any way. And we should not attempt to control them by any other means because doing so won't do anybody any good. Naturally we need to do work [to educate them]. Without [education] no cooperative can be consolidated. Yet if no consolidation is achieved after [education], then it would be better to let them go. They can come back again after we run good cooperatives. Just as I have said above, we will use the measure of friendly dealing.

Some APCs may become less capable because of the withdrawal of part of their membership. We will offer them our help. Or a few small APCs can merge. In short, we should first explain clearly to cooperative members that there is no need to worry about too many people withdrawing. After we lay bare to the masses the policy of voluntary participation and mutual benefit they can feel completely free to withdraw if they so choose. [But] does this indicate that most of our APCs are badly run? Not so. If we do not clarify this issue beforehand then we will encounter more problems. Therefore, we should not fear clarifying [the issue]. We need to consider that we will be caught in a very passive position in the future if we do not do some contraction at present. If we fall into an awkward position in the future there will be little we can do at that time. If today we take the initiative to contract it can only mean that our work [on the dissolved APCs] had not been done well. But once we become passive, in the future people would say that cooperativization itself is failing, which in turn would be advantageous to the activities of bad elements and leave room for counterrevolutionaries to spread rumors.

In the course of consolidation we should straighten out our cadres' thinking and protect their enthusiasm. We should talk them around if they cannot figure out what is going on. We should also help by explaining things to those cadres who suffer humiliation or lose face. We will say that the responsibility is ours; they are not the ones to blame. We will help them to shoulder the unhappy burden. Of course, there are some cadres with bad work styles. We should be critical of them and we are not going to shoulder the full load for them. Some cadres [commit the mistake] of commandism in their work. They are really bad, even corrupt. For these people we are not going to share their blame at all. They should be criticized and make public self-criticism before the masses in order to save their own reputations. Whenever cadres' work style is seriously wrong, and among them are even bad elements who unsuitably set up cooperatives using all sorts of means, there can only be unsatisfactory APCs. We must cautiously handle this type of cooperative during the course of consolidation. Bad elements must be brushed away. Since at present we are facing the task of production, whether these people should be dealt with immediately or later is open for further study. We may even handle them flexibly. In any case, we must take a cautious approach. During the consolidation period we must deal with them carefully, not evasively.

4. Mutual aid teams should be run well and consolidated well in order to take good care of individual farmers so as to make a good job of production and for the expansion of cooperatives in the future. Those cooperatives that have been developed from mutual aid teams are relatively stable and easy to run well. For the sake of current production, mutual aid teams should be run well and individual [private] farmers should be given assistance to overcome their problems so that they can keep their minds on production. If you help them to have good crop yields this year, mutual aid teams will in turn be run well and from there will develop further next year, providing a good foundation for the establishment of cooperatives. For this reason certain cadres should be assigned to take special charge of mutual aid teams from now on. There must be clear and specific assignments especially regarding which cooperatives [are to be dealt with], or which cadres have specialized responsibility. Some people have reported that because so many APCs are being set up, in some areas cadres in charge of mutual aid teams are transferred away. As a result the mutual aid teams are a big mess. If the latter are not overhauled our current production and the future development of cooperatives will be obstructed. All these matters warrant our attention. Therefore, we should give certain cooperatives the assignment of spurring on the mutual aid teams and individual farmers.

13

Mao Zedong

Speech on the Question of Agricultural Cooperativization (Excerpt) (May 17, 1955)*

There are not a few disturbances involving cooperatives, but on the whole they are good. If we do not emphasize that point we will make mistakes. There is a passive sentiment about the issue of cooperativization. In my opinion it must be changed; otherwise, we will make a big mistake. Regarding cooperativization [I say] first stop, second shrink, third develop. As far as contraction is concerned, there can be complete contraction, half contraction, big contraction, and small contraction. If the APC members are determined to withdraw from the cooperatives, what can anyone do about them[?] Contraction should be done in the light of practical conditions. One-sided contraction will inevitably dampen the enthusiasm of the cadres and the masses. In the areas that were liberated later, [cooperatives] simply must be developed, not stopped or contracted, but [I say] basically they should be developed. In some places [the movement] may need to be halted, but in general it should be developed. Even in some old liberated areas in North China and the Northeast there is the need to expand. Take Shandong as an example. Thirty percent of its villages do not have cooperatives. [The cooperativization movement] should by no means either stop or contract [in such areas]. There are no cooperatives there, what should we stop? There [the catchword] is simply to develop. [To summarize], wherever the movement ought to be stopped, we should stop it; wherever it ought to be contracted, we should contract it; wherever it ought be developed, we should develop it.

The principle for the development of cooperatives is voluntary participation and mutual benefit. Whenever livestock (even that of the

*This is a reprint of a part of Mao Zedong's speech at the conference of secretaries of fifteen provinces and municipalities convened by the CCP center, from *Nongye jitihua zhongyao wenjian huibian* (A collection of important documents on agricultural collectivization), vol. 1, edited by Office of the State Agricultural Commission, October 1981.

landlords and rich peasants) are turned over to the cooperatives, a fair price should be set and the poor peasants should not take petty advantage of the owners. Poor peasants should not take petty advantage of others' land, farm tools, and livestock. Mutual benefit can bring voluntary participation. There will be no voluntary participation without mutual benefit. Since [the principle of] mutual benefit does not harm middle peasant interests, [we should be able to] get them to join the cooperatives voluntarily. This would be, first of all, beneficial to the poor peasants, and of course beneficial to the middle peasants themselves as well. Therefore, we should adhere to the above principle. [The terms] semicompromise or semiconcessions should not be interpreted to harm middle peasant economic interests. Some people say that I made the remark, "Let the middle peasants suffer small losses." I do not remember whether I did or not. However, neither Marx, Engels, Lenin, nor Stalin ever said it. The state should provide more loans for the poor peasants so that they can straighten their backs. [You see,] within the cooperatives the middle peasants own livestock and farm tools, [yet the poor peasants have nothing]. Once the poor peasants have money, their voice can be heard. Regulations for the cooperatives should be made quickly to ensure that middle peasant interests are not harmed at all, so that cooperatives can develop rapidly.

Regarding the development of cooperatives, the targets of 70,000 in Henan, 45,000 each in Hubei, Hunan, and Guangdong Provinces, 35,000 each in Guangxi and Jiangxi, and 65,000 in Jiangsu should be set, once again, on the principle of voluntary participation and mutual benefit. The development of APCs is beneficial not only to the state, but also to each of your areas. If you are willing, we can strike a deal and fix the above figures. As far as the Northeast, Northwest, Southwest, and North China are concerned, we will have Lin Feng, Ma Mingfang, Song Renqiong, and Liu Lantao convene meetings [upon their return] at which time they will relay the gist of this conference and discuss the solution. What has been agreed on at this conference on the whole is correct and should be implemented. However, we must guarantee that 90 percent of the APCs that are developed are reliable.

14

Tan Zhenlin

Comrade Tan Zhenlin Reports on the Grain and Cooperatives Situation in Zhejiang (June 21, 1955)

Comrade Xiaoping for transmission to the center and chairman:

I have returned to Shanghai. During my ten-day stay in Hangzhou I spent most of my time investigating the issues of agricultural production cooperatives and state monopoly purchase and marketing of grain in Zhejiang. In Zhejiang the number of cooperatives has been decreased from 53,000 to 38,000 while the percentage of peasant households with cooperative membership the has declined from 28 percent to 18 percent. At present APC production is going very well. For most of them an increase in output can be assured, and [cooperative] operation and management is also good in most of them. However, the policy of mutual benefit has not been thoroughly implemented. Not only do cadres and activists in cooperatives bear resentment, but so do county, district, and township cadres. The investigation found the reason to be mainly that since the class line was implemented last year the idea of taking advantage of middle peasants had already emerged and nobody was willing to treat middle peasants equally and share benefits with them. According to my understanding, unless this problem is solved, the existing cooperatives cannot be fully consolidated and a batch of them will collapse after the fall.

The provincial committee has done something to deal with the problem by formulating some principles and conducting various kinds of model experiments. The prefecture party committees have straightened out their thinking but do not have time for implementation. Besides, because of their still insufficient understanding of the issues, they have not paid enough attention to them. After my investigations, it was decided to follow the method used by the Ningbo Prefecture Committee of selecting a group of cadres to concentrate on setting up and running cooperatives. It has already been decided at the provincial level to select 12,000 cadres and to have them sent down in July in order to start full implementation of the policy and to have it done well before the fall harvest. If this job is done well, not only can this group of old cooperatives be fully consolidated, but also new members can be recruited into them. At present, on average one cooperative has twenty-four households. It is expected that after the fall, on average the households in one cooperative will increase by ten and the new households in cooperatives will reach 380,000. These households will constitute 7.6 percent of the total households. Adding the households already in cooperatives, the total households in cooperatives will be 26 percent of all peasant households.

The grain situation in Zhejiang has not completely improved. According to materials available by the end of May, in only 13 percent of townships has the three fix [policy of setting quotas for production, purchase, and sales before spring planting] been implemented, while 78 percent of townships only carried out two fixes (fixed quotas in production and purchase or in purchase and sale), and the other 9 percent of townships only fixed one quota, i.e., for production. In addition to the fact that the tasks for tax levies, grain purchase, and sale have not been assigned, the other cause for the above situation is inadequate understanding of the political significance of the three fixes and as a result the cadres dare not determine the output quotas for this year or the criteria for the four retentions. Through investigation and provincial committee research, it has been decided that: output should be set about 10 percent lower than actual output and that a sufficient amount of the four retentions should be allowed. On the basis of this principle, a decision was made to start experiments on households in several townships. It appears that the results are very good, that work can be carried out smoothly, but that there exists a danger of failing to fulfill the grain collection task. In order to be prudent, it has been decided that the stage of model experiments starts now and will last until July 15, and that each county will select several key and six supplementary townships for experiments to find out whether or not the grain task can be fulfilled under the new policy.

If we still end up 200 or 300 million jin of grain short, it will be announced to the grain producing peasants that while the fixed quota for their grain output is affirmed and the four retentions will not be changed again, in order to fulfill the state's general task of grain collection each person should sell another 20 jin of grain to support national socialist construction. Such a measure will be much better than obstinately raising the quota for output and cutting down the four retentions. It is estimated that after the three fixes have been implemented at the household level, the amount of grain to be sold can be reduced. When the provincial committee distributed [the grain sales] to the lower levels, 300 million jin was retained (i.e., only 3.5 billion jin was distributed). If we make a good job of it, it is entirely possible for us to reduce the amount of grain sold. (For example, the originally planned amount of unprocessed food grains to be consumed by each urban dweller, that is, 472 jin, is too large and has been reduced to 420 jin. Take another example. The original planned amount of grain for the food processing industry, that is, 370 million jin, is too big and can be decreased by 100 million jin according to stipulations by the center concerning the use of grain in the food processing industry.) As long as model experiments turn out to be successful, three fix work can be implemented down to the household level by the end of September. If a good job is made of the task, not only can state monopoly purchase and marketing of grain for this year be easily done, but the current situation regarding grain can also be fully stabilized and the peasants' production enthusiasm will be enhanced. (This has started to be verified in two model townships in Jiaxing County.) If this task is smoothly fulfilled, party committees can devote their attention to the development of cooperatives. Since in Zhejiang there are still 6 percent of all townships without cooperatives and another 21 percent with only one or two cooperatives, it is possible to develop another batch of new cooperatives. The provincial committee has tentatively decided to develop another 15,000 APCs on the basis of the completion of the three fixes in grain work.

I am planning to go to Nanjing on June 24 to investigate the cooperatives and three fix work in Jiangsu, and then return to Beijing by the end of the month.

Tan Zhenlin
June 21, 1955

15

CCP CENTER

The CCP Center's Comments While Transmitting the Hebei Provincial Committee's "Directive on Several Policy Issues During Overhauling Agricultural Producers' Cooperatives" (July 6, 1955)

Shanghai Bureau and party committees of all provinces, municipalities, and autonomous regions:

The directive of the Hebei Provincial Committee on several policy issues during overhauling APCs is basically feasible. The experience in applying private ownership and collective use of livestock in APCs in Xingtai County in the appendix to the directive is also very good. Now we transmit them to all regions for reference. It should be pointed out emphatically that the policy of mutual benefit between the poor and middle peasants in the cooperative economy is the basis for the implementation of the principle of voluntary participation. An inspection of the concrete policies of each cooperative, especially the implementation of the policy of mutual benefit and the principle of voluntary participation, should be carried out in a planned manner in order to further consolidate the cooperatives established between last winter and this spring.

1. Experience shows that in the early stage of cooperatives, or before cooperative production has significantly increased and the members' economic strength is still weak, with regard to the APC members' livestock to be turned over to the cooperatives there is more advantage in adopting the method of private ownership and feeding by individuals while [the animals] are rented and used by the APCs. Having studied the experience in Xingtai County, the Hebei Provincial Committee has decided to promote and popularize this method step-by-step in a guided manner. It also decided

200

to educate and persuade according to separate circumstances those cooperatives whose members' livestock have already been turned over at depreciated prices [to adopt this measure]. These APCs [often] end up with heavy debts and a shortage of fodder that in turn seriously affect the livestock that become emaciated and sick or even die. This method will allow either private ownership and feeding with rent and use [of livestock] by APCs, or turning over part [of the livestock] to the cooperatives and transferring part of it to individuals. Such a measure is practical.

When the above method of hiring and employing livestock is adopted, it should be stipulated as a general rule that the rent should be equivalent to the local social rent enabling the owners of livestock to make some profit after paying for livestock expenses. However, when promoting and shifting to the method of private ownership and collective use, attention should be paid to avoiding arbitrary enforcement and formalistic adherence to uniform rules made by superiors. [Our cadres] should also avoid merely following orders to change [things] at one stroke without any preparatory work. [Doing things that way] will result in many disputes that, if they remain unaddressed, will in turn affect the consolidation of cooperatives. Private ownership may not need to be applied uniformly to some APCs where the organizational basis and economic conditions are fairly good and the regulations concerning payment and the terms of repayment for livestock turned over to cooperative ownership are relatively reasonable, as long as members from the poor peasants can afford it. In those cooperatives where repayment has not been made in line with agreed deadlines, they should be urged to fulfill the agreement in order not to break promises to their members and to eliminate the doubts and worries of the common peasants concerning the development of livestock.

2. On [the issue of] land remuneration, regardless of whether the system of proportional shares or fixed shares is adopted, there should be a set applicable period. In order to make land remuneration more reasonable, consideration should be given to changing the practice of simply treating the levied output as the output [for determining remuneration] upon joining the cooperatives. The reason is as follows. Levied output in calculating agricultural taxes is assessed on the basis of land quality. However, because of successes or failures in management, land with the same degree of quality may not produce the same output. Therefore, peasants (mainly middle peasants) who own land with high real output are dissatisfied with simply taking levied output as their output upon joining the cooperatives. If output is assessed on the basis of actual annual output with favorable treatment to owners of land with lower output than [that produced by] land of the same quality because of their insufficient management capabilities, it will receive support from most cooperative members. Please conduct further studies on this issue.

3. The share fund for production collected on the basis of the members' land turned over to cooperative ownership should not be too much and should be within the limits of what most cooperative members can afford. Once this is done, with the state's aid to poor peasants in the form of long-term low interest loans, the problem of poor cooperative members being unable to contribute to the share fund can be largely solved. The Hebei Provincial Committee's instruction that "contributions to the share fund required from some particularly poor members can be reduced or waived after consultation with all cooperative members" should be deleted since allowing payment over a longer period is acceptable whereas reduction or exemption of payment will readily arouse middle peasant discontent.

This document and its appendix can be published in party journals.

The Center
July 6, 1955

16
Comments by the Party Center on Provincial Reports and Directives concerning Cooperativization together with Excerpts from the Appended Local Documents

16a

Mao Zedong

The CCP Center's Directive to Party Committees of All Places While Transmitting the Hubei Provincial Committee's Report concerning Deployments for Agricultural Producers' Cooperatives (August 13, 1955)*

Shanghai Bureau and all provincial, municipal, and autonomous region party committees:

Now we are transmitting for your reference a report of August 5, 1955, by Hubei Provincial Party Committee concerning deployments for APCs. The center considers that the policy proposed by the Hubei Provincial Committee is correct. On the issue of why "in the course of socialist transformation some cadres have lost the vigor and enthusiasm displayed in the land reform period and instead harbor a kind of dangerous passive sentiment and dread of difficulties," you should conduct appropriate analysis and come up with unambiguous answers. We also expect that you, along with many other com-

---

*This comment was personally written by Mao Zedong—Eds.

rades, will look into the matter of how many cooperatives can be established in all provinces and autonomous regions in light of the practical situation before fall 1956. We expect you to draw up a plan and report it to the center.

At this moment all prefecture [party] committees in Hubei are calling conferences of activists above the level of members of district [party] committees to discuss the plans and arrangements [for APCs] of the prefectures, counties, and districts. The Hubei [Provincial] Committee is now preparing to call a joint conference of prefecture secretaries to study further and draw up a plan for the whole province. The center hopes that all provinces and autonomous regions can follow suit by the end of August or early to mid-September so that the plans for whole provinces and autonomous regions will be looked into and drawn up, preferably prior to September 20, 1955. It is a very important issue to overhaul the existing cooperatives by stages with a massive effort and not superficially. However, this is not mentioned in the report by Hubei Province. The center hopes that you will pay great attention to [this question], be sure to draw up a practical deployment plan before September 20, 1955, and send it in with the plan for development in the whole province. We are looking forward to them.

The Center
August 13, 1955

**[Appendix: The Hubei Report
(August 5, 1955)]**

The Center:

On August 3 we called an enlarged conference of the provincial committee attended by 340 party member cadres at and above the level of provincial and municipal office (bureau) director at which Comrade Wang Renzhong relayed the chairman's instructions in "On the Question of APCs." This was followed by a meeting of standing members of the provincial committee on August 4 to study and discuss the chairman's instructions. All the comrades attending the meetings expressed their full support for the instructions of the party center and the chairman. They were all very excited. They conducted conscientious self-criticism and examined the work and guiding thinking of the provincial committee for the past half year.

The provincial committee considers that we had harbored right-deviationist thinking on the issue of the socialist transformation of agriculture as reflected in our fear of having too many cooperatives and too much trouble. [Indeed, at the time] we were not clear concerning whether there were too many or too few cooperatives and on what basis we should judge [this question]. In fact, we still failed to understand fully the spirit of the center's view of the situation in our province, more cooperatives could have been set up by the end of 1957; however, at the conference of provincial party representatives [in June] we still decided to set the target of having [only] 35 percent of the peasant households join APCs. This shows that our thinking was still like a pot of half-cooked rice. In the past we always took for granted that [cooperativization] should be slower in the areas liberated later than in the old [liberated] areas. We thus lacked the enthusiasm to catch up with the old [liberated] areas.

Of course, it was wrong to "hurry to be the first." But it was equally wrong to be haunted by right-deviationist conservative thinking, for we failed to do enthusiastically what we could. The reason why we had this wrong idea was that we were bad at applying class analysis from the standpoint of the working class. Although at the joint conference of county secretaries in January and the provincial party representative conference in June we managed to analyze the enthusiasm of the poor peasants (including the absolute majority of new middle peasants) for socialism, the dual character of the middle peasants, and the reactionary nature of the rich peasants, we still failed to look into the matter profoundly and to work out thoroughly our reasons, still less to figure out on the basis of our analysis whether there should be a big or small development of cooperativization. This shows that our level of Marxism-Leninism is still low. We should step up our study to avoid blindness.

We failed to understand fully the situation that "a big storm in the new socialist mass movement is imminent." At the conference of provincial party representatives in June we made an examination of the fact that "in the course of socialist transformation some cadres have lost the vigor and enthusiasm displayed in the land reform period and instead harbor a kind of dangerous passive sentiment and dread of difficulties." We also looked into its causes. However, we failed to see whether or not [our] provincial committee had allowed a free hand in leading the movement, and whether or not we were daring enough to lead a big movement. For example, our position was ambiguous and uncertain in handling the issue of spontaneous cooperatives. Hence we committed some deviations in implementing the relevant policy. No wonder that at the time, upon seeing the cadres coming, some members in spontaneous cooperatives cried out "Here come the spies." We also made the mistake of imposing too rigid restrictions concerning the requirements for establishing a cooperative. This obviously hampered the initiative of the cadres as well as the masses. We believe that after the chairman's instructions are passed on to the lower levels, the vast number of cadres and relatively poor peasants will all be jubilant. In addition, on these extremely important issues we, as responsible comrades of the provincial committee, failed to consult enough with each other, think hard enough, and listen enough to the opinions of the lower levels.

hard enough, and listen enough to the opinions of the lower levels.

The provincial committee now holds that the chairman's instructions in "On the Question of APCs" are the guiding principles for all our work during the transition period. It also holds that our full potential should be mobilized in all work to overcome difficulties and to accelerate socialist construction as much as possible, and that we should oppose the passive and wavering right-deviationist attitude when facing difficulties.

On the basis of the criticisms of right-deviationist thinking and the analysis of various conditions, we now decide that our plan for developing APCs in our province is this: to increase the number of cooperatives to 70,000 by fall next year, with [APC membership] amounting to about 25 percent of the rural population, and to increase the number to 120,000 by winter 1957, accounting for 50 percent of the rural population.

[The report concluded with an instruction to the prefecture level to convene activists' conferences and indicated the intention of holding another provincial meeting at the end of August.]

The CCP Hubei Provincial Committee
August 5, 1955

16b

Mao Zedong

The CCP Center's Comments While Transmitting the Liaoning Provincial Committee's Report on the Agricultural Producers' Cooperative Question (August [16,] 1955)*

Now we are transmitting for your reference the August 12, 1955, report by the Liaoning Provincial Committee on the question of APCs. The center considers that the policy of the Liaoning Provincial Committee is correct. Concerning the interrelationship between socialist industrialization and the socialist transformation of agriculture, we should emphasize the close linkage between the two rather than emphasizing the former and playing down the latter. If we do not keep the pace of the socialist transformation of agriculture in step with that of socialist industrialization, socialist industrialization cannot be accomplished in isolation and will inevitably run into tremendous difficulties. However, right up to this moment many people in [our] party still do not understand this point. Concerning various preparatory work for overhauling, establishing, and expanding cooperatives, the Liaoning Provincial Committee pointed out that this work should include the following: "mobilize people's thinking level by level, criticize and overcome right-deviationist thinking, enthusiastically utilize the broad cadres' and masses' enthusiasm and initiative; make a good job of overall planning at various levels, especially at the village level (that is, at the township level, since in the provinces of the Northeast this level is yet to be called the township level) where the cooperativization plan in terms of the class composition of APC membership must take priority; continue doing well the work of overhauling and consolidating the existing cooperatives; carry out a step further the various concrete policies for cooperativization, and investigate, clean up, and purify cooperative organizations; strengthen

---

*This comment was personally written by Mao Zedong—Eds.

leadership over mutual aid teams so as to lay a good foundation for establishing APCs; closely integrate the work of overhauling and establishing cooperatives and that of strengthening party organizations at the grassroots level." These [measures] are all appropriate.

The Liaoning Provincial Committee has decided to convene a joint conference attended by secretaries of county and district [party] committees from the entire province in early September to discuss the issue of cooperativization. Other provinces can follow this method in light of their local conditions. There is no prefecture level in Liaoning Province. We regard it necessary to set up immediately institutions at this level in order to strengthen leadership over cooperativization.

[Appendix:] Report of the Liaoning Provincial Committee on Relaying and Discussing Chairman Mao's Instructions in "On the Question of Agricultural Producers' Cooperatives" (August [12,] 1955)

On August 8 the provincial committee convened an enlarged conference of the provincial committee at which Chairman Mao's instructions of July 31 on the question of APCs given at the conference of secretaries of provincial, municipal, and [autonomous] region party committees were relayed and discussed. [The report then briefly referred to who attended the conference and to the positive impact of Mao's instructions, and began a review of cooperativization in the province during the preceding year.]

The cooperativization movement in our province has been basically normal and healthy. At the provincial conference on mutual aid and cooperativization held in January this year, the provincial committee affirmed the achievements of the earlier period, emphasized the importance of and difficulties in establishing [new] cooperatives, and proposed a policy of concentrating on running well the existing cooperatives so as to consolidate positions for further advance, create favorable conditions, and prepare for development after the fall. All the above measures were basically correct. However, because of tension emerging in some rural areas, we later failed to understand fully the overall situation and for some time attributed the tension to the "too rough and too fast" development of the cooperativization movement. Therefore, for a time in March and April we carried out the decision to "halt the expansion [of cooperatives] and devote all our efforts to consolidation."

As a result, we failed to champion the high tide of cooperativization to an even higher level through our work on consolidation and thus violated the law of the development of the movement and failed to live up to the masses' demands. Fortunately, prior to the formal circulating of the decision to "halt the expansion," Comrade Lin Feng came to Shenyang on May 20 to relay the chairman's instructions. This enabled us to turn away from the erroneous thinking. However, when discussing the expansion of cooperatives in June, we were still acting [timidly] with bound hands and feet, were not bold enough, and lacked the necessary enthusiasm. Consequently the enthusiasm and initiative of many rural cadres concerning cooperativization has been frustrated and depressed for the past few months.

As the chairman points out, we were scared of success and thus failed to see the essential and principal aspects of the movement, and were misled by the partial, temporary, and nonessential aspects. If it were not for the chairman's correct and timely instructions we would have done even greater damage to the cooperativization movement. Why did we make such a mistake? The reasons are as follows: First of all, we failed to understand fully the party's general line for the transition period in that we only realized that industrialization was the main part, yet failed to see that the socialist transformation of agriculture is highly relevant to and will facilitate industrialization. In this way we failed to link closely industrialization with the socialist transformation of agriculture. [Second,] we were influenced by right-deviationist sentiment. This was reflected in the fact that we had underrated the party's high prestige and capable leadership in the countryside, and that we underestimated the enthusiasm for socialism on the part of the broad [masses of] the poor and not well-to-do peasants. [Finally,] we fell into the trap of one-sided thinking that tends to treat partial phenomena as the whole, takes nonessential aspects as essential ones, and therefore we only saw the difficulties and problems in the movement yet not its achievements and positive factors. In our future work we are determined to draw lessons from the aforementioned mistakes with feelings of deep remorse.

[The report concluded with revised APC targets and a call for strengthening various aspects of work toward that end.]

MAO ZEDONG

The CCP Center's Comments While Transmitting the Anhui Provincial Committee's Report on the Agricultural Cooperativization Question (August [31,] 1955)*

Now we are transmitting for your reference the Anhui Provincial Committee's August 21, 1955, report on agricultural cooperativization. The center considers that the policy proposed by Anhui Province is correct. The Anhui Provincial Committee sharply criticizes right-deviationist opportunist thinking concerning agricultural cooperativization. Such criticism is completely necessary. The Anhui Provincial Committee also raises its own opinions on ten concrete issues. The center holds that Anhui Province may now proceed with its work in accord with these opinions whose validity can be tested later in the course of experiment. We can still make revisions if such revisions are required in the future. The center considers that these opinions should be put forth to all provinces, municipalities, and autonomous regions. They should discuss [these views] and offer their own opinions at appropriate conferences before reporting to the center by National Day this year.

[Appendix:] Report of the Anhui Provincial Committee on the Question of Agricultural Cooperativization (August [21,] 1955)

At the first-level conference of prefecture and municipal party secretaries and heads of rural work departments held between August 6 and 10, 1955, we first relayed and discussed the chairman's instructions in "On the Question of APCs" and the chairman's concluding speech given at the conference of secretaries of provincial, municipal, and autonomous region

---

*This comment was personally written by Mao Zedong—Eds.

party committees. We also made a preliminary examination of our work. Now we would like to report concerning the conference as follows:

I. Those at the conference unanimously considered that the chairman's instructions were absolutely true and correct: "A high tide in the new socialist mass movement is imminent," "this high tide is already evident at the local level." These observations can be fully justified by the following facts.

1. For the past few years the development of APCs has fallen far short of meeting the masses' demands and our leadership has lagged far behind the mass movement. This can be seen from the expansion of cooperatives during the past four years: In the first year (1952, the years to be mentioned below can be calculated on this basis) when we first established 56 cooperatives on a trial basis, 277 more cooperatives appeared spontaneously. [Of these APCs,] only 106 were left after reduction. In the second year 361 trial cooperatives were set up while another 465 spontaneous cooperatives came into being. All these APCs, 932 in total including those of the previous year, were later reduced to 676. In the third year 3,351 formally approved cooperatives were established while 2,847 spontaneous cooperatives were set up. Adding the number of original cooperatives from 1953, the total number amounted to 7,054 [sic] that was subsequently reduced to 6,827. In the fourth year we approved the establishment of 31,622 cooperatives but 11,875 spontaneous cooperatives were set up separately. Adding those existing in 1954, the total number of APCs was 50,324. This was later reduced to 46,919. [The report continued with some county statistics.] Generally speaking, at present on average 15 percent of the peasant households in the whole province have joined cooperatives. This percentage could well have been increased to 20 or 30 percent if we had not been obstructed by "too much carping, unwarranted complaints, boundless worries, and countless taboos."

Fact show that where there is a big growth of cooperatives there is a considerable increase in crop yields, better consolidation, and trouble free [development]. Conversely, in those areas where there is little growth of cooperatives the consolidation of APCs and growth in crop yields always remains number two due to the cadres' lack of zeal as well as the low enthusiasm of the masses.

2. There has been a large number of spontaneous cooperatives. Those of 1953 were 1.7 times more than those of 1952, while those of 1954 were more than 6 times greater than those of 1953. In 1955, due to the growth in the number of cooperatives, spontaneous cooperatives are [only] 4-plus times more than those of 1954. Most of the spontaneous APCs were set up by the masses themselves. Some of them simply refused to be dissolved even if we attempted to dissolve them. For example, four spontaneous cooperatives in Jinshi Township, Tongling County, although not approved for three years are were still running (now they are approved). [The report then noted

briefly the success of one spontaneous APC.] The masses were so unhappy with our restrictions that they complained "[it is ridiculous that] even practicing socialism is restricted." They also remarked: "Since practicing socialism does not violate the law, if they do not approve, so be it."

The masses set up spontaneous cooperatives for the following three reasons: (1) Cooperatives, especially in areas troubled by natural calamities, are able to increase production. Even those devastated by severe calamities such as the one last year could still maintain cooperative production and pull themselves through the calamities. In the end the masses were able to feel profoundly the advantages of the cooperatives. (2) After being educated by the propaganda on the general line, the masses' socialist consciousness has been raised dramatically. They realize that mutual aid and cooperativ-ization have become the general tendency and the only road ahead; thus they understand that it is better to take the road earlier rather than later. (3) The broad masses have already accepted the cooperative's organizational form, its relevant concrete policies, and the measures for setting up a cooperative.

3. Now, establishing cooperatives has already become a mass movement. Not only are [new cooperatives] set up in batches around the old cooper-atives, in areas without APCs the masses are also seeking enthusiastically to establish cooperatives. The masses explore every way to find out how to set up cooperatives, such as by visiting their relatives and friends, seeing for themselves old cooperatives, and inviting old cooperative members to help them set up their own APCs. The advantages of cooperatives have struck root in people's hearts and establishing cooperatives has become a public desire.

By the same token these facts show that "too much carping, unwarranted complaints, boundless worries, and countless taboos" as expressed by women with bound feet have indeed done damage to our socialist enthu-siasm. At the conference there were abundant materials aiming at exposing such mistakes. Participants at the conference were particularly critical of the "Report on the Rash Advance Tendency in the Mutual Aid and Cooper-ation Movement in the East China Region and on the Situation after Our Preliminary Work of Overhauling and Consolidation" issued by the Rural Work Department of the East China Bureau and transmitted with a comment by the East China Bureau on October 31, 1953. Everyone considered the major mistakes in this document were:

First, in the document some individual shortcomings were treated as if they were common mistakes. For example, the slogan "whoever joins mutual aid teams is a hero and whoever does not is a chicken" and the isolated practices of relatively low monetary compensation for farm cattle and tools or unfair land remuneration were treated as if they were acts of impetuosity and rash advance, or as if they were the main trend of the

movement and thus had to be opposed. This in the end led to the phenomenon of "giving up eating for fear of choking."

Second, good things were treated as bad ones. For example, the "open
establishment of secret cooperatives" was seen not as due to the masses'
enthusiasm but as a sign of chaos; the "labor-contract and output-contract
teams" or the "three turnover teams" (land, farm animals, and farm tools
were turned over to the collective ownership of the team) were labeled
"spendthrift teams"; the legitimate development [of cooperativization] was
alleged to be committing the "serious mistake of impetuosity and rash
advance"; the fair evaluation of work and allotting workpoints (the "four
fixes," "standard labor," etc.) was treated as "the blind implementation of
complicated work assessment and accounting methods to the neglect of the
masses' customs and experience as well as the needs of production"; the
"step-by-step implementation of the [socialist] principle of distribution,
[i.e.,] to each according to his labor," was criticized as unwarranted.

Third, wrong things were taken to be good ones. For instance, it was
regarded as a good thing that in slack farming seasons some team or
cooperative members and their families engaged in producing, transporting,
and selling private goods such as beancurd and sesame cakes. [In this way]
everyone was encouraged to develop individualism and capitalism.

Fourth, various kinds of restrictions were imposed on [APC] development. (1) Too strict restrictions were imposed on the pilot scheme for
establishing APCs only at certain levels. For example, in 1952 cooperatives
were allowed to be set up on a trial basis only down to the prefecture level,
in 1953 only down to the county level, and in 1954 only down to the district
level. Once such a plan was exceeded it would be judged as committing the
mistake of rash advance. (2) Only appointed cadres were allowed to
establish cooperatives on a trial basis whereas the masses were restrained
from doing so even under the party's guidance. For example, in the first and
second years only the cadres were asked to set up cooperatives, yet in the
third and fourth years it was still the cadres but not the masses who were
asked to set up cooperatives. (3) The existence of a great number of
spontaneous cooperatives was seen as evidence of mistakes, hence as a
target for criticism. For all these reasons enthusiasm for setting up
cooperatives was dampened.

The above materials sufficiently prove that the chairman's use of the
metaphor of "a woman with bound feet" to describe this situation is indeed
incisive, graphic, and extremely profound.

II. It was agreed unanimously at the conference that although the provincial committee had played the role of "a sluice gate" concerning the
following three crucial issues, [we] did not close the sluice gate tightly
enough.

First, in 1952 the provincial committee went beyond the stipulation of setting up cooperatives only at the prefecture level and proceeded with setting up cooperatives at the county level. For this we were criticized. However, the facts show that it was correct to do so.

Second, in 1953 the provincial committee did not accept the instruction to concentrate on opposing blind rash advance; instead it emphasized opposing the laissez-faire tendency. This was because at the time all party committees at various levels had not yet placed the setting up of APCs on their agenda. Their problem at the time was [the danger of] the laissez-faire attitude, hardly the question of blind rash advance. Now it has been proven that the provincial committee was correct in taking a realistic approach and in not blindly accepting the instruction to oppose rash advance. [The provincial committee's position] has played an important role in the normal development of cooperatives in Anhui after 1953.

Third, in spring 1955 the provincial committee rejected the opinion of cutting down 20 percent of the cooperatives. Instead, the provincial committee suggested the following solution. Being practical and realistic, we would make every effort to consolidate all cooperatives except those that could not be consolidated at all and would be reorganized, [i.e., scrapped]. But unlike the plan for development, no number for the reduction of cooperatives would be set in advance. Due to [our] policy, now over 90 percent of the existing cooperatives are consolidated and all have managed to increase their crop yields. Had the policy of axing [the APCs] been carried out [by us], the ever flourishing cooperativization movement would have suffered severe damage and the cadres' and the masses' enthusiasm would have been dampened.

In short, everybody agreed that the reason why the provincial committee, despite being criticized, still had the courage to close the sluice gate and thus avoided committing mistakes in principle, and even dared to push for big development, is mainly due to the chairman's instructions at the Third National Mutual Aid and Cooperation Conference [in October-November 1953] that greatly increased our intestinal fortitude and enhanced our courage. However, this does not mean that the provincial committee had not made any mistakes or was free of shortcomings. [The report went on to list some of the shortcomings in the work of the provincial committee pointed out at the conference. The first item concerned not allowing spontaneous APCs.]

Second, although the provincial committee had rejected and altered the erroneous measures, it had done so not out of complete rational knowledge but largely out of perceptual knowledge and thus failed to make adequate theoretical criticism of the viewpoints and measures on which it disagreed. It could only realize that mutual aid and cooperation should and could be further developed, but stopped short of picking up signs of the imminent socialist upsurge in the countryside due to the lack of a Marxist-Leninist perspective and the failure to analyze this issue in light of rural class relations. Our effort thus was short of educational and persuasive appeal. Therefore, [the provincial committee] was unable to solve problems in some comrades' thinking. Certain kinds of disagreements or complaints existed inevitably [among our cadres]. For example, when the Rural Work Department of the East China Bureau criticized us for rash advance for the second time, some comrades began to grumble at and blame the provincial committee.

It was also agreed at the conference that in Anhui there indeed existed "women with bound feet," a "reorganization clique," yet also "big feet." In order to liberate the bound feet and equip the "reorganizationists" with a pair of natural feet, we must engage in further [self-]examination in conjunction with the study of the chairman's instructions to expose further and criticize the buffoonery of the women with bound feet. Only by doing so can we correctly implement the chairman's instructions.

III. Everyone at the conference unanimously maintained that we are confident about accomplishing the task and will strive to overfulfill the target assigned by the center of "doubling cooperative membership." We plan to set up another 36,000-odd cooperatives by this winter and next spring. Adding this to the old cooperatives there will be in total 80,000 that would account for 33 to 35 percent of all peasant households [in the province] having joined the cooperatives. Although this task is arduous we are all confident concerning its fulfillment.

[The report concluded with detailed discussions of deployments to complete the above task, and of opinions on various concrete questions such as the handling of farm animals and tools, the distribution of land and labor, sideline activities, etc.]

16d

MAO ZEDONG

The CCP Center's Comments While Transmitting the Fujian Provincial Party Committee's Report on the Agricultural Cooperativization Question (September 7, 1955)*

Shanghai Bureau and all provincial, municipal, and autonomous region party committees:

Now we are transmitting for your reference a report of August 31, 1955, by the Fujian Provincial Committee on the question of agricultural cooperativization. The center considers the policy of the Fujian Provincial Committee is correct. At present the slogan "Rely on the poor peasants (including all the new middle peasants who were formerly poor peasants) and firmly unite with the middle peasants" remains basically correct. However, [certain qualifications are in order for the following reasons]: (1) There has emerged from the new middle peasants [a new class of people who should be categorized as] well-to-do middle peasants (i.e., upper-middle peasants) who are not willing to join the cooperatives for the time being with the exception of a small number of them who are politically conscious. (2) The lower-middle peasants among the old middle peasants are in general interested in joining the cooperatives because their economic status is similar to that of the lower-middle peasants among the new middle peasants as they were originally not economically well-off and some of them suffered unduly from encroachment during land reform.

For these two reasons, wherever the upsurge of cooperativization is yet to come and the well-to-do middle peasants still lack consciousness, it is better to draw into the cooperatives first the following three types of people: (1) the poor peasants; (2) the lower-middle peasants among the new middle

---

*This comment was personally written by Mao Zedong—Eds.

peasants (in the revised version of Comrade Mao Zedong's report the middle peasants are divided only into two sections, the upper and lower-middle peasants, and the middle-middle peasants are not mentioned so as to avoid being too fine in differentiating them. It should be clear that what is here referred to as the lower-middle peasants actually includes two groups of people, the lower-middle peasants and the middle-middle peasants, formerly categorized as middle peasants); (3) the lower-middle peasants among the old middle peasants.

These three types of people should be suitably recruited into cooperatives (in batches in accord with their levels of consciousness; the higher the consciousness the higher the priority). Those well-to-do middle peasants, that is, the upper-middle peasants among the new or old middle peasants who are not willing to join the cooperatives, should not be dragged in against their will. Currently, in many places well-to-do middle peasants are forcibly dragged into the cooperatives simply because other people are attempting to obtain their farm animals and tools (at unreasonably low monetary compensation with payments over unduly long periods). In so doing we are actually infringing upon their interests and violating the principle of "firmly uniting with the middle peasants." To be sure, we should under no circumstances violate this Marxist principle. Yet leadership over any cooperative must be provided by the poor peasants and lower-middle peasants.

At present wherever cooperatives have been recently set up or are not in a predominant position, those well-to-do middle peasants with strong tendencies toward capitalism must not be allowed to assume APC leadership regardless of whether they have been recruited by us to join the cooperatives or they themselves sneak into the APCs in an attempt to grab the leadership (not out of their real political consciousness), or in some cases by setting up cooperatives of poor quality as discovered in Shuangcheng County, Heilongjiang Province. Otherwise the situation would be very unfavorable for establishing the leadership of the poor and middle peasants over the cooperatives.

Now some people say that the slogan "Rely on the poor peasants and firmly unite with the middle peasants" seems to have been abandoned in our present formulation. This is not true. We have not given up the slogan but rather made it more precise in light of the new conditions, that is, we count the lower-middle peasants among the old middle peasants as a section of the people on whom we should rely, but not the well-to-do peasants among the new middle peasants. This new distinction is made in view of their [current] economic status and whether or not they take an active attitude toward the cooperativization movement. In other words, the poor peasants and the two groups of lower-middle peasants who correspond to the old poor peasants are now taken to be those we should rely on, whereas the two groups of upper-middle peasants who correspond to the old middle peasants, are now taken to be those with which we should firmly unite. One way of uniting with them at present is not to drag them into the cooperative against their will as well as not to violate their interests.

In addition, several more points should be made clear regarding the question of whom we should rely on in the countryside. First of all, we should rely on party and Youth League members. It is wrong for our [party] committees at and above the district level or for cadres sent to the countryside not to rely primarily on party and Youth League members, but to mix them up with the nonparty and non-League masses. Second, we should rely on the more active elements among the nonparty people who should account for about 5 percent of the rural population (for example, there should be about 125 activists in a township with 2,500 people). We should make efforts to produce through training such a group of activists and should not mix them up with the masses either. Third, we should then rely on the masses composed of the poor peasants and the two groups of lower-middle peasants. The cooperativization movement is bound to make mistakes if we are not clear about the problem of who we should rely on and how to rely on them.

The Center
September 7, 1955

**[Appendix: The Fujian Report
(August 31, 1955)]**

The Center:

The provincial committee has come up with the following opinions in its discussion of how to carry out the chairman's instructions given on July 30 [sic] at the conference of secretaries of provincial and municipal committees concerning the two issues of the imminent high tide of socialist reform and of class policy. Please enlighten us concerning whether or not they are appropriate.

**I. Concerning the issue of the imminent
socialist high tide in agriculture**

We fully agree with the chairman's instructions that a high tide of socialism in the countryside has already reached some places and is going to [over-whelm] the whole country. In light of the situation of the APC movement in our province, we think that after we implement the chairman's instructions, mobilize people's thinking at each level, and overcome and criticize right-deviationist thinking, the enthusiasm of the broad cadres and masses will be greatly promoted and through our work between this fall and the coming spring the high tide of the socialist mass movement will reach our province.

[The report continues with statistics and description concerning the previous years' development of the movement, and a call for preparations for the coming high tide.]

II. Concerning the issue of class policy

Due to the lack of clarity and certainty in our thinking concerning how to rely on and give support to the poor peasants, we made mistakes in implementing class policy in the countryside after the publicizing of the general line. As a result the well-to-do and the relatively well-to-do peasants dominated the backbone [posts] of some cooperatives. More seriously, in some rural areas the poor peasants did not dominate the backbone [posts] of the party branches whereas the well-to-do and relatively well-to-do peasants constituted the majority of membership in party branches. Also, since we had talked loosely about "relying on the poor (including new middle) peasants and uniting with the middle peasants" and failed to distinguish the new middle peasants and still not well-to-do peasants among the old middle peasants from the well-to-do or relatively well-to-do middle peasants, we mistakenly took the negative sentiments of a small number of well-to-do or relatively well-to-do peasants to be those of the broad masses. We therefore underestimated, or failed to see, the enthusiasm [for cooperativization] on the part of the vast number of poverty-stricken or not well-to-do peasants. If this viewpoint is not rectified and clarified we will be likely to make further mistakes in the future. Our understanding of the chairman's instructions is as follows. The party's class policy in the countryside should be to "rely on the poor peasants (including the new middle peasants) and unite with the middle peasants. . . ." However, in terms of concrete implementation, it should be clear that those on whom we should rely are the poor peasants, the lower-middle peasants, and the middle-middle peasants among the new middle peasants, and the lower-middle peasants among the old middle peasants; and that those with whom we should unite are the upper-middle peasants among the new middle peasants, and the middle-middle peasants and well-to-do peasants among the old middle peasants.

Our reasoning [for such a proposal] is that if we still stick to [the old formulation that we should] "rely on the poor peasants (including the new middle peasants)," then we would have a problem with the upper-middle peasants who are usually categorized as part of the new middle peasants (and account for about 6 percent of the middle peasants), who are obviously not those we should rely on. But if we merely rely on the poor peasants without including the new middle peasants, then we would also have the problem that the poor peasants could easily be isolated due to their moderate numbers (accounting for about 25 percent of the total peasant population in our province) and the problem that [we could be seen as] abandoning the lower-middle peasants and the middle-middle peasants, both being in the category of the new middle peasants and both having enthusiastically supported the party in taking the socialist road. [Such an implication] is obviously unwarranted. Moreover, concerning the issue of uniting with the middle peasants, [the old formulation tends to] treat the lower-middle peasants of the old middle peasants equally with the well-to-do peasants. Based on this understanding and the situation of the class composition of rural party members in our province, we therefore suggest that we should clearly articulate the following points for building rural party branches:

1. At present prospective party branch members should be primarily confined to poor peasants, lower-middle peasants, and middle-middle peasants among the new middle peasants, lower-middle peasants among the old middle peasants, and working people in the countryside (handicraft workers, etc.). The well-to-do peasants will not be drawn into the party branches for the time being.

2. We must ensure that poor peasants dominate the core leadership of the party branches. Other elements among the poor peasants and farm laborers should also be actively sought and trained for backbone leadership in the party branches.

3. Class education, such as "lest we forget our class origins," should be conducted and intensified for the well-to-do or relatively well-to-do peasants. Furthermore, concerning the class composition of the APCs, we would like to propose in full accordance with the chairman's instructions that within the coming two or three years the prospective members of the cooperatives should be composed primarily of the current poor peasants, lower-middle peasants, and middle-middle peasants among the new middle peasants, and lower-middle peasants among the old middle peasants, and that initially the active members of the aforementioned groups of people should be organized and promoted to fill the major leading positions in the cooperatives.

Please enlighten us on whether or not the above formulations and interpretations are appropriate.

The CCP Fujian Provincial Committee
August 31, 1955

16e

Mao Zedong

The CCP Center's Comments While Transmitting the Zhejiang Provincial Committee's Report on the Agricultural Cooperativization Question (September [8,] 1955)*

Now we are transmitting for your reference the Zhejiang Provincial Committee's report of August 15, 1955, on the question of agricultural cooperativization. The center considers the Zhejiang Provincial Committee's policy is correct; [its self-]criticism of this spring's erroneous policy of "resolute contraction" is also correct. Yet because this erroneous policy was proposed to the Zhejiang Provincial Committee by the Central Rural Work Department, the latter should therefore shoulder the main responsibility. Now the comrade [in charge of] that department has already acknowledged his mistake and has made self-criticism accordingly.

Appendix: Report of the Zhejiang Provincial Party Committee
on the question of agricultural cooperativization
(August [15,] 1955)

Upon his return from the conference of secretaries of provincial, municipal, and autonomous region party committees called by the center, Comrade Jiang Hua [presided over] conferences of secretaries of provincial and prefecture [party] committees, of directors of the prefecture and county departments of mutual aid and cooperation, and of cadres of the provincial bureaucratic organs to convey and discuss the chairman's instructions. All comrades at the conferences maintained unanimously that they were profoundly enlightened and greatly encouraged [by the chairman's directives]. They expressed their wholehearted support for the chairman's instructions

---

*This comment was personally written by Mao Zedong—Eds.

and pledged to carry them out resolutely in their practical work. At these conferences, equipped with the chairman's instructions, we reviewed the work of agricultural cooperativization in Zhejiang Province and made a preliminary plan for the further development and consolidation [of APCs]. In the following we now report on our [self-]examination as well as our opinions concerning overall planning.

I.

The agricultural cooperativization movement in Zhejiang has gone through three stages of development in the past four years. The first stage was a period of establishing cooperatives on a trial basis at the county level and above. After receiving the center's (draft) resolution on mutual aid and cooperation in agriculture of December 15, 1951, the provincial committee immediately set up on a trial basis the Xu Guirong Cooperative in Xindeng County. In spring 1952 all prefecture committees and some county committees set up altogether 63 cooperatives, all of which were basically successful. After the provincial committee decided to trial-establish cooperatives widely at the county level at the end of 1953, the number of APCs started to grow to 247 by spring 1953. In addition, 602 spontaneous cooperatives were set up. After the "antirash advance" campaign, 231 APCs were still operative. The second stage was a period of trial-establishment at the district and township levels. From the fall 1953 propagating of the general line for the transition period to fall 1954 the number of APCs grew to 3,298, an increase of 14.19 times over the original 231 cooperatives [sic]. The third stage was a period of a massive development. In summer 1954 the provincial committee planned to increase the number of cooperatives to 25,000 by spring 1955. Yet by April 1955 it had grown to 53,114, an increase of 16.1 times over the existing 3,298 APCs. But due to the April 1955 adoption of the erroneous policy of "resolute contraction" this number was reduced to 37,507 APCs (a decrease of 15,607 cooperatives), according to the statistics at the end of July. The peasant households in the cooperatives dropped from 1,311,857 to 879,000, constituting 17.6 percent of all peasant households.

In the past four years the agricultural cooperativization movement in Zhejiang Province was basically healthy except for suffering two severe setbacks that were to teach us profound lessons. It should be affirmed that in the period 1951–53 the decision of the provincial committee to ask all party committees at and above the county level to trial-establish cooperatives was correct whereas the spring 1953 "antiimpetuosity and rash advance" campaign and the subsequent dissolution of 618 APCs were wrong. In June 1954 the provincial committee decided to speed up cooperativization, drawing up an overall plan to increase the number of cooperatives to 110,000-plus by 1957. It also rightly proposed to make a good job of preparing for the forthcoming massive development of agricultural cooperativization. Following this massive development, the provincial committee proposed at the enlarged meeting of November 1954 that "positive leadership should be provided and consolidation carried out with great effort in order to lay a good and solid foundation and to prepare [ourselves] well for the forthcoming [further] massive development of agricultural cooperativization in the next two to three years." Then at the February 1955 conference of the provincial committee we made the proposal that "great effort should be devoted to running well the existing cooperatives, current development should be stopped temporarily until the summer, while [favorable] conditions should be created earnestly in preparation for further development." The estimation concerning the agricultural cooperativization movement in our province and the measures adopted at the above two conferences [have been proven to be] basically correct, whereas the policy of "resolute contraction" adopted at the conference of the provincial committee and at the enlarged conference of the provincial committee, both held in April 1955, is erroneous.

[There are several reasons for saying that] the acceleration of the agricultural cooperativization movement is correct. First, socialist industrialization cannot proceed in isolation without agricultural cooperativization. The advance of socialist industrialization urgently requires the corresponding development of agricultural production. If the socialist transformation of agriculture is not in step with socialist industrialization and agricultural production is conducted on the basis of the small peasant economy, the ever increasing national demand for commodity grain and industrial raw materials will not be met and our nation's undertaking of socialist industrialization will encounter tremendous difficulties. Only through accelerating agricultural cooperativization can these contradictions and difficulties be solved step by step. We consider that our country's key construction projects for socialist industrialization can be better supported only when local party committees below the provincial level are determined to facilitate vigorously the early arrival of the high tide of agricultural cooperativization, strengthen the party's leadership of the movement, and ensure an increase in crop yields.

Next, from the viewpoint of the peasants' situation, after the completion of land reform in Zhejiang the poor peasants still constitute about 30 percent of peasant households and economically remain poverty stricken. [Furthermore,] the new middle peasants, formerly the lower-middle peasants, and the lower-middle peasants among the old middle peasants still encounter some degree of difficulty both in production and in their daily lives. All of them have seen with their own eyes the superiority of APCs. Having been exposed to propaganda and education on the general line, the state monopoly purchase and marketing of grain, and the State Constitution, they become all the more clear about the socialist direction. In order to shake off poverty, improve their lives, and fight calamities, they earnestly demand to take the path of cooperativization.

[The report continued with a discussion of party organizations in the province.]

The policy of "resolute contraction" that we adopted in April 1955 was wrong. As Chairman Mao pointed out, "it was decided on in a state of panic" [and a result of] "being scared and panic-stricken by success."

At that time the first kind of erroneous thinking was [reflected in the following statements]: "The development of cooperativization is too fast!"; "Such a rapid expansion goes beyond the level of the masses' consciousness and constitutes a fundamental source of tension in the countryside. If we do not get off the horse right away we will run the danger of breaking up the worker-peasant alliance"; "Such a rapid expansion in Zhejiang goes beyond the pattern of the whole country and of the Soviet Union as well." Dominated by such false thinking, [some cadres] have thus exaggerated the problems that emerged within the cooperatives at that time. [The report then noted some of the shortcomings of the period but stated they were not the main trend.] Yet the fact is that agricultural cooperativization has received enthusiastic support from the majority of the peasants and the rich peasants and relatively well-to-do peasants who were dragged into the cooperatives constitute only a minority. In the wake of overhauling [APCs] and implementing the principle of voluntary participation and mutual benefit, there were still 20 percent of the rich peasants and relatively well-to-do peasants willing to stay in the cooperatives. As a result, the cooperatives were further strengthened and the masses' enthusiasm for establishing cooperatives grew stronger. Therefore, the problems that emerged within the cooperatives at the time were not so serious as some people had imagined. The tension in the countryside had not come from the rapid development of cooperatives but rather was caused by rich peasants making a fuss over the grain issue. [In any case,] the big development of agricultural cooperativization not only will not break up the worker-peasant alliance, but it will [actually] consolidate this alliance all the more.

Another line of mistaken thinking was that "such a speedy development goes beyond the level of the cadres' experience and therefore [the movement] could not be consolidated," and that "compelling them to keep [APCs] would only result in a drop in crop yields." As a matter of fact the party committees at various levels had already gained preliminary experience in the course of trial-establishment. There were more than 1,400 cadres who worked full time on cooperatives, 3,000-plus old cooperatives serving as leading examples, and a large number of cadres at the grassroots level who enthusiastically demanded the establishment of cooperatives. As long as effective measures are taken, the level of the cadres' experience will be gradually improved and the problems within the cooperatives can be gradually solved in work. The idea of waiting for the cadres to gain experience before establishing cooperatives was [sheer] idealism that goes against the theory of practice. Meanwhile 90 percent of APCs have experienced an increase in this year's output of spring cotton as well as in early and mid-year rice harvests, 3 percent of the cooperatives maintained their levels of output, and only 7 percent registered a drop in output (including the factor of natural calamities). The hard fact that most of the cooperatives registered a general increase in output also shows that the above thinking was wrong.

One more line of wrong thinking was due to the failure to differentiate the various strata of the new and old middle peasants and due to the sweeping style of emphasizing the wavering attitudes of the middle peasants (including the new middle peasants). For example, one of the arguments on this line was that "the new middle peasants are those on whom we should rely politically, yet economically we could [do no more than] unite with them." It was thus believed that up to 70 to 80 percent of the peasants would waver. Such a misleading analysis significantly reduced the class basis for agricultural cooperativization. The facts show that the lower-middle peasants among both the new middle peasants and the old middle peasants have enthusiastically supported cooperativization.

In short, the root of the above false thinking and loss of direction lies in mistaking the nonessential and minor aspects as the essential ones. This is the concrete manifestation of idealism in practical work and the concrete reflection within our party of the well-to-do peasants' resistance to socialist transformation.

It is hardly accidental that we had already voiced opinions representing the above wrong thinking. [The report then briefly noted failures in analysis and research since land reform.] As early as February this year, in an analysis of the tension in the countryside at the provincial committee conference, some comrades already voiced opinions representing the rich peasants' thinking. Yet the provincial committee, due to its lack of clear views, failed to confront resolutely the erroneous thinking despite some criticism attempted in the concluding session of the conference. The [false] thinking was thus allowed to have its way and subsequently led to the adoption of the policy of "resolute contraction" at the April 1955 conference.

Next, in terms of organizational principle, we were not serious enough in that we went ahead with such a major policy without the center's consent. When sending messages both by telegraph and envoys the responsible department of the center made it clear that its opinions were [merely] suggestions and that it would be up the provincial committee to make final decisions. However, the provincial committee mistakenly took the instructions of the responsible department as those of the center. Having adopted the policy of "resolute contraction" and having further noticed that the comrades sent as envoys had already reported to the responsible department, the provincial committee failed to make a special report to the center in time so that the center could discover and rectify our mistakes more quickly. During the discussion sessions, comrades of the provincial committee have already made serious self-criticisms concerning the above mistakes.

The consequences of dissolving over 15,000 APCs are indeed serious. [They include the following:] our socialist positions in the countryside were reduced; counterrevolutionaries grabbed the opportunity to engage in sabotage activities; the peasants' spontaneous inclination [toward capitalism] developed for a while; and the enthusiasm of the vast number of cadres and the peasant masses for socialism was so seriously dampened that they lost their way forward for a time. All these [factors] helped engender fairly serious pessimism and the laissez-faire tendency. [The report then elaborated on this situation and claimed that Mao's instructions provided the strength for overcoming difficulties.]

II.

In order to carry out resolutely the policy of "comprehensive planning and more effective leadership" as instructed by the chairman, we have looked again into the matter and come up with a new plan for the development and consolidation of APCs.

There are about 494,000 peasant households in Zhejiang Province. If all of them are to join the cooperatives and on average there are about 40 households per cooperative, then about 110,000 APCs should be set up. Our preliminary plan is as follows. In the period from fall 1955 to before fall 1956 we intend to increase the number of cooperatives to around 65,000 (including the existing 37,500 APCs), accounting for 40 percent (including the present 17.8 percent) of peasant households joining the cooperatives. By fall 1957 the number will be increased to around 100,000 APCs [sic], accounting for 70 percent of peasant households. By fall 1958, given [our party's shifting emphasis on the size rather than number of APCs, namely] the principle of expanding existing cooperatives first and establishing new cooperatives second (with another 3,000 to 5,000 APCs set up), 85 percent of peasant households will join the cooperatives. By fall 1960 more than 90 percent (including some former landlords whose class status would be changed according to law and law abiding elements among the rich peasants) will join cooperatives and thus the semisocialist transformation of agriculture will be basically accomplished.

Plans for the coming two years:

From fall 1955 to before fall 1956, in the relatively well developed townships in the whole province with a good basis for mutual aid and cooperation (accounting for 52 percent of the total number of townships), 52 percent of peasant households will join cooperatives. In ordinary townships where there are only three or four cooperatives (accounting for about 20 percent of the townships), 40 percent of peasant households will join cooperatives. In relatively backward townships where there are only one or two cooperatives (accounting for about 20 percent of the townships), 20 percent of peasant households will join cooperatives. In blank and backward townships without cooperatives (accounting for 7 percent of the townships), 10 percent will join cooperatives.

Prior to fall 1957, in the first kind of township 80 or 85 percent of peasant households should join cooperatives; in the second kind of township 65 to 70 percent; in the third kind of township 50 percent; in the backward townships 30 percent.

[The report concluded with specific measures and general exhortation to achieve these plans.]

For Product Safety Concerns and Information please contact our
EU representative GPSR@taylorandfrancis.com Taylor & Francis
Verlag GmbH, Kaufingerstraße 24, 80331 München, Germany